D0611242

Theology for Today

Theology for Today

by *Charles Davis*

SHEED AND WARD
New York

NIHIL OBSTAT: JOANNES M. T. BARTON, S.T.D., L.S.S.
CENSOR DEPUTATUS
IMPRIMATUR: E. MORROGH BERNARD
VIC. GEN.
WESTMONASTERII: DIE 25a JULII, 1962

The *Nihil obstat* and *Imprimatur* are a declaration that
a book or pamphlet is considered to be free from doctrinal or moral error. It is not implied that those who
have granted the *Nihil obstat* and *Imprimatur* agree with
the contents, opinions or statements expressed.

This book was published in England under the title,
THE STUDY OF THEOLOGY

MANUFACTURED IN THE UNITED STATES OF AMERICA

CONTENTS

FOREWORD

There is such a dearth of theology written in English and the time available for such writing is so restricted that a theologian must be excused if he tries to gain a wider public for his occasional writings and so to increase their usefulness. Hence the publication of these essays.

"Our Knowledge of Christ" and "What is Original Sin?" are published here for the first time. "The Resurrection and the Atonement" first appeared as the introduction to the English translation of Père Durrwell's book, *The Resurrection: A Biblical Study* (London, 1960), and I must thank Messrs. Sheed and Ward for permission to reproduce it. "The Theology of Preaching" first appeared in *Preaching: The Papers of the Maynooth Union Summer School 1960,* edited by Ronan Drury and published by Messrs. M. H. Gill and Son, to whom my thanks are due also. The other essays, some first read as papers to various audiences, were all published in different periodicals, namely, *The Clergy Review, The Downside Review, The Dublin Review* (now *The Wiseman Review*), *The Furrow, Liturgy* and *Worship*. I am indebted to the editors and proprietors for permission to republish them. All, however, have been checked over and several have been considerably rewritten. It will be noted that certain key ideas are repeated throughout this book. It was decided to let such repetitions stand; experience both as a student and teacher has convinced me that repetition, while seldom graceful, is rarely superfluous.

CHARLES DAVIS

CHAPTER I

INTRODUCING THE THEME

We read in the opening chapter of *The Imitation of Christ:* "What is the use of talking profoundly about the Trinity, if you displease the Trinity by a lack of humility? In truth, fine words will not make a man upright and holy; it is a virtuous life that draws a man close to God. I would rather feel compunction than know how to define it. You may know the text of the Bible from end to end and all the sayings of the philosophers as well, but what is the use of all that without grace and the love of God? Vanity of vanities, and all is vanity, except to love God and to serve him alone."

That statement is undeniably true—as far as it goes; but, because of what it leaves unsaid, it grates on us today. Few will want to question—and rightly so—the permanent value of *The Imitation* in leading men to take the interior life seriously, but our generation is more sensitive to the inadequacies of the book because we are more aware that reflexion on the Trinity and on the other doctrines of our faith is really important for a mature Christian. The present stirrings of renewal in the Church could be well described as a striving for a more explicit, a more conscious faith. And for that reason many experience a real hunger for theology. Today a theologian is called upon again and again to give lectures and courses to people who are eager to possess some measure of theological knowledge. These may not be able to express clearly their reasons for seeking it, but they realize intuitively that theology is what they need for their Christian life and apostolic work.

Nowadays, then, a theologian has no need of sales talk to secure an attentive audience. It might seem pointless in these circumstances to urge at length the practical relevance of theology. Why preach to the converted? But what seems obvious to many a layman is not always, I am afraid, so obvious to a seminarist. Seminarists are a captive audience; they are compelled to study theology without necessarily having a personal perception of its value for their future pastoral ministry. For them, it is essential to put directly the question: Why study theology? To attempt some remarks in reply might also help those devout and apostolic laymen who, muttering to themselves the words of *The Imitation,* remain doubtful about the present enthusiasm of their companions for theology. And busy priests, too, might welcome the reassurance that it is worth while to keep in touch with the present burst of theological activity in the Church. Such preliminary remarks are also needed to guide us in our approach to theology. If theology is to be truly relevant to the Christian life and apostolate, it must be studied in the right way.

So, what is wanted, I take it, is some introductory remarks of a personal and concrete character on theology. Not the careful analysis of the nature and functions of theology which is given in a special treatise called *Introduction to Theology,* but a brief glance at theology and its value for the priest, the seminarist and the layman. Why study theology? Is it worth putting oneself out in order to study it and study it well? What is the connexion between it and the apostolic ideals of the ordinary priest and layman? In other words, the sort of treatment the *Reader's Digest* would entitle *Theology and You.*

Nevertheless, even within these terms of reference, the scope of the present work is limited. It is directed primarily at seminarists, and is concerned more with the apostolic function of theology than with the relation between theology and a personal growth in faith. All the same, the wider bearing of its observations should be fairly evident, and maturity of faith and apostolic zeal are inseparable.

How may we best conceive the purpose of a general course of theology? Simply as this, to make apostles. Is the answer unexpected? Surely, it may be thought, what the lectures must aim at is the imparting of theological knowledge, the giving of that information and book-learning which the Church insists upon for her priests and which is increasingly needed by educated lay people. Obviously such a purpose is included, but it is inadequate, seriously inadequate, to see the study of theology merely in that way. It is not a question of injustice to the ideals of the lecturer; injustice is done to theology itself. To repeat, then: the purpose of any ordinary course of theology is to make apostles, to form bearers of God's Word.

It is not the function of the seminary, nor will it normally be the function of theological lectures to laymen, to form learned theologians, men capable of theological research. The concern is with the pastoral ministry and the lay apostolate; the aim is not academic but apostolic. Certainly, learned theologian and apostle are not incompatible ideas, and the work of the apostolate sorely needs at the moment all the theological learning that is available. It must be added also that theology can no more be separated, in any degree of its development, from the apostolate than it can be separated from the faith. The fact, however, must be recognized that the average student has not the ability to become a specialist in theology, and his needs must be served by a primary and general course of theology. Now, in the general teaching of theology, as distinct from the research and special studies engaged in at university level, the apostolic character of theology, together with its religious value for the student, stands out, or should stand out, with unmistakable clarity. This first and general teaching of theology, if true to itself, will have a close and evident connexion with the mission of the Church to proclaim and make known to men the Good News of Christ.

Very often students seriously underestimate the value of theology because they do not realize the intimate relationship between theology and the apostolate, and, indeed, between theology and their spiritual life. To seek from the dogma course in a seminary merely the acquisition of basic professional knowledge is to miss all that makes theology live, and to miss too that which will make one's future preaching and instruction a rich and fruitful presentation of God's Word. No, not the acquisition of information— that does not express the aim; the matter must be put instead in this way: the purpose of a theology course is to give students an understanding and awareness of revealed truth such that they will want and be able to impart it to others. To do this is unquestionably something that is at the heart of the training of an apostle. The task is nothing less than that: to impart that developed grasp and loving awareness of the Christian message of salvation that will impel the future priest and the lay apostle to go out and tell it to men and make them able to do so. That should be the effect of theology itself, properly taught and properly studied; in that role, theology can be assisted but never replaced by pious exhortations.

"An understanding and awareness of revealed truth"—the word that comes at once to mind is "vision"; but we must remember that revelation unveils for us a reality that remains unseen. Nevertheless, the word "vision" expresses well the quality, the force and integrity, of that grasp of revealed reality that is required. The phrase "theological knowledge" is misleading here. Theological knowledge may be but a mass of unconnected information about Christian teaching. The mind may be cluttered up with historical details and abstract notions and technical terms; it may be loaded with the erudition of the centuries and trained to manipulate with logical skill the many concepts; but with all that there may be no real possession of the revealed truths and no deep awareness of the shape of revealed reality. Knowledge worthy of the name is something else. There must be the vision of the whole. The structure of the divine message must stand out clearly; its lines should be clear-cut and not obscured. The central truths must be seen as central, and all the rest placed in harmonious relationship to them. The individual truths must be possessed as living truths; they must be entered into and assimilated—indeed it is rather they themselves that should possess the mind.

Theology, however scientific, remains a work of faith; without faith there is no theology. It does not study God's truth with indifference but with commitment, and that commitment should animate with charity all the intellectual labours of the student. His scrutiny of God's Word in theology should form a unity with his approach to God and with all his spiritual aspirations. If Catholic preachers and teachers have done their work well, the student will already have a vital and balanced possession of revealed truth. Yet it may be through a course of theology that there is first gained that synthetic grasp of the Christian message which gives order and harmony to the mind's knowledge of Christian doctrine. But, in any case, the lectures in theology must deepen and strengthen, widen and enrich the vision of the whole and the understanding and awareness of each individual truth. It would be lamentable if the study of theology should obscure that vision or blunt that awareness by multitudinous details and unassimilated information; or if the believing mind's equilibrium and the force of its faith be lost by the disproportionate treatment of the lecturer's pet themes at the expense of other truths. A course of theology, especially a seminary course, must be an integral, ordered and living presentation of revealed truth. The scientific solidity of the treatment does not mean that erudition can run riot and that side-issues can be allowed to prevent the imparting of an ordered and finished synthesis; nor does it imply that God's message of salvation must be viewed as a series of remote abstractions.

The understanding and awareness of revealed truth gained by theology must be such that the students will want and be able to impart it to others. The desire to communicate truth comes from its possession. "The very essence," wrote Frank Sheed, "of being possessed by any truth at all is a desire to tell it. To be possessed by a truth and not to long to communicate it would be impossible. The mark of the teacher who is possessed by truth is an almost anguished desire to convey to others what is so rich a treasure to her."[1] If a student studying the great Christian truths does not end by saying to himself that others must be told about them; if he does not feel the desire to go out and make them known to men; if he does not experience anguish that so many Catholics are unaware of these saving truths and so many unbelievers ignorant of them: if this is so, then there is beyond question something wrong with the teaching or with his study. No amount of earnest exhortation to the apostolate can replace theology in giving this lasting impetus to proclaim the Christian message. Such exhortation will remain superficial and its effect will soon fade. The source of the enduring and inescapable longing to bring men to the divine truths is the possession of them by oneself.

But am I not claiming too much for theology? An unlettered man can so possess Christian truth that he longs to communicate it to others. He can lead other men to embrace the faith by the testimony he bears to it. Is such a man to be denied a share in the apostolate? Certainly not. The most simple believer can act as God's witness and thus communicate his faith. The student,

---

[1] *Are We Really Teaching Religion?* (New York, Sheed and Ward, 1953), p. 10.

however, cannot be treated as a simple and unlettered man, for
the very good reason that he is not a simple and unlettered man.
This is particularly true of the seminarist. He is subjected to a
course of theology; for four years he studies the Christian message.
If this intellectual contact with revealed truth does not impel him
to go forth and make it known to others, it will instead prove a
hindrance to his spiritual development. Yes, it will tend to deaden
his faith and damp his apostolic zeal; it will produce a spiritual
malaise that will call for remedy. The only cure will be to study
once more revealed truth at the level of his mental development
and make those barren notions and arid theses that are clogging
the mind and preventing fruitful activity become what they should
be: vehicles of living truth. (I have assumed that the course has
left some impression on the mind and has not left this entirely
unaffected.)

Again, while an unlettered man may act as a witness to his
faith, he cannot teach and instruct the converted in that faith. To
teach another the faith requires that rational understanding of its
message and that ordered grasp of its constituent truths which,
beyond an elementary stage, pertain to theology. The activity of
theology and the activity of bringing the Christian message to men
are not the same, and they should not be confused. In preaching
and in catechetical instruction the person makes known to men the
saving Word of God. In doing this, he is sharing in an event that
is in itself a supernatural mystery. The message he proclaims and
teaches is no merely human message and his words have a divine
power and force. When we bear God's Word to others, we know
by faith that Christ is the living author of our message and that it
carries with it the power of his Spirit to move and change the
hearts of men.

This does not justify any carelessness in our human preparation
and our attempt to adapt our teaching to our hearers; does the
invisible efficacy of the sacraments justify a neglect of the visible
rite, its vehicle? Theology, though resting on faith and penetrated
by its influence, is a more human and less exalted activity than
preaching. It is the human mind's study of that saving Word
which preacher and teacher bear to men in the name of Christ.
Its laws and methods are not those of catechetics and preaching,
and for that reason a diluted theological thesis does not make a

doctrinal sermon. Nevertheless, the teaching activity of the Church leans heavily on theology. This is true of the preparation of a papal document, it is true of the preacher in the pulpit, and it is true to a large extent of the ordinary teacher. Certainly, at least the priest needs a solid theological formation if he is to be adequate to his task as preacher and teacher. The stress on the apostolic orientation of the seminary course implies no plea for superficiality. There is a pressing need for priests with a thorough grasp of theology. They must be able to proclaim Christ's message as well; they must be equipped to present and explain the truths of the faith to men of differing mentalities; they must not be confounded by the objections and difficulties that are raised. A long solid intellectual formation is essential for them. All the same, mental agility is not enough. There must be the right attitude to God's Word—the commitment and the desire to make it known. No intellectual ability can replace that, and with it a less able student will often become the greater preacher, the finer teacher and the better student.

What, then, is required of the student of theology? Here, to omit others, are four things that are necessary. First, reflexion. How often a student neglects to think! He must think in order to enter into the truths and penetrate their meaning and significance. He must grasp their inwardness. They must become his own. He must endeavour to see the problems, to feel them and weigh them. It shocks to see problems so far-reaching that they have caused untold anguish to men, truths so liberating that they have produced inexpressible spiritual joy, treated by the seminarist as paltry mental counters to be played with and their markings memorized. It is a sight of mental degradation. Think, for heaven's sake, think; you are not studying a grocery list or a Bradshaw, but problems that have racked the human spirit and the staggering responding message of God's Love.

Theology is not the memorizing of notes or the amassing of information; it is the reflexion of faith. It should also for that reason be at the heart of the student's spiritual development and not outside of it. Theology should transform one's piety, which should become increasingly based on the great central truths. Thought must enable these to sink deep into the mind and exert their influence. Then, second, diligence is needed. To study earnestly is not easy; it demands persevering effort. Discipline helps us to do what we want to do. It secures our deep choices from the pressure of the immediate distraction. It is regrettable that there is so little external encouragement and social support for the priest in his study of theology, but at least in the seminary these are there. Let the student co-operate with that discipline and study zealously and perseveringly. A wishy-washy enthusiasm is not enough. But, third, enthusiasm is important. The enthusiastic are often naïve and amusing and misguided, but at least they have generosity of spirit. Let us avoid like the plague that deadly cynicism that can begin in the seminary and leave still-born the seminarist's apostolic ideals. Fourth, giving life to all the rest, the apostolic spirit. Let there be a burning desire to impart God's truth to others. That does not imply that we make God's truth a means. It is not a means but an end. No one has expressed this important point better than Mgr. Romano Guardini in this passage:

The deepest significance of dogma lies not in its practical applications but in safeguarding the fullness and freedom of sacred truth. Truth, in itself, has no purpose, only meaning. It does not serve life but shines by its own light. . . . For us men of an age wholly set upon utility and expedience, of achievement and power, of intensification of living and increase of production, understanding of this point is extremely important. There is nothing at all which truth should be made to serve. It stands above all purposes, all designs. If it really holds this sublime place in a man's mind, it will construct an order in his existence from which issue right desires and acts. Truth is like light. A man does not desire it primarily in order to see his path or to enable him to work better, but just because it is light—ask a blind man what it means to be deprived of it. Truth is the light of our proper existence, the space and order in which we live. By standing above all practical aims it guarantees that they can be rightly viewed and achieved.

Much too long Christianity has been beset with practical purposes. We have moralized it, made it active, and in so doing have lost sight of its true nature. We must perceive that the truth of revelation is not given to us, primarily, that we may do something with it, but that we may adore it, and live by it.[2]

2 *The Faith and Modern Man* (New York, Pantheon, 1952).

We do not, then, approach God's Word so that it may subserve some practical scheme in a superficially conceived apostolate. We come before it with the adoring reverence due to God the First Truth communicated to men; but it is precisely our initial possession of this Supreme Good that generates the zeal to lead others to It.

Now suppose a student convinced of all that I have said. He opens the manuals and listens to the lectures. A wave of disappointment passes over him. The expectation aroused has been dashed to the ground by encounter with the reality. Theology in practice, he complains, lacks the qualities that have been extolled. Such complaints from a student are rightly treated with suspicion. It is endemic among students to seek for quick results. They will not bother to peel the orange to get the fruit. The true value of any science cannot be appreciated without patiently working through the difficult period of initiation. Likewise, theology must be studied for some time before it really comes to life. Granted all this, there is some justification for the complaints. Theology is gradually emerging from a state of impoverishment. It is this impoverished theology that largely explains the decadence of preaching, and also the reaction of many priests against theology and their failure to use it to nourish their ministry and their spiritual life. A renewal of theology is with us, and a renewal implies a prior unsatisfactory state of affairs. The story is a long one, too long to relate here. Enough to point out that it is principally three great trends in the Church today that are revivifying theology and helping to remove those defects that deprive theology of this vitality and impact.

In the first place comes the movement of return to the sources of theology, the biblical and patristic revivals. The first, by far the more important, is doing immeasurable good by restoring a more biblical, more concrete, more historical and less abstract conception of the Christian message; and theology is being guided once more by a vision of this history of salvation. Further, the great biblical themes that can nourish our preaching and teaching are receiving more and more their due place in the treatises, and Christian truths are being studied as expressed in the language and imagery of God's inspired Word. Meanwhile, there is the use of a more critical exegesis. None of this means a neglect, let alone any undervaluing, of the later developments of Christian teaching, due in the Church to the abiding presence of the Holy Spirit. But the Scriptures are given to us as an inexhaustible source, and the Church is rightly turning to them to refresh and revivify the reflexion of its faith.

And then, the liturgical movement has given new life to the whole field of sacramental theology; but more than that, acting concurrently with the movement of biblical theology, it has brought back to its central position in the Christian message the mystery of Christ's Resurrection. The new appreciation of the mighty saving event of the Pasch and of the lasting role of the risen Christ has given new spiritual strength and joy to many individual Christians; it is acting like a leaven in the dough of theology. The restoration of the Paschal Vigil will probably remain as one of the momentous spiritual events of this century, and we still await the full fruits of its repercussions on the Christian consciousness.

At the same time the catechetical movement is having a beneficial influence on theology. This movement is concerned increasingly with the content of what must be taught. The saving truths of the Christian message must be presented to the mind by the teacher. But where must the stress be laid? Which are the central truths that must stand out clearly? How must the body of revealed truth be presented, so that the divine message is in no way distorted but rather its beauty and value made apparent? Theology and catechetics are closely related, since theology must study the message that the catechist teaches, and these heart-searchings among teachers are helping to give back to theology a sense of proportion that in some respects was lost by the stress of controversies, both domestic and with heretics.

In some ways it is impossible to distinguish the influence of these three trends, because they interact and form but one upsurge of life in the Church of today, a fresh sign that the Holy Spirit is still with her. It has brought an immense enrichment of theology, particularly on its positive side. Less progress has been made in the difficult task of making contact with modern thought. It is not sufficient for the theologian to refute false theories; he must endeavour to see the problems that people are trying to solve and then to rethink them in the light of the Christian faith. The surge of vitality due to the return to the sources is not enough. True, a more biblical approach is in many ways more acceptable to the modern mind, but it does not answer all needs. The Christian message must still be presented in a language that the modern pagan can appreciate, and his difficulties and objections must be resolutely tackled. Catholic theology is still too much of a closed world; and the theologian is not sufficiently in touch with modern thinking.

It is well to have some idea of the task and the present state of theology; it helps one to make contact with its wealth and to overcome initial difficulties. Present-day theology has its problems and its defects. The Church—and the theologian under her guidance—moves slowly in these deep and vital matters. But theology has more than enough life at the present time to give the student all that he needs for a fruitful apostolate. If the study of it is wholeheartedly embraced, it will transform and enrich the spiritual life and it will make apostles, eager and able to bring to men the living Word of God.

CHAPTER II

THE DANGER OF IRRELEVANCE

It is now a commonplace to observe that the distinctive character of modern theology is its return to the sources. The renewal this marks has been stimulated by the biblical, liturgical and patristic movements. Biblical scholars enjoy a new freedom in the Church, which enables them to pursue in a vigorous though Catholic way the critical study of the Bible. But what is more important from a theological point of view is that they have turned from an exclusive concern with the minutiae of exegesis and the aridities of critical problems—vital as these matters are—to an examination of the doctrinal content of the Bible. There has been a fresh flowering of biblical theology, and many studies have appeared that set forth the riches, say, of Old Testament thought or Pauline teaching for the nourishment of the believer. This cannot leave the theologian unmoved, for the Bible is the source of his theology, and the influence of biblical theology on dogmatic theology is being felt in many ways. The jejune treatise on the redemption is being fertilized by the new understanding of Paul's soteriology; the still young treatise on the Church is finding strength in the Old Testament themes of the covenant and the kingdom of God and the Pauline theme of the body of Christ; the individualistically conceived treatise on the last things has been recast in the perspective of the community and the history of salvation; and so on.

Meanwhile, the liturgical movement has been busily renewing the theology of the sacraments. And its influence has been felt in other directions too. The ministry of preaching, studied in the treatise on the Church, is now being seen in a sacramental context. Our knowledge of the liturgy has supported the biblical understanding of redemption, with the prominence it gives to the resurrection. The effects of the patristic revival are more difficult to assess. Its general result has been a widening of outlook. The development of the doctrine of the mystical Body in modern times has been largely due to the discovery of the patristic outlook on the Church. The treatise on grace is overcoming its one-sidedness, arising from the excessive preoccupation with actual grace, through a knowledge of the teaching of the Greek Fathers. The patristic approach to the Bible, with its grasp of the essential biblical themes, is receiving new attention.

Anyone who comes into contact with this ferment of renewal is filled with a sense of freshness, of wonder and of richness. He is excited by what is taking place. He reads some of the recent writing and compares the wealth offered there with the barrenness of the theological manuals of the recent past or, indeed, of the present. Theology has come alive, he feels. Here is no longer the detritus of past controversies but a message relevant to the present.

But is this so? Is not the conclusion too hasty? The warmth of such optimism will soon be dissipated by any real contact with the cold, harsh reality of the modern world. In *The Screwtape Letters,* Uncle Screwtape, writing to his nephew Wormwood, tells the story of an atheist who began to follow a "dangerous" train of thought while reading in the British Museum. The tempter broke it by suggesting lunch. "Once he was in the street the battle was won. I showed him a newsboy shouting the midday paper, and a No. 73 bus going past, and before he reached the bottom of the steps I had got into him an unalterable conviction that, whatever odd ideas might come into a man's head when he was shut up alone with his books, a healthy dose of 'real life' (by which he meant the bus and the newsboy) was enough to show him that all 'that sort of thing' just couldn't be true."[1] Although it means giving it a different twist, the story may be used as an illustration of what I said. When I read the recent work of the biblicists, the liturgists, the patristic scholars and the dogmatic theologians, I am filled with wonder and delight at all they have to offer. But when I rush down the steps of the cultural museum in which they are

[1] New York, Macmillan.

found and enter the arena of the modern world, what they say seems curiously remote and sometimes pathetically irrelevant.

In the passage quoted, Professor Lewis is considering the way the familiar stream of sense experiences can prevent a man taking seriously the unfamiliar and make the latter seem unreal. Here is certainly a problem, especially in this noisy age. The spiritual needs silence in order to make its reality felt, but from morning to night people are subjected to an endless bombardment by aggressive visual and aural impressions. Higher realities get little chance to show themselves, and, when they do break through, their lack of sensual colour makes them seem unreal. But that is not our present problem. The fact that the climate of modern life is inimical to spiritual development is only the symptom of a deeper trouble. We deceive ourselves if we think that it is only those immersed in sense-experience who are out of touch with Christianity; it is also the thinkers and writers of our time. Not only the daily atmosphere but also the thought and creative imagination of the modern world have lost contact with the Christian faith.

An age is reflected in its literature. There we shall see the moral vision, the patterns of thought, the emotional temper and the motives of action characteristic of our period and interpreted by the more perceptive of our contemporaries. What do we find today? Modern poetry, fiction and drama belong to a world with which part of ourselves is in sympathy, because we live in it and are influenced by it, but which is far removed from the Christian part of ourselves, which we are trying to make dominant and pervasive in our lives. We have made much of exceptions. The Christian vision of T. S. Eliot: but how influential has that been when compared with his poetic theory and technique? The Catholic novels of Graham Greene: but the Christian concepts with which he works are very thin. There are scraps of Christianity around, which are used in the building of themes and the formation of images, but the general picture is that of a culture alien to us as Christians. Theology and literature have long been divorced. This statement does not spring from a naïve wish to see slabs of Christian doctrine inserted into imaginative literature. There must be the artistic process of assimilation and creation. But in a Chris-

tian culture there is a living contact between theology and literature. It does not exist at present.

When we turn from literature in the narrower sense to the
more general writing of our time, we find the same situation. Nowadays, people turn to science for an account of reality and an answer to the riddle of the universe, and most have some smattering
of science and scientific ideas. The conflict between science and
religion used to be a subject of great interest. It is no longer. Why?
Because scientists and people generally are no longer interested
in what religion has to say. Science has won by monopolizing
the attention; the case for religion goes by default. We do not
get very far by solving individual difficulties. The fundamental
trouble is the attitude which looks to science for salvation and
regards religion as irrelevant. And what of philosophy? It is chas-
tening for anyone trained in the Scholastic tradition to look
through a number of *Mind*. Bewildered, he finds himself in a world
of thought which he does not know and which does not know
him. And apart from the present situation in England and the
United States, can we say that we have made as yet fruitful contact theologically with modern philosophy as it has developed since
the Renaissance? On every side we find the same. We need not
go very deep. It is enough to read regularly a periodical like *The
Listener* or *The Kenyon Review* to realize with sadness that we
are aliens in the world of today.

And so, what happens to our enthusiastic student of modern
theology? His own Christian thought is enriched immeasurably.
Truths which had no meaning for him before come now to life.
The Christian faith takes on a new vividness for him. And that
makes him feel the urgency of the Christian message. He wants
to make it known. He would like others to share in his discoveries.
But unless he preaches only to the already converted or predis-
posed (and not all Catholics are in these categories), he will face
an uncomprehending stare. It we contrast Catholic religious books
with other writing, the difference is apparent. We do not use the
same language. We do not write in the same way. We do not invoke the same concepts. We do not share the same preoccupations. I am aware of the element of exaggeration in this diagnosis.
But there is a serious maladjustment here and we need to perceive it sharply. We have been busy gathering the materials for

our Christian message. It is time we began to interpret them for
our contemporaries.

Let us now look again at the biblical movement with this in
mind. Some of the biblical ideas it has brought to light have an
affinity with modern thought. The history of salvation with its
gradual unfolding is a notion that harmonizes well with the modern sense of history and modern ideas of evolution. So, Teilhard
de Chardin can bring together evolution and redemptive history
into one vision of reality. There are probably other examples of
such affinities. But the general result of the biblical revival has
been to reveal a world very different from our own. The difference
goes very deep. It extends not merely to the content of thoughts
and images but also to the general mentality and modes of thought.
A set of strange literary forms and procedures accompanies it.
Biblical scholars are quite aware of this and insist upon it. We are
told that we must become Semites mentally and spiritually if we
want to appreciate the Bible and not misunderstand it. At the
same time, they—and all of us to a lesser extent—live so continually with it that they tend to forget how strange this biblical
world is to those without their special interests and training.

If modern men are to assimilate Hebrew thought, the gap
has to be bridged between that thought and the thought of our
present age. A man only understands what he can grasp in its
relationship with the general content of his mind. In other words,
a work of interpretation must intervene. The interpretation will
re-express the same truths in a different way, in a way that is
adapted to the modern mentality, with its different outlook, ideas
and preoccupations, which presupposes an understanding of that
mentality in its qualities and deficiencies. Now, this work of interpretation is not being done in the Catholic biblical movement.
The fine studies of biblical theology produced up to now are in-
ventories of biblical data. This does not mean that they are arid
lists of biblical doctrines without the nobler qualities of synthesis;
in fact, they include some excellent syntheses. What it does mean
is that they are accounts of biblical teaching in biblical terms, without any attempt to make contact with the modern mind.[2] As such,
they are admirable for those with an innate historical sense or those

---

[2] Fr. J. L. McKenzie's popular *The Two-Edged Sword* (Milwaukee, Bruce,
1956) is an exception.

whom long study has made familiar with the Semitic world, but they remain inaccessible to others. We cannot demand in all men the mental power to resurrect an ancient culture before we bring them to the truths of revelation. Further, if the biblical message is intended for every age, it must be possible to state it in terms relevant to every age, including this one. It is not part of my purpose here to enquire how far such an interpretation comes within the scope of biblical theology. I am not blaming biblical scholars for not doing something that they may well consider not one of their functions. I am simply ascertaining the fact that the work of interpretation, in the sense I have defined it, is not being done. To assemble and order the biblical data is only the first stage and is not sufficient by itself. The excesses of Bultmann with his programme of demythologization should not blind us to the fact that, as Fr. Malevez observes,[3] he has seen a real need. We cannot be content to repeat the biblical message in biblical terms. We must transpose it in a way that will make it intelligible today. And the task is unavoidable.

We must be careful that our enthusiasm for the doctrinal rediscoveries of the biblical movement does not generate in us a false biblicism: an unwillingness to go beyond what the Bible states and the way it states it. This, by the way, has nothing to do with the question whether the Bible contains the totality of the deposit of faith or not; it concerns the way God gave us that deposit and the validity of a development of doctrine. Since the unwillingness mentioned is basically un-Catholic, it can be seen most clearly in Protestant writers.

A good example of the tendency is the work of Dr. Cullmann—good, because his analysis of biblical teaching is so sane and balanced. His recent book on the Christology of the New Testament[4] is a magnificent account of biblical doctrine that can be recommended with few reservations. Now, he rightly insists on the perspective proper to the New Testament itself, which always views Christ in relation to his work. But he then shows a reluctance

[3] L. Malevez, S.J., *Le Message chrétien et le mythe: la théologie de Rudolf Bultmann* (Bruxelles, 1954), pp. 116–17. Eng. trans., *Christian Message and Myth: the Theology of Rudolf Bultmann* (Westminster, Newman, 1960).

[4] *Die Christologie des Neuen Testaments* (Tübingen, 1957). Eng. trans., *The Christology of the New Testament* (Philadelphia, Westminster, 1959).

to endorse fully the emergence of a different perspective which gave rise to the discussions about natures and person and led to the definition of Chalcedon. He admits a certain historical necessity for this development, but he is clearly unhappy about it and indifferent to its results. The discussion about natures is not a "biblical problem"; the Bible neither is able nor intends to answer such questions. This attitude supposes that all that we can or should do is to repeat the statements of the Bible in the way the Bible makes them and bow down in silence before the mystery they express. It refuses that activity of faith seeking understanding, which, while respecting the mystery, seeks to penetrate its meaning, asks without fear the questions to which the teaching of the Bible gives rise and which it implicitly answers, and hammers out new formulations to express its fresh insights and exclude subtle errors. The ultimate reason for the refusal is the denial of an infallible Church, which alone can guarantee the soundness of such a process and the validity of its results. But, more immediately, we must insist that the further questions that arise are indeed "biblical problems," unless the biblical doctrine is there only to be repeated and not to be interpreted for each age. The Bible is the source of Christian thinking, not its abolition. Dr. Cullmann manifested the same attitude in his earlier, again admirable book *Christ and Time*.[5] He explains how the Hebrews thought of eternity as endless time, but then he refuses the introduction of a more philosophical concept of God's eternity, oblivious that this is demanded by the biblical teaching itself on the relation of God to time. It is not the way the Bible puts it, he argues. Once more we have the obscurantist refusal to face any question that is not directly answered in the biblical text.

I would not have spent so much time on this point, did I not fear that the same attitude affects some Catholics, though in a more hidden and unconscious way. In this respect, it is significant that several eminent Catholic reviewers of Dr. Cullmann's book on Christ failed to observe its intensely Protestant setting in their enthusiasm for the quality of its biblical analysis. The attitude referred to shows itself in the *malaise* felt by some biblical scholars, when theologians discuss biblical doctrines in terms other than those of the Bible and in their too exclusive insistence on the

[5] Philadelphia, Westminster, 1951.

biblical formulations as they stand. It is only fair to these scholars to recognize that the present situation is rather complicated. In the tension sometimes felt between the biblicist and the dogmatic theologian, I find myself nearly always on the side of the biblicist. The biblical knowledge deployed in our dogmatic treatises has for long been poor in quality. Whatever the labour involved, the theologian must bring his treatises into line with the better biblical knowledge now available and at least overhaul thoroughly his use of biblical texts. Moreover, he has been far too prone to see in the immediate wording of the Bible what was only made clear by later development, a mistake which, paradoxically, often has an impoverishing effect by narrowing unduly the meaning of the relevant texts. All the same, he must vigorously maintain his right to go beyond the expression of revealed truth found in the Bible, to ask and answer questions about biblical doctrine which are not raised in the Bible itself and to transpose that doctrine into different terms. It would help if such efforts were more warmly endorsed by biblical scholars than they are. Biblical theology, understood as the assembly and ordering of biblical data, cannot stand by itself. The biblical movement is not enough. It is a mistaken optimism in the modern world to suppose that it is.

When viewed in the light of a need for interpretation and adaptation, the liturgical and patristic movements are easier to deal with. It is tempting here to go off at a tangent and consider the practical problems of a living liturgy. The liturgy is a sacred heritage handed down to us which we must not manhandle in favour of a passing fashion. At the same time, the preservation of the splendour of an ancient, and often feudal, ceremonial does not rank high among the purposes of the liturgy. But all this is beside the point at the moment. Our concern is doctrinal. The liturgical movement has brought to light the basic themes and symbols used in the liturgy. Like the biblical movement, it has produced many books displaying the riches it has discovered. But what has been done to interpret these for men today? We should not hide from ourselves that the initial result of this activity has been to place before people a mass of strange ideas and symbols, many of which are not readily assimilable by the average modern man. It is not enough to repeat and analyse what we find in the liturgy; we must also bring it into contact with the rest of the mental make-up of twentieth-century man. The attempt to do so might make us better able to distinguish between that in the liturgy which is traditional in the strict sense and incidental features left over from past fashions and hindering the present impact of it. All that needs to be said on the patristic movement, in this respect, is that it is more important to catch the spirit of the Fathers, immersed in their own age and boldly tackling its problems, than to make ordinary people acquainted with the details of their opinions. The revival of a past age, however valuable to the theologian and scholar, is not itself the immediate answer to the problems of this one.

What has been said must seem ungrateful grumbling to many. We must indeed be deeply thankful for the wonderful results of the present renewal and its transforming influence on Catholic life and thought. But it would be cowardly to flee from an honest appraisal. The renewal has remained of domestic interest among Christians and falls short of a powerful movement of thought with a significant impact on the modern world. Why? The question nags: why with this fresh abundance are we not a greater force in the world of today? There are grounds, I suggest, for thinking that the reason is the weakness of our speculative theology. The biblical, liturgical and patristic renewals have not been accompanied by any comparable renewal on the speculative side of theology. There we might find what is still lacking.

The interpretation of revelation in terms accessible to the modern mind cannot be a hit-and-miss affair, a hasty adaptation based on superficial knowledge. That way leads to relativism and modernism. Of itself truth is neither ancient nor contemporary; it is timeless and, in that sense, always relevant. But what matters is the level at which it is grasped. What we really want to know here is what happens when a truth, first expressed in terms of a particular audience, moves out into a wider field and meets other audiences. The process is this. Thinkers try to see the truth from a standpoint higher than its initial setting, if possible from a standpoint that is universal, one valid for all human thought, and, in doing so, they search for more general concepts of permanent validity in which to formulate it. To the extent that they succeed, they reach a new understanding of the truth. This new understanding makes it possible, not merely to keep the truth in relation to its first expression, but also to express it for new audiences. The higher the standpoint from which the truth is seen, the more easily can it be related to the contents of different mentalities and the more surely can the discrimination of what is true and false in these be effected.

Such a process can be observed in the development of doctrine. Revealed truth was expressed in Scripture in relation to a given people and culture. It was not expressed in the abstract terms of speculative thought but in a concrete and descriptive way, in terms of ordinary human and religious experience. Since that expression is inspired and divinely chosen, it must remain central to Catholic thought. First, its comprehensive richness makes it the theologian's permanent source and norm; he returns to it repeatedly to seek new aspects and avoid onesidedness. Second, it was intended by God to be a permanent vehicle of religious experience within the Church; people must be brought to it and cannot leave it aside. Hence we must heartily endorse the conclusions of the catechetical movement on the essential role of the Scripture in teaching and preaching.

But the revealed truth thus expressed would not have lived on in the world of thought and become accessible to men of different cultures and mentalities unless a development had intervened. This development did not consist in the mere succession of different particular formulations, one being left aside as the other succeeded. To look at it in this way would be equivalent to denying the power of the mind to reach objective truth and would make dogmas but symbolic expressions of religious experience. The development was a search for a higher, universal standpoint and an attempt to formulate revealed truth in the objective, universal, permanent categories of human thought, while never forgetting the limitations of these, and every other human expression, in the face of mysteries. It was in the light of the deeper understanding and more general formulations obtained in this process that revealed truth was interpreted for different men and errors excluded. In other words, a real progress has been achieved in the understanding of revealed truth, and in that achievement speculative thought has played an essential part.

But what has been done so far is still imperfect. Not all that has been defended by theologians in the past is equally permanent, and we must strive for new insights. Fresh progress will be made by meeting the challenge of new problems, and these problems will be met only by fresh progress. When in the great Trinitarian and Christological controversies the Fathers met the needs of their own age, they also permanently enriched our understanding of revealed truth. If we face up to the problems of our own time at the deepest level, we shall produce, not a superficial adaptation of revelation to modern thought, but a lasting progress in our understanding of the Christian faith. And that deeper understanding will have its repercussions on the more superficial and practical aspects of our attempt to bridge the gap between Christianity and the modern mind. Speculative thought is for the few, but we are always in danger of underestimating the extent and ramifications of its influence on the many. Unfortunately, speculative theology is in a poor state at the present time. There is a great deal of mere repetition of past thought. The dazzling advance in the positive part of theology is accompanied by a certain lack of confidence in the "arid speculations" of the theologians. This is justified in part, but perhaps we should be more careful to distinguish between what is being done and what could be done in the field of speculative theology. We must not lose our confidence in its essential task. The necessary work of interpreting all the fresh data of positive theology is lagging behind. But without that work of interpretation we are unarmed in encountering our contemporaries; it is not enough simply to display the data before them.

A theologian who has seen the full scope of the task of theology is the Jesuit, Fr. Bernard Lonergan. His great book, *Insight: A Study of Human Understanding*[6] is a philosophical work. But the author is a dogmatic theologian and his ultimate aim is theological. It is precisely because he has seen the full dimensions of theology that he has found it necessary first to rethink his philosophy. All who had worked their way through this difficult but immensely powerful work and have gathered as well the hints he has given elsewhere about his views on theological method will earnestly hope that the theological counterpart of *Insight* will not

[6] New York, Philosophical Library, 1957.

be too long delayed. It would take a separate chapter even to outline Fr. Lonergan's approach, but it was impossible to speak of
speculative theology without paying tribute to his work. It is a
sign that a renewal of speculative theology may well be on the
way.

The argument of this chapter will have been misunderstood if
it is taken to mean that we must busy ourselves with every passing
fashion of modern thought and upset the immanent development
of Catholic theology by an excessive concern to relate it to modern culture. Dogmatic theology must exist in a certain retirement
from immediate issues where truth is pursued for its own sake and
from the simple desire to understand. But that very desire to understand demands that we bring modern thought into relationship
with our theology. Now this chapter arose from an experience
which perhaps others have shared. The first reaction to the modern
renewal of Catholic thought is one of undiluted enthusiasm. One
is simply overwhelmed by the riches that are set before one. As
time goes on, there is no diminution in the appreciation of the
new insights, but there is a gradual realization that they exist in a
cultural enclave. Wider reading outside theology makes abundantly
clear the gap that exists between all the new data and the modern
mind. Since we live in the modern world and inevitably share its
outlook to some extent, the dichotomy is felt even in our own
minds. We suffer from the absence of a sustained effort to bridge
the gap. We ask ourselves: what is missing? It was reflexion on
the relationship of dogmatic theology to biblical theology and the
stimulus of Fr. Lonergan's book that brought me personally to
the conviction of the role of speculative theology and the need
that exists for its revival. Only with a vigorous speculative theology
behind us can we go forward to meet the modern world and interpret Christianity to it.

There is no easy answer to the present need. A strong speculative theology cannot be created overnight nor can it develop
with the momentum of the positive branches of theology. It depends on the emergence of thinkers of stature, working with wide
horizons in view. But the situation can be helped by facing honestly
all questions that arise. We should not be content to ask theology
and theologians questions that can be answered by simply turning

up the index of a theological manual. Such questions are due ultimately to our ignorance of present theology. We must ask real questions, questions that cannot be met without fresh theological thought. A real confidence in the activity of faith seeking understanding would create a climate in which a strong speculative theology could grow.

CHAPTER III

WITH OR WITHOUT FAITH?

It is not that science has disproved religion; it has simply made it irrelevant. There is no cause for excited talk about this; let the inevitable
take its time. The conviction grows that the age of religion is past, that
faith is an incongruous feature in our modern mental landscape—a
Gothic church embedded in a new town; some still cling to it, most
ignore it, and eventually the far-seeing will be able to have it quietly removed. The pitched battles are past; the real conquest is being achieved
by the general change in mental climate. The unimaginable immensity
of the universe reduces the God conceived in function of the cosy
universe of the past to an unimportant figure projected by man's mind.
If man had so little idea of the real universe, he is hardly likely to have
achieved much accuracy in conceiving the Power that governs it.

Man himself formerly held the centre of the stage. He was lord of
the material creation; his God looked down on him in love or in anger
and became incarnate in his nature, anxious to save him from his folly;
the destiny of the entire universe was correlative to his own. This now
looks as out-of-date as an ancient myth. Man, though a wonderfully
interesting organism, is but a fragile and insignificant unit in the cosmos as a whole. His origin and his future are bound up with remote
cosmic forces of which he is a lesser by-product. He might eliminate
himself or be eliminated without repercussions of any magnitude. Why
inflate man's understandable concern with himself to cosmic proportions? Why, too, hold on to the postulates of his past ignorance?

The ever-increasing knowledge of matter in its complexity and
potentialities is making it more and more unnecessary to demand a
fiat of a Creator to explain the origin of man or of life or of the cosmic
process. In the cosmological field religion has nothing to offer and,
despite the ingenuity of theologians, it still bears all the marks of an
outlook long since surpassed. Nor need it claim our attention in the

moral order. Christians are not noticeably better than others in their
personal lives and relationships, and if technical progress has not immediately brought a more civilized behaviour—well, religion has no cause
to boast. What is clear and what is seeping into the consciousness of
ordinary people from every side is that it is applied science and not
religion that is determining man's way of life. It is to science that we
must look to draw mankind from its poverty and misery, and many
research workers and technicians have in the contrast between their
own lives and those of their parents a private support to their confidence
in what their knowledge and skill can do for the human race.

That does not mean a facile optimism. There are fools who may
destroy all in a senseless war. But risk often accompanies human enterprise. A climber on a dangerous ascent recognizes the risk that all
may end in disaster, but feels within him the strength of his limbs,
experiences the thrill of the climb and is spurred on by the thought of
the summit. And there is no easier way. Religion is not going to stop a
war, and the Christian moral code was never intended for this technical age. It will be even more out of place when man not only changes
his environment but also, by his knowledge of genetics, begins to change
himself. No wonder, then, that any news of a notable advance in science, from whatever quarter it comes, is received with a firm satisfaction. Political issues are secondary. What matters is the continual
reassurance that science retains its power to transform human existence
and that this power is gathering in momentum. Religion? Why mention
it? It is no longer relevant. And if there is much talk of a religious
revival, it is because eddies always make more disturbance when the
current is strong.

The above, I think, represents fairly a widespread attitude.
Often it is unformulated, and more practical than theoretical. The
details too may vary, but in some such way many a modern looks
out on a universe without faith. It is easy to dub it shallow from the
standpoint of one's own experience of the Christian life; easy but
ineffectual. Again, the metaphysician and the theologian can
rightly point out its defects and refute one by one its individual
assertions; it remains surprisingly undislodged. Its strength lies
in that it is a general attitude of mind which does not rest on any
one particular objection. Yet nothing imposes it. Impressive as it
sounds, it is a freely chosen stance before reality, not demonstrated
truth. It is possible to represent the relationship between the

Christian faith and science in an entirely different way. The old antagonism was never more gratuitous than it is at present.

Development within science itself has brought home to scientists the limited function of scientific hypotheses, and there is nothing in modern scientific thought that need cause the believer or the theologian any distress.[1] Conflict has purified our grasp of the faith and helped us to distinguish it from the adventitious elements with which it gets mingled. The scientist who is a Christian can go about his task without any sense that his faith is a hindrance. Thus, the acknowledgement of an infinite, transcendent God is more likely to be strengthened than weakened by a study of the immensity of the universe. And man's material insignificance drives home man's nothingness before God and the utter gratuitousness of God's love—a central theme of the Christian message. Again, to reject creation on scientific grounds is crudely to misunderstand its meaning. The evolutionary process with its display of what is relative and finite demands, not excludes, the unfailing presence of the Absolute or Creator; but this does not necessitate any break in the continuity of phenomena, upsetting or hindering scientific investigation into the workings of the universe. Creation is not an object of scientific observation or induction.[2] Further, the doctrine of the direct creation of each human soul expresses a truth about man's nature which is supported by the data of his consciousness. Man transcends the material; and for that reason his origin even as an individual cannot be explained exclusively in terms of material antecedents. The creative influence of God can alone account in man for the presence of a spiritual principle—but that does not modify at all the findings of embryology.

We could continue along these lines, but this is not the place to run over once more the individual objections. The point is clear: in theory, the scientist has no reason to fear faith as an obstacle and the believer has no cause to fight shy of science. Tension, here and there, will always occur; it is part of the condition of human

[1] For a detailed and balanced study of some individual problems, see *Christian Theology and Natural Science: Some Questions on their Relations,* by E. L. Mascall (New York, Ronald, 1957).

[2] A profound treatment of the meaning of creation is given by Fr. Sertillanges, O.P., in *L'idée de création et ses retentissements en philosophie* (Paris, 1945).

knowledge. But it can be a fruitful tension. The limited scope
now allowed to scientific theories by the scientists and the sifting
of traditional data accomplished by the theologians make unlikely
any attempt to weld together into one whole the teaching of revelation and contemporary scientific thought. Each has its own order
with its own certainty, and it is better to keep the two orders
clearly distinct. All the same, they are bound to make contact at
a number of points, and why should not the ensuing discussion be
profitable to both? And science is not self-sufficient. Its very
progress has given rise to a situation about which the scientists
themselves are concerned and where the Christian teaching about
man and human destiny is very much to the point and cannot be
dismissed as unworthy of serious consideration or as out of place
in this technical age. Faith opens up a vast universe of another
kind, which leaves intact for man but transfigures with the new
meaning the universe before his eyes. Why, then, do so many
prefer a universe without faith to a universe with faith? It seems
a preference for loss rather than gain.

To deal with this question on the individual level is for the
pastor of souls. He has to co-operate from outside in the work of
God's grace within men. God alone knows the secrets of the
heart, and the workings of his grace are intricate as it acts to
open the mind of man to the call of faith, against the forces, including but not alone sin, that shut him upon himself. Unwise to
simplify in this matter. The personal background of unbelief can
vary considerably. But when this has been said, it still remains
of interest and importance to take this reaction from faith as a
general problem and attempt to analyse it. What do we find?
That it is exactly that: a reaction from faith, a turning away from
the kind of knowledge faith offers. What causes offence is not any
particular doctrine but the very idea of faith. Many are bewildered over what it is supposed to be, and what they hear about
it makes them mistrust it. Others realize better what it involves and
they dislike this. Whether vaguely or more clearly understood,
faith is refused as unpalatable. Behind this rejection stands the
contrast between scientific knowledge and faith. Scientific knowledge is knowledge. People think they know what it means and how
it works. What is faith? How can it claim my mind? It demands
an absolute and categorical assent to doctrines as true, yet that

assent, it is said, essentially depends on a free choice by me, a free commitment on my part; and this itself is only possible, it is alleged, by the grace of God. Is this genuine knowledge or a mere forcing of the mind? Can thought be the fruit of a choice and remain thought? The contrast of the personal commitment required in faith and the impartial objectivity of scientific thinking leads many to turn aside from faith as unworthy of a mature mind. Undoubtedly, any effective apologetic today must go beyond the immediate arguments for the Christian claim and answer the basic question so insistently asked: What is faith?

One thing at least is correct in the unbeliever's estimate of faith: faith is very different from scientific knowledge, and, for that matter, from any knowledge within man's own range. Faith is a unique act; it takes man outside his own order and gives him entry to a higher one. The legitimate desire to find analogies to faith among the ordinary activities of human knowledge, for example in our acceptance of the statements of trustworthy witnesses, should not make us forget that faith in the theological sense has no exact parallel in normal human knowing. It is *sui generis;* every analogy falls well short of what it is. Small wonder, then, that the mental process implied is disconcerting and that some find it more comfortable to remain where they are.

A unique act, but still an act of the mind. Christians will not allow any explanation that puts faith outside the mind. To attempt, as some have done, to save faith or to disparage it as a blind emotion or sentiment is a grave error. Faith takes man higher not lower; it is not below ordinary human thinking but above it. Faith, indeed, is dissatisfying intellectually—that is why we shall pass from it to the clear vision of God; yet, already in its painful obscurity it is a gift of divine light. We are given a share in the divine knowledge.

But to the statement that faith is an act of the mind, an intellectual assent, we must add the statement that faith essentially includes an act of man's will. Part of the structure of faith is the pursuit and choice of what is spiritually desirable, and without this the assent of the intellect could never be achieved. Here it is regrettable that there is no unambiguous language in which to express the reaction of the spiritual depths of man when what is good is presented to him. The inclination of man's spirit to the good carries with it an intellectual awareness that puts this spiritual affectivity poles apart from an irrational urge or sentiment. The common use of words such as "affection," "love" and "desire" to describe mere emotion must not lead us to suppose that an appeal to the will and its affections in explaining faith immediately destroys its objectivity and reasonableness. They are used here of what is an indispensable element in man's search after reality and possession of it—the search and possession proper to him as a spiritual being. All intellectual activity is closely associated with man's spiritual affections; for intellect and will are not two independent subjects or agents, but simply two principles by which the one subject, the person, acts. Both take part in all his spiritual activity. Admittedly, the freedom of faith means that the affective side of man's spiritual make-up has an unusually large role in it; but that does not make it an unreasoning emotion. Faith, with all its peculiarities, is a reasonable intellectual assent. But we must examine more closely its peculiarities. How does it differ from scientific knowledge?

A first, manifest difference lies in its object, in what is believed. The content of faith seems very disparate, but it possesses in fact a close unity. All its truths are connected with man's destiny, or rather, to put it more precisely, with man's vocation to a higher destiny. Faith essentially concerns the calling of man by God to eternal life or supernatural beatitude. That is important, as we shall see, in understanding the process of faith, which is an initial movement of man towards God as his last end. It is a wrong idea that faith can bear on any truth whatsoever that God may arbitrarily draw out of the treasure of his omniscience and make known to us. Whatever may be the possibilities of other communications of knowledge by God to man, faith as we know it is related of its very nature to a divine message about man's supernatural destiny, and without that relationship its workings are inexplicable. Fundamentally what is made known to us is the gratuitous love of God for man: that unexpected love that did not limit itself to creation but poured itself out on man, calling him to share as a son in the very life of God. But that love has been revealed to us in an order of sin and redemption, in which Christ, God the Son incarnate, has been sent to us by the Father as the supreme manifestation of his love and the source of our power to respond to it. We reach our life in God through Christ, by being incorporated into Christ. When we consider sin and redemption and all that they involve, we see the reason for an unavoidable complexity in the object of faith in the present order. It was not enough for God simply to tell man about the final happiness open to him. Many truths had to be revealed in order that man should have a sufficient knowledge of a destiny now given as a gift of salvation in Christ and of the means he needs to overcome sin and make that salvation his own. Nevertheless revelation is not a list of heterogeneous truths but a single message, and that message is the good news about man's destiny as a son of God. What it announces goes beyond mere human knowledge; the divine saving love of which it speaks is by definition undiscoverable from creation. The response it demands is even in its first, basic act, which is faith, beyond mere human ability. Faith lies on a higher plane than that of scientific knowledge.

However, in being surpassed, human knowledge is not supplanted. Faith is not an easy way of giving man all the answers. There is a temptation to expect at once too much and too little from faith. Too little: people can so easily reduce the Christian faith to a bunch of moral precepts with some teaching about a supreme model to be imitated, without realizing the staggeringly unexpected and far-reaching character of God's plan and its inevitable repercussions on man's entire life and activity. Too much: the possession of ultimate truth through faith is a temptation to forget that the more laborious processes of human knowledge still have their place. Faith, however helpful its influence, does not of itself give the answer to all problems, even human problems. Our faith tells us what should be our attitude as Christians to the poor of India; it does not show us how to build an irrigation system to relieve their need. The Christian teaching on the requirements of justice and charity has an intimate bearing on the conflict between nations; it provides no political solution for the present deadlock. And so on. Man still needs to think and improve his knowledge. Faith does not diminish the usefulness of science. There is every reason to look to science for a greater alleviation of poverty and for a greater knowledge and control of man's environment; but to know why he exists and how he must live a man must turn to God in faith. The force of God's love has given him a destiny that in its reality and implications lies well outside the range of his unaided reason.

But it is when we turn from the object of faith or what we believe and ask what is the motive of our faith or why we believe that the full strangeness of the act of faith becomes apparent. What moves the mind to accept the message? In science what we accept is what we see as true. The statement or hypothesis may have but a limited truth and we qualify our assent accordingly, but our assent is measured by the truth laid bare before the mind in its investigation of reality. In faith we do not see the truth of what we believe. We accept the message as true, but we do not see its truth. Since revelation is objectively true, what it tells us enriches the mind. We can reflect on revealed truth present in the mind and gain more and more insights into its meaning. Our acceptance of revealed truth and our penetration into its meaning can have a stimulating and fruitful influence on other branches of knowledge, for example on philosophy. But when we are questioned about its truth, we must admit that we do not see this. We cannot prove what we believe, we cannot demonstrate its truth. We believe something, not because we see its truth, but because in it we encounter God. Faith is called in technical words a theological virtue. That means in simpler language that in faith there is a personal encounter with God. The motive of our faith is God himself as the First and Absolute Truth. God alone, not the truth of what he tells us, moves us to assent.

If in the light of this we now ask about the workings of faith, we find that what we reach and affirm by our act of faith is the presence before us of a word or testimony of God. We accept a message in its, perhaps detailed, content by assenting to the testimony it bears from God. A message comes to us by preaching, it carries signs of its divine origin or authenticity, and the mind responds by faith when it acknowledges in the message the word or testimony of God and thus accepts its truth. The mind is not confronted with the truth of the message but with the marks it bears of a divine communication. And faith is not an inference. It is in one simple movement, which is the act of faith, that the believer assents to the divine origin of the message and, in doing so, affirms the value it thereby necessarily has as divine truth. So, across a contingent structure of preaching and signs, man comes into contact with God as Truth and moulds his thought on the word of God.

That is all very well, the agnostic might rejoin, but how is God made present to us in our act of faith? In what way do we encounter the First Truth, so that it becomes the norm of our thought? It would be easier to answer this if we could say that the mind sees God as Truth and conforms its knowledge to what it sees. That, however, would be the intuitive vision of God, reserved to the blessed; it would not be faith. Faith is essentially a knowledge in obscurity, and its motive, the First Truth, remains unseen. The paradox of faith lies here. We judge in faith with unhesitating certitude that a message is a communication to us of God as Truth and, in doing so, accept it as divinely true, but without in any way seeing the divine Truth that motivates our assent. God does not become present to us in faith by showing himself to our intellect.

But how, then? By arousing in us an inclination towards himself. It is the Supreme Truth that we encounter, but as an object of desire not of vision. This is where the will and grace enter into faith; let us remember that they are an essential part of its structure. Without them there neither is nor can be an act of supernatural faith. What is their role? Seen or unseen, God is in reality the supreme good of an intelligent being, and in the present order, he offers himself to man to be known and loved as he is in himself. The direct possession of him by man's intellect and will has become man's ultimate destiny and final happiness. Faith is the first radical turning of man towards that destiny. Now, through the gift of grace there arises in us an active desire for communion and direct intellectual relationship with God. We are no longer content with our human and restricted mode of thinking; we aspire after the vision of God with a restlessness that can no longer be assuaged by anything less. It is God himself who draws us toward himself in this way, awakens in us the, perhaps uncomprehended, longing. And it is this longing that makes faith possible.

It does so by giving us a higher set of values. We have, it has just been said, a desire aroused in us which the beatific vision will alone fulfil; we are drawn by grace towards a full and direct intellectual union with God. Now, this inclination is a factor directing our present judgements. We already seek beyond the ordinary limits of human knowledge for some beginning of our union with God as Truth. This seeking acts in us as a guide. When we are confronted with a divine message, our desire serves as an inner light or testimony that illuminates the external revelation and gives the mind the power to discern the divine character of what is put before it. The revelation that comes to us from without meets the desire that is within us, and the mind perceives the correspondence between them. A revelation is an initial communication of himself to us by God. Aroused by God's grace to pursue eagerly all that we can discover and assimilate of the content of that Supreme Truth which we desire to contemplate later in its totality, we seize upon this initial bestowal. The external message comes before the mind with objective signs of its divine goodness and value. It is the grace within us that gives us the inclination towards it that is necessary if we are to respond to and discern such transcendent goodness and value. What, then, alone explains the particular and original intellectual process of our act of faith is the existence in our grace-endowed wills of this efficacious desire for union with the First Truth. It is an impulse that makes us want to develop in ourselves from now, in the measure possible, a relation and intimate union of our thought with God. When the divine call comes from without, the will with its desire carries us beyond what we see into the darkness of faith. To be docile to God in faith implies that we allow our intellect to be guided by our will when this is drawn to the First Truth. Faith, indeed, can be described as the virtue by which the intellect is rendered disposed to obey the will as it moves towards the divine Truth.

There is no denying that in faith we sacrifice our intellectual independence. This mental autonomy of ours was always limited, but there is an undoubted attraction in relying exclusively on our own mental processes, on the native light of our own mind. It is a sacrifice, too, made in a darkness that is bound to be mortifying to man's mind, avid for clarity. Yet, it is an enriching sacrifice. Already in this life the believing mind feeds on a higher truth and, as this truth is assimilated into its thought, it comes to realize that the darkness of faith is worth incomparably more than the brightness of ordinary knowledge. The sacrifice, however, is but a preparation for the clear vision of God. The free homage of our faith is to be rewarded by a possession of Truth that will satisfy our intellectual natures to the inmost recesses of their being.

Faith is meritorious because it is a free homage. It is well to recall this freedom of faith, despite the difficulty it seems to add to the understanding of this assent. We freely accept the message as from God. It is indeed stamped with the marks of its divine origin. These are enough to make it worthy of belief, but they are not such as to compel our minds to acknowledge it as divine. They show us clearly that we ought to believe, but they do not remove our freedom to refuse. The response of man to God's love is fittingly left free even in its basic act—faith.

But freedom must not be confused with uncertainty. There is perhaps some excuse for confusion. The intellect was not made freely to pick and choose among truths but to conform itself at once to any truth presented to it. In the ordinary run freedom of knowledge comes only from a lack of the strict evidence that justifies and causes an absolute certitude. It is only then that the will may intervene and cause a limited assent on the ground of suitability, usefulness or value; but in such instances it cannot force an absolute assent without doing violence to reason, because any motive to justify this is absent. Faith brings together the seemingly incompatible requirements of an absolute and unreserved assent and freedom to give or refuse it. This unique combination of freedom and absolute firmness is due to its motive. Although this remains unseen by the intellect, which assents to it only when moved by the will, it is a motive that excludes of its nature any possibility of error and demands for that reason an absolute and unconditional assent. To give less to what is divine is unthinkable. All the same, the peculiar character of faith means that its certitude, with its supreme firmness, comes not from what the intellect sees but from the movement of the will under the impulse of grace.

There is little doubt that the picture of the act of faith thus outlined presents many aspects that disconcert the scientific mind. It is tempting to try to lessen such an effect. This can be rightly done by pointing out the impoverished character of the views on human knowledge current today. Scientific method and reasoning have their place; they do not embrace the whole of human knowledge even in the natural order. The claim that no knowledge is

valid unless it is gathered by man as a detached spectator with no
personal commitment that would influence his judgement cannot
be sustained of all branches of human thought. The affective side
of man has its part to play in the acquisition of truth. Again, the
prejudice that everything can be expressed in clear and distinct
ideas and that what is not knowable in that way is not worth knowing serves to cripple man's thinking. These are but hints that man's
relation to truth is richer and more complex than many allow.
Were this realized, some features of the entry by faith into a higher
order would seem less starkly incongruous.

A much less happy way of making the idea of faith more
acceptable is to reconstruct the act of faith in a quasi-scientific
form. Many have thought that we can in that way reduce the distance between faith and science. This is how it is done. The key-
stone in the structure is the establishment by natural reason of
the fact of revelation. The arguments of apologetics are considered to prove beyond question the divine origin of the Christian
religion, even to a man unaided by grace. Armed with a natural
certitude of the fact of revelation, a man can go on to believe the
revealed truths with every confidence in the reasonableness of his
act. He knows by his natural reason the existence of God and his
unfailing veracity; he knows by his natural reason that God has
revealed these truths; based on these preambles, the act of faith
whereby he accepts the truths concerned is manifestly the act of an
intelligent and reasonable man. What cause here for even the most
exacting intellect to jib?

The vogue and influence of this view in modern theology make
it a surprise to learn its comparative novelty. For Capreolus,
Cajetan and all the older Thomist school, for Suarez, de Lugo,
Bellarmine and other writers, the fact of revelation was an object
of faith, not of ordinary knowledge. We accept the divine origin
of the Christian revelation, or of a given truth in it, by our act of
faith. That is, in fact, what we primarily assent to when we believe.
The act of faith is an assent by which we acknowledge a communication as divine and whereby, in one and the same movement, we
acknowledge its truth. As an object of faith the act of revelation
remains inevident, that is, without that evidence that would motivate an absolute assent. We "demonstrate" it only in the sense that
we "demonstrate" the divinity of Christ or the other truths of faith;

namely, we show that it is credible or worthy of the free assent of
faith. We do not and cannot make it evident. The more recent
analysis of faith was introduced under the influence of Cartesian
philosophy. Put forward for the first time in the seventeenth century it was immediately opposed as a daring innovation, but it
later gained that ascendancy that is only gradually being thrown
off.[3] Its straightforwardness is only deceptive, and it leads to in-
superable difficulties when we try to save the essential characteristics of faith.

What are its implications? Faith ceases to be an encounter with
God in which he himself is the motive of my belief and the light
of my thought; it is reduced to a natural knowledge in which my
assent rests ultimately on my own reasoning and on the light of my
own mind. What I accept may be supernatural truths, but the
reason why I accept them is evidence assessed by the mind using
its own power and resources. It is in this way that St. Thomas
explains the faith of the devils.

And how can this process account for the free yet absolute
character of faith? If the arguments adduced for the fact of revelation are apodictic, then the mind has no choice but to accept the
divine truth of what is revealed. It does not help to appeal to the
fact that what is revealed is established only indirectly; it is still
decisively established. No sane man can doubt the existence of
America on the ground that he has never seen it. But if the force
of the arguments is limited, then the assent which rests upon them
must be limited also, and faith loses its absolute character. This
shows us how little this view of faith helps us to defend the reasonableness of that unique act. Faith is reasonable wherever it is
found; if it deviates at all from right reason, to that extent it ceases
to be a virtue. The faith of the peasant or child is not a whit less
reasonable than the faith of the theologian. It is also, wherever
it is found, an absolute, infallible and irrevocable assent. There
is nothing provisional in the faith of a child or unlettered person.
Now, whatever the value of the arguments of our natural reason
for the fact of revelation, they are not known by all believers
with sufficient understanding to justify an absolute assent; they

[3] A fuller account of this will be found in *La vraie notion thomiste des
"praeambula fidei,"* by G. de Broglie, S.J., *Gregorianum*, 34 (1953), pp.
341–89.

cannot then be the essential factor in the reasonableness of faith.

What is justified by the quasi-scientific process of faith is in fact only a natural assent proportionate to the known force of the arguments. Such a process is already bewilderingly inadequate to explain, the existence in the theologian of a free, yet absolute, supernatural assent, caused by the gift of grace; it faces an even more impossible task when it is a question of the faith of children and uneducated people. It is true that these—like all of us—must receive the object of faith from others through preaching and instruction, but their act of faith cannot rest on another person's certitude. No absolute and irrevocable assent may be accounted for in that way, and to make a child's act of faith dependent for its reasonableness on that of its parents is to make it a provisional assent.

So, the advantages of this quasi-scientific approach turn out illusory, and the attempt to cut the act of faith to suit the Cartesian cloth has led to some very unsatisfactory theological patching. And many a mind has unnecessarily tormented itself by thinking of faith in that way and suffered anguish by supposing that the essential reasonableness of faith rests on the perceived cogency of the rational arguments in its support.

Does that mean we refuse the scholar his right to investigate the Christian fact? Certainly not. The Christian religion does offer a natural credibility, that is, a credibility before natural reason itself. It is a historical religion with historical claims that can be tested at the bar of history. The truths about Christ and the Church involve features that are patient of rational investigation, and that is also true of the many created signs with which God has accredited his revelation. The Christian religion defies a natural explanation. But more than that. Looking at the abundant marks it bears of its divine origin, we can say that even were God, which he never does, to leave a man without grace before the Christian message, the mind could come by a natural knowledge to discern there his handiwork; always provided, however, that we do not claim that the arguments are of such force as to compel assent and bring an absolute certitude, because this would exclude the possibility of the mind responding by the homage of a free faith. Further, the body of Christian doctrine presupposes many philosophical truths. These by definition are fully capable of rational proof, and that the existence of God can be proved in this way is an article of faith. The apologist, then, has much to do. He must rebut the objections made against the Christian faith from every side—a work that clears away obstacles that keep many back from adequate contact with the message of Christ. There is also a positive task: to display the signs of credibility that accompany divine revelation—a work that confronts people with the external testimony that conveys the object of faith. The activity of apologetics never ends, since each human generation with its prejudices and ignorance has to be brought to look fairly at the Christian claim. Our age certainly needs to do so. But the nature of the act of faith forbids us to look to the rational force of the apologetic arguments for that essential credibility that justifies the act of faith and makes it reasonable wherever it is found.

Are we not in a quandary? Faith is reasonable. That means it must be guided in some way by evidence. Unless we would fall into a blind fideism, we must find in faith some element of vision which enlightens, directs and justifies our belief. But what we cannot see cannot be the truths of faith themselves nor their divine origin; all that is precisely what we accept in obscurity by faith. What, then, do we see? The evident knowledge that guides our faith is the knowledge of credibility. What is necessary in order to believe reasonably? It is that our minds perceive that the Christian revelation is sufficiently guaranteed by divine signs for us to have the right and duty of believing it. To perceive that we should believe something is not the same as to perceive its truth. To demand that what we are asked to believe be established as undeniably true is equivalently to refuse faith. The object of faith cannot be made evident, but there is made manifest to the mind that it is good and obligatory to give to it the assent of faith. With that the mind has what is sufficient and necessary for an act of faith to be reasonable; namely, an actual, concrete, individual perception, however unformulated, that it can and should believe this revelation as divine and true. With that it must be content.

But how can we perceive this credibility, and perceive it clearly, without seeing the truth of the object of faith? In other words, is it possible in the last analysis to reconcile the darkness of faith with its reasonableness?

The Scholastics had at their disposal for this problem a richer conception of human thought and its working than many modern writers. The mind, they saw, has more than one way of perceiving a value. But the knowledge of credibility is in fact the perception of a supernatural value. To know that a mesage is credible is to know that the act of faith is the only appropriate response to it, which means that we perceive it as an appropriate object of supernatural desire—in other words, as a supernatural value. St. Thomas, therefore, brings the perception of credibility under what he calls knowledge by connaturality. This kind of knowledge is had when the mind knows a good or value by its harmony with the inclination of the knowing subject. How are we personally aware of what is morally good? The will with its virtuous strivings is present to the mind and, consequently, the mind judges what is good by the way it accords with the inclinations of the will. In this way a virtuous man knows what is virtuous by its conformity with what he is. Now, grace puts in us an inclination towards God as First Truth, a desire for direct intellectual union with him. This inclination draws us to him when offered to us already in an initial way in a supernatural revelation. When the message, with its expression of supernatural values, is presented and examined, the mind perceives its accord with the grace-produced inclination present to it and sees the act of faith as good and obligatory, because the only suitable response to such an object.

The knowledge of credibility essential to faith comes to this: the perception in the concrete way that my act of faith is a virtuous act because demanded by my inclination towards the supernatural good which constitutes my ultimate end. It is hardly necessary to add that the believer can have this without the ability to analyse and formulate it. A man does not have to analyse in the abstract the dictate of his conscience before recognizing its validity. Such a concrete perception of credibility is present by God's grace in the simplest believer. He may be unaware of the process, but his conscience tells him clearly enough that he should believe.

The pursuit after the meaning of faith has led us very far from the reflexions on the present state of unbelief with which this chapter opened. Yet, is it not very much to the point to recall the essential character of faith? It is important to remind ourselves that it is a free and humble submission of the mind made in darkness. How easy under the pressure from unbelief unwittingly to forget this and go forth to meet the unbelieving mind on its own terms instead of calling it to conversion! The incessant labour of taking up individual objections and removing misunderstanding must always continue, but the primary requirement for the genesis of faith is the integral proclamation of the Christian message. Argument has its place, but fundamentally men are offered faith, not argued into it. So often what prevents faith is an inadequate presentation of the message, so that the grace of faith lacks its corresponding external object.

Valuable study has been done in recent years on the nature and structure of the Christian message. This can help us in our task of bringing it to others. What is the core of the Christian message, its central theme? What should be the characteristics of that missionary proclamation of the Gospel that calls men to faith and gives rise to faith?[4] The Christian message can be described briefly as the proclamation of the salvation given by God in Christ and offered to all men who repent and believe. The word "proclamation" is used deliberately: the announcement of the Good News must resound, be public, solemn and dynamic. When it proclaims the salvation wrought by God, it is proclaiming an event, a history. The Christian message is not just a body of truths and precepts but the telling of a history. The preacher makes known the mighty deeds of God, his actions for men, and unfolds the history of salvation in which God reveals himself as Lord, Saviour and Father. But the salvation was given in Christ. All this history is centred in Christ, and so is the message. It is the proclamation of the Good News of Jesus Christ. It announces the salvation, the new order, brought about by the death and resurrection of Christ. Centred on Christ, its heart is his paschal mystery. This salvation is offered to all men who repent and believe. The message is essentially a call to conversion. It tells sinners of their salvation and calls upon them to put away their sins and be converted. They must repent and believe. Such is the basic proclamation that gives

---

[4] Information and excellent reflexions are given in *L'Annonce missionnaire de l'évangile,* by P. Hitz, C.SS.R. (Paris, 1954). Eng. trans. in preparation, New York, Sheed and Ward, 1963. The next chapter in this present volume will deal more fully with the points touched on here.

rise to faith. When it is placed before men by the ministers of the Gospel, it is not merely a human utterance. Christ is the author of it, not merely its theme. When the message of Christ is preached, it carries with it the power of his Spirit to move and change the hearts of men.

Christ relies on men for the spreading of his Gospel. The Christian revelation, though illuminated for the person by grace, must be presented from outside. Within its content it already has signs of its divine value, but if its presentation is to be adequate it must be accompanied by some manifestation of divine and supernatural life in its witnesses. What is offered is not mere abstract teaching but a message of salvation. How can this be delivered effectively, if its bearers show no sign in themselves of the new life they proclaim? What God offers to man in revelation is holiness: a union with him as he is in himself, a share in what is proper to God; and that holiness comes not only as a gift but also as a deliverance to sinful man. The offer finds expression in the lives of his witnesses as well as in their words; otherwise it would be but half-made. We are often too facile in attributing a sense of emptiness, frustration and restlessness to unbelievers. Experience should teach us caution; many, perhaps an increasing number, feel quite satisfied and content with what this world with its achievements has to offer. The fact is that the revelation of man's inadequacy and sinfulness is correlative to the revelation of what is offered him by God's gratuitous love. That must be proclaimed by preaching; but it must also be shown forth by Christian lives. If the present situation demands the ceaseless presentation of the Christian message, it demands just as imperiously Christian holiness. That Christian lives are no different from others is an unanswerable objection—at least, it can only be answered by pointing to Christian lives that are.

"At that time Jesus said openly, Father who art Lord of heaven and earth, I give thee praise that thou hast hidden all this from the wise and the prudent, and revealed it to little children" (Matt. 11.25, KV).[5] A well-used text, but still relevant. It sum-

[5] KV: *The Holy Bible,* trans. by Ronald Knox. Copyright 1944, 1948 and 1950, Sheed and Ward, Inc., New York. Quoted with the permission of His Eminence, the Cardinal of Westminster.

marizes all that has been said. Humility and simplicity are required for faith; this is inescapably a surrender of the mind to God, in which a man goes beyond what his own mind assures to rely in darkness on divine truth. The paradox is that nothing is lost but all is gained.

CHAPTER IV

THE THEOLOGY OF PREACHING

The title may puzzle many. People are used to talks and essays on theology *and* preaching, dealing with the doctrinal content of sermons—but, the theology *of* preaching? The phrase is new. What does it mean? Simply, theological reflexion on preaching itself. Or, in other words, an investigation, at the theological level, of the ministry of the word. For some years now on the Continent, particularly over the last decade, much writing has appeared on this new theme. It has become a commonplace to observe that the present crisis of preaching—everyone seems agreed that there is a crisis—can only be met if theologians take up the question of preaching and discuss it seriously in all its aspects, so that eventually they succeed in creating a treatise on preaching to stand alongside the treatise on the sacraments.

Discussing practical techniques, it is said, is not enough; what is wanted is a genuine theology of preaching. When we enter the pulpit, we are ministers of a mystery, engaged in a saving event that is part of the history of salvation. Only theology, faith seeking understanding, can do justice to an activity that cannot be understood or exercised as if it were an affair of human eloquence. Handbooks on preaching should not be mere manuals of sacred rhetoric but should give a theology of the mystery of preaching. Seminarists have been taught preaching merely by means of practical exercises. No one would dream of dismissing the sacraments in that way. Just as seminarists are taught the doctrine of the sacraments as well as given practical lessons in their administration, so they must be taught about preaching, its meaning and efficacy, and not receive only practical advice on technique. Remarks such as these are evidence of a change of outlook. What has brought it about?

There has been a general change of approach to the pastoral work of the Church. The change of attitude to preaching is part of this. Recent years have seen a renewal in the life and work of the Church; examples of it are the lay apostolate, the liturgical movement and the catechetical revival. As this renewal has gathered force, the conviction has grown that practical techniques are of no use without doctrinal reflexion. The promoters of the lay apostolate found themselves compelled to rethink the doctrine of the Church. The liturgical movement would have come to a halt long ago had it been simply an affair of practical ritual reform. It is moving on irresistibly, because of the profound reflexion it has stimulated on all the truths connected with liturgical worship. In the catechetical revival, the question of methods has given place to the more basic question of the structure and content of the Christian message. Everywhere, the realization has been the same. Practical techniques of themselves will get nowhere. We must re-examine the doctrinal basis of the work of the Church.

What the common conviction comes to is this. Not only the permanent structure of the Church, but also its activity is supernatural. The work of the Church is a mystery of grace, dependent on the other great mysteries of our faith. It is the task of theology to give us an understanding of it. If our active work is to be fruitful, we must know what we are doing. Otherwise we may find ourselves on the wrong track altogether; at best our work will be superficial. Hence we must go to theology for the insights we need to guide our work, a work that cannot be planned and carried out as if it were purely a human activity.

Is our theology ready for this task? The loud lamentations heard about its defects would seem to indicate not. But the urgent demand for more and better theology, coming from those engaged in active work, is having a healthy influence. Treatises are taking on a new look: forgotten riches are being unearthed. And besides the general repercussions on theology, a move has been started to give it a new dimension. This new dimension is a genuine pastoral theology. We all know what pastoral theology has been up to now. Little more than a discussion of the problems of the ministry at the practical level. Such a discussion is very useful, but

it is not theology. The pastoral theology now in process of formation reflects theologically on the mystery of the Church at work.
Using all the resources of theology, it examines the Church as a
supernatural reality at work in human history, gradually penetrating mankind and growing during this phase of its existence until
the Second Coming. It attempts to uncover the basic laws and
characteristics of pastoral work. Such a reflexion on the Church
precisely as living and working will supplement the more familiar
treatises of theology, while being dependent upon them. We are
not concerned here with the architectonics of theology, so we
cannot treat the place such a genuine pastoral theology will have
within theology as a whole. But the theology of preaching certainly
comes within its scope. That is, then, the setting in which we must
place it. We may add that, apart from the trend towards a new
pastoral theology, other causes which have drawn attention to
the particular problem of preaching are the discovery of the
importance of the word in the liturgy and recent Protestant writings on the subject.

The conclusion of all this is clear. Preaching is an urgent practical problem. Most observers think that it is in a wretched state
at present. The inadequacy of preachers is not the only reason.
The modern world has put the hearers in a new situation. In various ways it has caused a disaffection towards preaching. What is
to be done? We must not rush at once to discuss practical
remedies. We must first refresh our ideas by recourse to a theology
of preaching.

A radical solution to our present difficulties would be to
abolish preaching. Man has advanced socially. New social relationships now prevail and fresh techniques of communication have
been evolved. Preaching, it could be argued, is no longer a suitable means of conveying truth to others. Why not replace it by
discussions or conversational dialogues? Let us have an end to
monologues uttered from the height of pulpits by authorized
speakers to quietly listening congregations. Nowadays we like to
learn in the give-and-take of discussion and debate, even if a
particularly qualified person acts as guide. Is then preaching, the
proclamation of a message by lawfully commissioned witnesses,
an outmoded way of getting across the Christian revelation? The
answer—the reader will have guessed—is No. Preaching is abso-

lutely necessary and completely irreplaceable. There is room for other forms of communication as supplementary aids, but preaching is the essential way in which the Gospel message is made known to men. It is part of the very structure of the Church. It goes back to Christ as instituted by him. At the outset of our reflexion we are confronted with preaching as a sacred fact, an element in the revealed reality of the Church. Some of the reasons for its place will emerge later. Notice, however, the significance of its institution by Christ. What comes from Christ historically and juridically may be taken as penetrated here and now with the active and present power of Christ.

We can understand preaching only in its relation to revelation and the Church. The Church may be called the Church of the Sacraments and the Word. Now, the two constitutive elements of the Church, the sacraments and the word, correspond to two components in God's revelation. Revelation has two components, though we often think of only one of these. We identify revelation with a list of statements, a body of words, coming to us stamped with the authority of God. There are such statements: there is a revealed body of doctrine. God has made himself known in the teaching of the prophets and apostles, and, above all, in the teaching of Jesus Christ. But God has revealed himself, not only in words, but also in deeds. He has made himself known by intervening in human history for man's salvation. The deliverance from Egypt, the theophany of Sinai, the conquest of the Promised Land, the liberation from Babylon and, above all, the events of the life, death and resurrection of Jesus Christ are essential constituents of God's revelation. Revelation then is twofold. We may distinguish revelation as a reality or as events and revelation as words. Revelation as a reality is the very reality of God's love inserted into human history and present there as a force bringing about man's salvation. It is God's saving acts as present in the world and causing the events that make up the history of salvation. This reality of God's saving love become fully and permanently present in Jesus Christ. And so, in what he was and what he did, Christ came as the complete revelation of God to man. This component of revelation is basal. Revelation as utterance or words is dependent upon it. The function of the words is to tell us of the existence of the reality and interpret its meaning to us.

An intimate connexion binds together reality and word in revelation. *Dābār,* which is Hebrew for "word," may designate an action or event as well as a word. And so, revelation in its entirety may be called the Word of God. Its two components imply each other. On the one hand, revelation as reality calls for revelation as word. The action of God is addressed to us as persons; it is intended to lead us to a personal encounter with him. But if God approaches us as persons, he must not simply act for us or upon us. He must tell us what he is doing in intelligible discourse. Language is among the highest endowments of man. God's revelation would not be adapted to the dignity of man as a person and an intelligent being if it did not find expression in language. When we reflect on the role of language in establishing spiritual contact with men at the personal level, we see that the reality of God's self-gift must be offered through the medium of language if it is to bring man as a person into communion with God.

On the other hand, we have already seen that revelation as word depends upon the reality or events which it is its function to express. But more than that. It includes within itself as word the action of God. God's word is never the mere handing on of information. It possesses a dynamic power; it carries an action capable of effecting what the word expresses. The Hebrew *dābār* and the Greek *logos* are not precise synonyms, although they are both translated as "word." The Greek term denotes the meaning of a thing; the *logos* is the expression of its inner nature. What was uppermost in the Greek mind was the intellectual content of words. The Hebrews were more concerned with words as the means of conveying a call, an invitation or command; a word was something addressed to the will, demanding a decision from those who heard it. And if the word was the word of God, it was never ineffectual. If a man accepted it, it saved; if he rejected it, it was a judgement upon him. Now, the revealed word of God is both an effective invitation and a doctrinal message. Neither aspect must be excluded. Though the dynamic aspect is more prominent in Scripture, the idea of a content of truth is not absent. We must bring both aspects into a synthesis. But since we have been inclined to stress onesidedly the intellectual content, it is well to insist here that the word of God, the Christian message, comes as a divine call with a power to save or judge. The response to it can never be an attitude of cool intellectual detachment. It will evoke either the surrender of faith, and save, or the rejection of unbelief and condemn.

Revelation lives on in the Church. The sacraments make it present as a reality. Symbolic representations of the mystery of Christ, they bring present the reality of that mystery, so that we can take part in it. And the primordial sacrament is the Church itself. The Church is a visible sign containing an invisible reality. Christ set it up as his sign, the extension of his incarnate life, and he remains one with it, acting unceasingly in the Church through his Spirit. The Church is as it were the fundamental sacrament in which the other sacraments are rooted. They exist in the Church, the body of Christ, as so many actions of the risen Christ. At the centre of the Church is the Eucharist, which contains the totality of the mystery of Christ and his substantial presence. And so, the Church of the Sacraments is the permanent presence among us here and now of that reality or self-gift of God which is revelation taken in its basic meaning.

Likewise, revelation as word is continued in the Church. The message of God is permanently present in the teaching and faith of the Church. Since this permanent presence of the totality of God's word is part of the structure of the Church, part of what the Church is, we may call the Church the primordial word, just as we have called her the primordial sacrament. The teaching activity of the Church and the various expressions of her faith have their origin in the Church as word; they come forth from her as from the deposit of living truth. They proceed according to the hierarchical structure of the Church. Although all must take part in the work of the Church, the mission of the Church with the powers this implies was not entrusted equally to all the members of the Church. Christ placed the Church under his apostles and gave them and their successors alone the power of teaching. What is this power?

Fundamentally, all the powers of the Church are one. They form a unity as the power to continue the mission of Christ. At first they were thought of simply as one, and it was some time before any clear distinction was made between them. We must never forget that basal unity. When we distinguish the different powers, we must keep in mind how intimately they are joined together.

But what distinctions shall we make? There is a debate here among theologians. Some prefer to distinguish three powers, namely, of order, of jurisdiction and of teaching. Others say there are only two, of order and of jurisdiction. The threefold division is comparatively recent, and the twofold division may lay claim to a far longer tradition. For a number of reasons I prefer the twofold division, and it is under that presupposition that I intend to discuss the Church's function of teaching.

Does the teaching activity of the Church belong to her power of order or her power of jurisdiction? To both, but in different ways. Through the Church the revealed message is put before men by official and authentic witnesses. Official witnesses are those publicly appointed. "Authentic" indicates that they have been invested with the power necessary for the fulfilment of their office. Since it is a question of revelation, the appointment and investiture must come from God through Christ. We find then in the Church men who are divinely appointed and qualified teachers. They have the right and power to declare the message of God, and thus they stand before men as witnesses to his word and teachers of his doctrine. These official and authentic witnesses or teachers are the bishops. They are such in virtue of the power of order, which they possess in full. Their power of order includes a charism of teaching which makes them ministers of God's word and ensures the graces required for this.

The bishops alone are teachers in their own right. Others, however, have a subordinate role. This is especially true of priests. They have the power of order as helpers of the bishop. As teachers they extend the range and intensify the effectiveness of episcopal teaching, which otherwise would remain too confined. This does not mean that priests are simply gramophone records of the bishop's voice. No one in the Church is merely a passive recipient. Not even the faith of the laity is a passive impress of episcopal teaching. The Holy Ghost is active in every member of the Church, giving him personal insights into revealed truth. The priest exercises his ministry under the movement of the Spirit. In his power of order he has a divine charism of teaching which brings him special graces. He is helper of the bishop, but as an assistant able to make a personal contribution that is itself due to the action of the Spirit. That is why the bishop may rightly call upon a priest for advice in matters of teaching. All the same, a priest is not an authentic witness in his own right; his role is that of a subordinate co-operator with the bishop.

Preaching, whether episcopal or sacerdotal, is an exercise of the power of order. The character given by Holy Orders makes bishops and priests, though in different degrees, ministers of God's word, just as it makes them ministers of the sacraments. They are representatives of Christ and instruments of the Holy Spirit for the proclamation of the Christian message. But the Church does more than preach in an official and authentic way. The hierarchy exists to teach authoritatively. That means that its presentation of revealed truth may take the form of a law binding upon our faith. Questions of faith may be judged authoritatively and the judgements imposed upon us as obligatory. The magisterium is entitled to demand by law our response of faith. It does so by the power of jurisdiction. Indeed, the power to make laws that bind our faith is the highest function of jurisdiction. Since the Church does not create the object of faith but draws it from the sources of revelation, this jurisdictional power in matters of faith is a declaratory power. Basically, what the Church does is to determine the obligation already present in God's revelation. But its determination makes effective an obligation that would otherwise be without force because of lack of clarity.

Jurisdiction in matters of doctrine is exercised in many ways. What I have said so far concerns definitive judgements that impose an act of faith as obligatory. Besides these, there are provisional judgements and administrative decisions. All bishops with jurisdiction over a diocese possess some jurisdiction in doctrinal matters. But in the Church faith is one and universal. When there is an obligation to believe, it must fall on all the members of the Church alike. For that reason, only a universal jurisdiction can issue a law that binds our faith. Hence, such laws must come from the Pope personally or from the episcopal body as a whole in union with the Pope. Severally, bishops are limited to provisional judgements and administrative measures.

It is the function of jurisdiction to control the exercise of the power of order. It governs both the administration of the sacraments and the ministry of preaching. But preaching is more dependent upon it than the sacraments. No one can lay claim to a

55947

part in the official and authentic witness of the Church unless he
has been authorized by the jurisdictional authority. Rejection by
that authority destroys the authenticity of preaching in a way that
it does not invalidate the sacraments. Anyone then who teaches
in the name of the Church must be duly authorized. He must receive what is known as a canonical mission, either in virtue of his
office or by a special act. And so we speak of bishops giving
priests the faculty to preach. At the same time, preaching as such
is an exercise of the power of the order, not an act of jurisdiction.

This point helps us to understand how the laity can receive a
canonical mission to teach, although they are incapable of possessing jurisdiction. A canonical mission is not required for the ordinary, unofficial passing on of the faith, which we urge upon all
Catholics and which is a particular duty of parents. But diocesan
catechists and teachers in schools cannot teach, as they do, in
the name of the Church without such a mission from the bishop.
And here also the authorization by the bishop presupposes a divine
endowment in the person authorized. It is the character of Confirmation that makes the Christian a witness of Christ and renders
him an apt subject to receive from the bishop some part in the
official work of bringing the Christian message to men. What I
have said about the charism of teaching given with the power of
order may be applied, though in a lesser degree, to the character
of Confirmation.

Our concern, however, is preaching. So far we have seen that
a priest has a sacred power making him a minister of God's word
as a helper to the bishop. The necessary condition of its exercise
is a canonical mission. Without this, his preaching is no longer a
witness recognized by the Church as her own. But it is the power
of order that comes into play when the priest, acting as an instrument of the Holy Spirit, makes actual before men the word of
God, which is sharper than any two-edged sword (Heb. 4.12).
But can we define more precisely the efficacy of preaching?

All are agreed that the word of God in the Church is living
and effective. As present in the Church, it has the dynamic quality
proper to God's word and so insistently ascribed to it in the
Bible. The word is rendered actual before a particular congregation by preaching. Hence, preaching cannot be a merely human
activity. It is a sacred action that goes beyond the level of ordinary

human discourse. Priest and faithful are engaged in a sacred event, a mystery; the power of the Spirit is there. The problem is to determine the exact connexion between the action of the preacher and the action of the Spirit. How far is preaching a cause of grace? Here there is no agreement. It is the key question in the modern theology of preaching, and authors are still fumbling.

Understandably enough, the biblical insistence on the power of God's word has made writers want to attribute to preaching an efficacy similar to that of the sacraments. Some, however, have stood firm against this. For them, preaching is an occasion, not a cause, of grace. The Holy Spirit acts on the listeners at the time of preaching, but the grace given is not caused by the preaching. Those who are dissatisfied with this must be careful. Preaching is not an eighth sacrament, first because there are only seven, and secondly because the part of the human minister is obviously greater than it is with the sacraments. A deceptive compromise has been to call preaching a sacramental. More subtly, it has been suggested that preaching causes actual graces, while the sacraments cause sanctifying grace. Needless to say, there have been different variations on these themes. The nub of the difficulty lies in the relationship between preaching and the sacraments. We can, then, tackle the matter best from that angle.

The sacraments are inconceivable without preaching. The Gospel must first be preached, because people are brought to the sacraments through preaching. And they are not merely told about the sacraments. Preaching arouses in them the required dispositions. It is essential to the liturgy as a mystagogy, a leading of the people into the mysteries celebrated in the sacraments. In return, the sacraments give point to preaching by bringing about what the preacher has proclaimed, by making present the saving events he has announced. But the union between word and sacrament is even closer. Words constitute the form of the sacraments. And these words are not magical formulae but expressions of the faith of the Church. They are intelligible utterance in continuity with preaching. So, in the sacraments, words have a sacramental efficacy, and the sacraments may be rightly seen as the highest exercise of the Church's ministry of the word. These intimate bonds between word and sacrament mean that the liturgical

assembly is the privileged setting for preaching. To use a biblical
term, the assembly is the *kairos* for preaching, the opportune time
when the word is preached in circumstances that allow its maximum efficacy. But when the word is not the form of a sacrament,
in what way is it efficacious?

Preaching, I maintain, is a direct cause of grace. It is a sign
which mediates grace to the hearers. The action of preaching does
not simply put before the congregation the external expression of
the Christian message; it does this, but, in doing so, it is a sign
that causes grace. Now, if we maintain this, we must face squarely
the question of the difference between preaching and the sacraments.

Putting the matter briefly, we can say that preaching is correlative to faith, the sacraments to sanctification. Preaching is a
ministry which serves faith. The grace that it gives is the grace
of faith. But the sacraments presuppose faith. Even baptism demands faith in an adult for a fruitful reception. The giving of faith,
then, is something that precedes the sacraments and leads to the
sacraments. So, the mediation of preaching goes before the sacraments and leads men to the sacraments. This fits in with preaching as a mystagogy.

We must examine more carefully the way faith is given. We
cannot believe unless the object of faith is put before us. By the
object of faith are meant the various truths that we have to believe.
We must also become aware of the motive of faith, which is the
reason moving us to faith and grounding our assent. The motive
is God himself as First Truth, and this motive must be offered to
the mind. Now, all would agree that preaching brings us the object
and motive of faith. As St. Paul says: "Every one who calls
upon the name of the Lord will be saved. Only, how are they to
call upon him until they have learned to believe in him? And
how are they to believe in him, until they listen to him? And how
can they listen, without a preacher to listen to?" (Rom. 10.13–
14, KV). But faith requires more than the outward presentation
of its object and motive. If we are to respond to this presentation
by an act of faith, we must be given an interior testimony by
grace. The object and motive of faith are attainable by us, according to their supernatural significance, only if our mind is
enlightened and our will drawn by grace. In other words, both an

outward presentation and an interior testimony are necessary, in order that we should be offered the Christian message in a way sufficient for faith.

Now, what I maintain is simply this. Preaching offers men the Christian message, not merely outwardly, but gives also at the same time the interior testimony, the grace needed for faith. Both elements are required for an adequate presentation of the word of God. The two are intimately connected and always found together in fact. Further, the preacher is joined to Christ and made an instrument of the Holy Spirit by the power of order. It seems reasonable to hold that the action of the divinely appointed minister of the word when he proclaims the Christian message causes the grace without which his hearers are unable to grasp by faith the saving significance of what he is saying. Moreover, only if we hold this, do we do justice to the biblical teaching that the preaching of the apostles was the very word of God, and not merely words about God. To quote again St. Paul: "And we also thank God constantly for this, that when you received the word of God which you heard from us, you accepted it not as the word of men but as what it really is, the word of God, which is at work in you believers" (1 Thess. 2.13, RSV).[1] The word the apostles preached, the word we preach, is the effectual, saving word of God. Preaching does not stop short at words about God. As his ministers, priests convey the word of God, understood as the action by which God turns towards men and addresses them, calls them and invites them to faith. They do not preach a dead word, which is then vivified without their ministry. They mediate the word in its fullness, the living word, which means the word illuminated by the action of the Spirit. With the external word, they offer the light of faith. Notice that the need for grace does not apply only to the unbeliever hearing the word for the first time. The believer needs grace in order to exercise his faith. Although he has the virtue of faith, he still needs the actual grace of God for his activity of believing.

But it may be felt that I have narrowed excessively the scope

[1] RSV: *The Holy Bible, Revised Standard Version* (New York, Nelson, 1953). Copyright 1946 and 1952 by the Division of Christian Education of the National Council of the Churches of Christ in the U.S.A. and used by permission.

of preaching. The preacher addresses the faith of his hearers, but
he does more than that. In the course of his ministry, he urges
them to the practice of all the Christian virtues. Does preaching
give the grace for the exercise of the virtues other than faith, at
least in so far as internal acts are concerned? There are no sufficient grounds for asserting this. But some distinctions must be
made. First, when preaching encounters a living faith, the response of faith it evokes is commanded by charity. It is by an act
of charity that the will moves the intellect to assent. The grace
for this particular movement of charity is mediated by preaching.
The reasons already given apply. As a ministry of faith, preaching is directed to a living faith as well as to an imperfect, dead
faith. Secondly, no Christian virtue is possible without faith, because only by faith can we perceive the objects and motives of
the virtues according to their supernatural value. And so, the
preacher promotes the exercise of all the virtues in two ways. He
exhorts his hearers by his words, and the efficacy of his preaching
causes the interior testimony, or grace, needed for them to appreciate supernaturally the Christian ideal he is putting before
them. Thirdly, since a person who opens his heart to one grace
receives further graces, one who listens to a sermon with faith is
offered graces to set in motion the other virtues. Preaching starts
the process by presenting the objects and motives of the virtues
under the light of faith. Hence, it may be considered rightly as an
occasion on which God grants an abundance of actual graces.
However, it seems excessive to regard the action of preaching as
the cause of these graces, apart from those immediately connected
with faith. Such an efficacy is not required in order to give to
preaching its full value as the mediation of the living word of
revelation. It is better understood as the ministry which serves
faith.

We have, then, a clear difference between preaching and the
sacraments. Preaching is a sign causing the grace necessary for
faith. It does not directly give sanctifying grace or its increase,
although it may lead to actions that draw down such grace *ex
opere operantis*. The sacraments are correlative to sanctification
and directly cause sanctifying grace *ex opere operato* in those who
receive them worthily. Therefore, preaching prepares for the sacraments and is completed by them.

A further and very important difference between preaching and the sacraments lies in the extent to which preaching depends on the minister. His personal unfitness can destroy the efficacy of his preaching. Why this contrast? The preacher has to compose the sermon and thereby construct the sign that causes grace. All that is necessary for a valid sacrament is exactly determined. No matter how careless and unworthy the priest, if he administers the sacrament correctly, it comes into existence with all its power of causing grace. With preaching, it is left to the preacher to form the word of God. It depends on him how far a sermon is the genuine word of God. His activity determines whether the word of God is presented in its full richness or in an impoverished form. It is not unknown for a preacher to spend his time putting forward his own ideas, and sometimes only faint vestiges of the Word of God can be discerned in a sermon. The interior grace given by preaching bears upon what is outwardly presented, and only on that. A defect in the outward presentation mars the efficacy of the sermon for grace. Preaching on the Mystical Body will give grace to believe in the Mystical Body, but people will only receive such grace if the priest does in fact preach on the Mystical Body. And likewise with the rest of the Christian message. The grace of faith is not an immediate revelation; it is a light illuminating what is externally expressed. The efficacy of preaching is dependent on the faithfulness and insight with which the preacher conveys the word of God. When a priest does faithfully preach the message of Christ, and in the degree to which he does, the essential power of his words comes not from human eloquence but from the Holy Spirit. Preaching is a divinely established cause of grace. But the sign that causes grace depends for its very existence on the priest, and it is a sign that can exist more or less fully according to how well the priest carries out his function.

So, the assertion that preaching is a direct cause of grace does not alter the fact that the learning and holiness of the priest are required for its efficacy. It simply makes more precise the reason why they are required. The essential efficacy of preaching is not given by the learning of the preacher or the merits of his prayers; it belongs objectively to preaching in virtue of its institution by Christ and the action of the Holy Spirit. But the sign which conveys the divine action is brought into existence by the priest. His learning and holiness do not directly measure the power of God's word, but they determine the extent to which the word of God emerges into existence here and now. Learning is necessary. Unless the priest knows the Christian message, he cannot preach it. Holiness does not abolish the need for sacred learning. For example, if a priest is unaware of the new insights gained through the liturgical movement, he will be unable to enrich the faith of his people with those insights. But holiness is supremely necessary. A profound insight into the revealed word of God comes, not from human erudition, but from faith and charity. A holy priest whose lack of learning is not due to any neglect will often have a truer understanding of revelation than a learned but worldly theologian. And if we ask which virtues are particularly relevant to a preacher, we shall not be far wrong in saying faithfulness to Christ as his minister and a humble self-effacement before God's truth. There can be no more damning verdict against a preacher than to say he preaches himself.

There is an added reason why holiness is necessary in the preacher. The presentation of the Christian message is adequate only if it is accompanied by signs of the life of grace in the witnesses. We preach a message of salvation, not abstract theories. By our preaching, God is offering to men holiness: a union with him as he is in himself, which comes as a deliverance to sinful man. The offer is only half-made, unless it finds expression in the lives of the witnesses as well as in their words. To put the point technically, the concrete manifestation of divine life in the witnesses is a sign of credibility that must accompany the normal presentation of the Gospel message. It is true that a lack of such a manifestation in the individual preacher can be supplied for his hearers by its presence elsewhere in the Church. But this remains an anomaly. Preaching is the full witness that it should be, only when the preacher is urging upon others a salvation which has come to himself and is fruitful in his own life. Only then is he adequately serving the faith of his hearers. At the same time, we must recognize that the ministry of the individual preacher is not isolated, but is supported under all its aspects by the Church. While, however, this is a consolation for the zealous, it is no excuse for the negligent.

After this lengthy analysis of the efficacy of preaching, we may glance again at some of the explanations recently proposed. To say that preaching is an occasion of grace is partly true, but it is not enough to save preaching as the mediation of the living word of God. The idea that preaching is the cause of actual graces is both too wide and too narrow. It is too wide if it means that preaching gives actual graces of all kinds. Preaching is directly addressed to faith. It is too narrow if one agrees, as I do, with those theologians who hold that the infused virtue of faith is given in the first act of faith, even before justification; for there is no reason to deny to preaching the power to bestow the virtue. I called the designation of preaching as a sacramental a deceptive compromise. It is easy to seize upon the term to express that preaching is not a sacrament but like a sacrament. However, sacramentals are instituted by the Church: preaching by Christ. Sacramentals can be changed or abolished by the Church: preaching remains essentially unchanged as part of her structure. Sacramentals derive their efficacy from the prayer of the Church: the efficacy of preaching is due to the objective power in the word when mediated by a divinely appointed minister. Since the merits neither of the minister nor of the recipient give preaching its divine power, we are justified in speaking of an *ex opere operato* efficacy. But the phrase is misleading. Because it is normally used of the sacraments, it gives the impression that the effect of preaching depends as little on the preacher as the effect of the sacrament on the minister. We have seen that this is not so. In brief, we can perhaps do no better than say that preaching is a direct cause of faith, through the action of the Holy Spirit, when it is the presentation of the word of God by a divinely appointed minister of Christ.

What has been said so far can be summed up by saying that preaching has Christ as its principle in three ways. He is its principle historically, since our preaching was established by him. He is its principle juridically, because preachers are his authorized spokesmen with a mission derived from him. He is its active principle, because its power is due to the present action of the risen Christ, who gives the Spirit. We must now add that Christ is the content of our preaching. Our task is to preach the mystery of Christ in its fullness. How are we to do this? Christian preaching has assumed many forms as the one message has been adapted for different times, places and situations. The need for adaptation has always been felt, and rightly so. But recent work has made clearer than before the existence of laws governing Christian preaching, which must be followed if we are to be true to the structure of preaching as instituted by Christ. These laws, which are inherent in the word of God as given to men, must be respected, whatever the situation of our hearers.

Preaching is of two principal kinds: evangelization and catechesis. The first is concerned with conversion. Its purpose is to convert the hearers, whether by a first conversion, involving the genesis of faith, or by a second or later conversion, requiring the renewal of faith. It is the missionary proclamation of the *kerygma* or message, the good news of Christ, first directed to the unbeliever and then repeated when a spiritual renewal is called for, particularly at the time of missions. Catechesis, the second kind, is concerned with communion, the strengthening of union with Christ. It consists in a deeper and more detailed presentation of the Gospel message, with the purpose of nourishing the Christian life of believers. They are led ever closer to Christ as the different facets of the Christian mystery are displayed before them.

Evangelization has certain basic characteristics. We can describe it as the proclamation of the salvation brought about by God in Christ and offered to all men who repent and believe. We speak of it as a proclamation, because the announcement of the good news must resound; it must be public, solemn and forceful. Since our message is a demand for faith, our preaching should be striking and bring into relief the telling power of the mystery, rather than superficially clear in a way that shows an over-concern to measure the message in terms of human reason. This form of preaching presents the Christian message in a global fashion. It is important that this global presentation should respect the structure of the message. If this is done, the preacher will not offer men a list of truths and precepts, but tell them a history and announce to them an event. His task is to recount the mighty deeds of God, his actions for men, and unfold the history of salvation, in which God has revealed himself as Lord and Saviour. But salvation was achieved in Christ. The preacher must proclaim Jesus Christ and his work as the definitive intervention of God, the saving event *par excellence*. Evangelization announces the good news, the salvation, the new order, brought about by the death and resurrection of Christ. At the centre of the *kerygma* is Christ in his paschal mystery. But the announcement is not made to add to our stock of information. It comes as an offer of salvation to those who repent and believe. And so the message must be delivered as a summons to conversion; it is addressed to men as a call imperatively demanding a decision. We tell sinners joyfully of their salvation and urge them to put away their sins and be converted.

Such is the preaching that corresponds to conversion and the genesis of faith. Since the need for conversion is always with us, our Christian people must hear such preaching from time to time. It is the kind of preaching that should predominate at a mission, because missions are intended to renew the basic conversion of men to the Christian faith. We owe the analysis of its character and content to recent biblical studies of the apostolic preaching.

Faith once engendered needs nourishing. This is done by introducing believers to the full content of the Christian message in its various elements and initiating them into the sacraments. To do this is the work of catechesis. This also has certain basic characteristics. Although the preacher deals with the details of the Christian message, dwelling now on one point now on another, the harmonious structure of that message must not be disturbed. Stress on individual doctrines should not be allowed to upset the balance of the whole. The preacher fails in his duty if he pays too much attention to peripheral points, neglecting what is central, or expatiates unduly on his favourite devotions. Even the necessity of explaining a newly defined doctrine or combating an error should not lead to a disregard of the proportions that determine the relationship among the truths of revelation. The history of Christian instruction would have been happier if this had always been observed. Hence, catechesis must be Christocentric, with the paschal mystery at its heart. Further, all catechesis is inseparably dogmatic, moral and liturgical, even though one or other aspect may be dominant in a sermon. A Christian dogma is never mere theory but a saving mystery that demands a moral response and is encountered in its reality in the sacraments. Christian morality is not merely ethical behaviour but a peculiarly Christian way of life, based on the truths of faith and finding its expression and source in the liturgy. The liturgy is not a set of traditional ceremonies to be explained to the curious but the mystery of Christ made present sacramentally as the object of our faith and the source of our Christian life. To isolate one or other of the three constituents of catechesis, which is a danger threatening especially our moral preaching, is to distort its meaning and weaken its appeal. A more detailed account of the themes of Christian preaching may be found in the writings connected with the catechetical revival.

Our initial conversion underlies all our Christian life. We never leave it behind, and our communion with Christ but deepens it. All catechesis includes, at least implicitly, a call to conversion. It springs from the *kerygma* or proclamation of the good news and is simply its organic development, the display of its full implications. This kerygmatic bearing of catechesis is particularly important in the instruction of Catholic children, who must be led to make their adherence to the faith a truly personal decision. The conversion of the unbeliever must find its counterpart at some point in the lives of Catholics. The failure to evoke such a conversion explains the ease with which so many Catholics lapse.

Both evangelization and catechesis must respect the objective structure of the Christian message. What enables us to achieve this is the existence of the Bible as the perennial centre around which the teaching of the Church always revolves. The Bible has given the mystery of salvation a primordial verbal expression, which is the exemplar and norm of our preaching. The value of its contents as a source lies not only in their fecundity but also in their divinely guaranteed balance and proportions.

If Christian preaching has permanent features, it carries with it an urgent necessity of adaptation. It is not enough to offer the Christian message in biblical terms. The task of a living voice is to preach divine truth to each generation in a way that it can understand. Preaching seeks to arouse a personal act of faith. Its fruitfulness presupposes an intelligent grasp of what is said. We do not preach to infants or unconscious adults. And a man cannot believe what has no meaning for him. We must make contact with the minds of our hearers. We must enter into their mentality and try to discover the thoughts and desires to which we can link the Christian message. That does not mean that we can leave aside entirely the biblical and traditional categories. There are certain ideas and themes that must be conveyed to every generation. We cannot change them, any more than we can change the basic symbolism of the sacraments. If they are no longer meaningful to our people, we must make them meaningful. Examples of these are salvation, glory, grace, the kingdom of God, the exodus, witness, mystery, life, resurrection and spirit. These cannot be replaced, but we must get them across. We must explain them in a way that means something to people today. An immense effort of adaptation is required. It demands a deep understanding of the Christian message itself and an insight into the minds of modern people. Only through such an effort will our preaching be a real preaching and not a fruitless sign.

Not much has been said in recent writing on the theology of preaching about the attitude required in the hearers. Place, however, should be found for an analysis of what is appropriate in those who listen to the word of God. Since preaching is addressed to faith, the qualities required for faith may give us our clue. First, an openness to God's grace. The attitude with which people listen to a sermon should not be that with which they listen to an ordinary talk on the radio. It should be similar to the one with which they approach the sacraments. Preaching offers them the grace of God, and their hearts must be ready to receive this. Secondly, such openness implies generosity. Faith is a surrender of ourselves to God; there should be no reservations, but a willingness to follow the suggestions of the Spirit, whatever the cost. Thirdly, faith is an obedience. It is an assent made in darkness as a homage to God. We sacrifice our intellectual independence and cease to rely exclusively on the native light of our own mind. The obedience characteristic of faith is intensified by the fact that the word of God comes to us through men. Obedience to the Church secures what is basic to faith, namely, the surrender of the autonomy of our reason, and thus offsets the danger of a reliance on our own unaided intellect, which is ultimately destructive of faith. Basically, the attitude of those who hear the word should be humble obedience, with a recognition of the priest as a divinely appointed witness. But we should want our faithful to be mature Christians, and Christian maturity includes an ability to discern clearly the human element in the Church. Preaching is often defective, if rarely frankly erroneous, and any failure of our hearers to perceive its defects is due to ignorance, not faith. Humble obedience is not the same as blind submissiveness. But, just as in our general attitude to the Church, recognition of its divine character is primary and a critical awareness of its human defects but secondary, so also in the attitude of our hearers, humble obedience to the word should be primary and a critical appraisal of the inadequacy of the preacher but secondary. As for ourselves, far from exploiting such an attitude by aggressive self-assertion, we should be able to say to our hearers what St. Paul said to his: "After all, it is not ourselves we proclaim; we proclaim Christ Jesus as Lord, and ourselves as your servants for Jesus' sake" (2 Cor. 4.5, KV).

We are living within the history of salvation. The present stage of that history is the age of the Church on earth. Now, preaching is the characteristic of this period, which will last till the Second Coming of Christ. The reason why the Second Coming is delayed is the preaching of the Gospel, for it is held back until the Gospel has been preached to men. Preaching is a sacred task. We are very conscious of our role as ministers of Christ's sacraments, but are we sufficiently aware of our role as ministers of God's word? Yet, we are given the ministry of the word by the power of order, and it is, as we have seen, a mediation of grace. Recent studies of the sacrament of Holy Orders have shown how the Christian priesthood is essentially related to the ministry of the word as well as to the Eucharist, a point comparatively neglected since the Reformation. The sacraments and the word are the two components in the structure of the Church. They are and must be the two concerns of our ministry as priests.

CHAPTER V

FAITH AND DISSIDENT CHRISTIANS

It is unfortunately true that Catholics sometimes call in question the existence and very possibility of a genuine Christian faith in those separated from the Church. On the popular level, the ambiguity of our language about the conversion of other Christians is a frequent cause of misunderstanding. When these return to the Church, we speak of them coming to the faith or receiving the gift of faith, and people are led to think that before conversion the converts did not have a true supernatural faith. But the refusal of faith to non-Catholics is occasionally maintained in a more learned way. Protestants, we are told, accept many Christian truths but they have not the right motive; their assent springs from private judgement, so that their acceptance of these truths is not the assent of faith. Or it is argued that without the infallible guidance of the Church a man cannot know with the certitude necessary for faith that a given truth is divinely revealed; his so-called faith becomes then a personal and arbitrary preference. Or it is urged that since one or other article of faith is denied the whole assent is vitiated; for divine faith is one and indivisible.

These attacks on the genuineness of the faith of dissident Christians have not been invented for this occasion; they have been heard. But it is to be doubted whether those who launch them realize the consequences of what they say. To deny the Christian faith to anyone is to deny him the Christian life. Faith is the fundamental act of the Christian life; on it all the rest depends. Without a genuine and supernatural faith, there can be no Christian life. To say that a person is without a true faith is to say that he is without the life of grace and in the state of sin. A compromise attitude which would question the validity of a non-Catholic's faith while admitting the sincerity of his Christian life makes no sense theologically; it is, in fact, untenable/Faith is the root of every Christian life; it is basic to the life of grace wherever this is found. To refuse the gift of faith to dissident Christians is to declare spurious their Christian life.

/ Such an attitude would be unjust and disastrous. There are no grounds for declaring it the attitude of the Catholic Church. A recent work[1] examines carefully the papal documents on Church unity and finds that Rome recognizes the presence of a true divine faith among Protestant Christians; this, besides the warmer acknowledgement accorded to the Christian life of the Eastern dissidents. Modern theologians do not hesitate in this matter. Many of the questions discussed in theology today would be meaningless, were it not for the assumption of a genuine Christian faith and life in those visibly separated from the Church. And, needless to say, Catholic ecumenical work is possible only because there exist real Christian values in other communions; and every Christian value is the fruit of faith./

Our separated brethren have a true Christian faith. Granted. No claim is being made here to judge any individual person. Only God knows the sincerity or insincerity of each one who remains outside the unity of the Church. All the same, we are entitled to conclude from the fact that their position is due to historical causes outside their control and from the many signs of Christian life among them that the multitude of separated Christians around us are sincere, and consequently enjoy a true Christian faith and life. Such a situation gives rise to various problems which are worth discussing. Faith is in truth one and indivisible; how can it be possessed by those who differ from us in creed? Has not the Church an indispensable role to play in faith? What is meant by conversion? Does not the convert receive the gift of faith? Can a false Church be said to mediate genuine Christian faith to its

---

[1] *That They May Be One: A Study of Papal Doctrine* (*Leo XIII–Pius XII*), by Gregory Baum, O.S.A. (London, 1958), pp. 40–64. (Westminster, Newman, 1958.) This essay was worked out in its main lines before I read Fr. Baum's work, but it proved most useful in the final stages of preparation.

members? To discuss such questions is the purpose of this chapter.

It seems best to begin by examining in a general way the part of the Church in our act of faith. The Church is not the motive of our faith. The motive of divine faith is, and can only be, the uncreated Truth of God. Faith always involves a personal encounter with God as Truth. Faith is a theological virtue, and that means that by it we must attain God himself. Our faith rests on nothing less than the reality of God, and by our act of faith we are brought into contact with God as the First Truth. The Church can in no way take the place of God as the motive of faith. We must never think of the Church as an intermediary in the sense of a substitute for God, as if our actual motive were the authority of the Church alone, which we could establish to our satisfaction to have the backing of God. No fear of illuminism must make us forget the theological character of faith and that the act of faith is, through grace, a meeting between God and each individual believer. Apart from being essential to any understanding of divine faith, a realization of the personal structure of faith and the divine encounter it involves will enable us to see something of the working of faith in those separated from the Church.

The Church enters in because of the way God has chosen to communicate himself to men. To develop this. Faith comes from without. That means that the object of faith, together with the signs that accredit it as from God, is presented to our minds from outside by preaching and by the testimony of witnesses. If we are to believe, God must speak to us. He must make a revelation. He does this by putting before us from without by the action of men and by external and perceptible means a message claiming to be from God and marked by signs of its divine origin. The total object of faith is presented in this way; in the economy of the Christian faith—we are not speaking of the process of immediate revelation —there is no direct action of God that places any new object of faith before the mind. But there is a direct action of God on the soul in faith. Faith is supernatural and requires the grace of God. To believe, a person must receive the interior grace of God. This grace of faith is a divine enlightenment of the mind that enables it to interpret what confronts it from without, to recognize the message as the Word of God and to give the assent of faith to it as the communication of God's Truth. It is interesting to note that this interior enlightenment also used to be called revelation. The divine revelation to which our faith is a response includes both the presentation of the object from without and the action of God from within. Such is the way God communicates himself to men. In and through such a revelation he offers himself to each one for the personal union of faith. He, uncreated truth, remains the motive which our act attains; the created means he uses—the external signs and testimony, the graces—form the necessary conditions on which faith depends.

And what is the part of the Church? God set up the Church as the universal and infallible witness of his total revelation. The Church in this role simply continues the work of Christ. When God the Son became man, the Word of God was made present in this world in the thoughts, words and actions of a man. Christ was the Word of God. Faith is always to surrender the mind to the Truth of God and to measure one's thought on the thought of God. Faith has now become surrender to Christ and also measuring one's thoughts on the thought of Christ. It is not simply a question of accepting a list of truths on the testimony of Christ. What is necessary is a surrender to the all-embracing authority of Christ as being the incarnation of the living Word of God and the total revelation of God to men. The Church is the extension of Christ. He established his followers as one community, hierarchically organized, and committed to this community the fullness of his revelation. That community was to persist in this world to the end of time and was to possess always and without fail in the unity of its faith the integral revelation of Christ. That is why the faith of the Church is infallible. It must be, as the permanent embodiment in this world of the revelation given in Christ. It is also the reason for the promise of infallibility given to the magisterium. In an infallible Church those who have the power and function to proclaim authoritatively and to judge definitively the deposit of faith possessed by the Church must be infallible.

The Church thus exists as the universal witness to the truth of Christ. Her faith always represents the integral revelation of Christ. To measure our thought on the thought of the Church is to measure it on the thought of Christ. To submit to the faith and teaching of the Church is to submit to the truth of Christ. We must surrender our minds in faith to the Church as we would surrender them in faith to Christ. Or, rather, we surrender them to Christ in the Church. To believe the Church is, in this sense, to believe God. Not that the Church is the motive of faith, or that we encounter only the Church, not God, in faith, but that God is present in the Church as he was present in Christ and we meet him in and through the Church. He comes to us across the testimony of the Church. The Church is the place of our encounter; it is the instrument of God's communication. The testimony of the Church conditions the manner in which we reach the motive of our faith. *Divine* faith involves a surrender to God as First Truth; *Christian* faith is essentially the same faith, but it adds the characteristic of a surrender to Christ as the Incarnate Word of God; *Catholic* faith is again essentially the same, but it adds the characteristic of a surrender to the Church as the permanent embodiment of the truth of Christ.

This mediation of the object of faith by the Church has two aspects. First, she has within herself all the signs of credibility designed by God to lead men to the faith. The Church has without fail in her faith and teaching the full truth of Christ. She is the extension of Christ—his Body, united to him in a mysterious union of life. For these reasons, the various signs of credibility are present within her and point to her. There are the signs inherent in her doctrine: its sublimity, harmony and divine wisdom; the signs manifesting the strength and fruitfulness of her life based on that doctrine: her holiness, unity, catholicity and stability; then, the miracles and charismatic gifts bestowed on her from time to time. The Church stands in the world, drawing men to the truth of Christ. Her own children are never left without abundant signs of her divine origin. Second, the Church is the guardian and rule of faith. The object of faith is complex; there are many truths to be believed. The individual believer tends to go astray, to mix error with the divine message and to be confused by the problems and questions to which the faith gives rise. The Catholic has in the Church an infallible guide. The closer he unites himself to the faith of the Church the purer will be his faith. Guided and instructed by the Church, his faith can steadily grow and become increasingly explicit. This greater explicitness will give him a fuller grasp of the truth of Christ and enrich his life of faith. Questions can be definitively settled when this is necessary. Ob-

scurities do arise and do create difficulties and cause harm, but
the divine message remains intact and the Catholic knows that in
the faith of the Church he has always the integral revelation of
Christ.

This account of the Church and faith may have seemed in-
ordinately long, but it allows us to tackle the question of the faith
of dissident Christians with greater ease. The principle which
governs their situation is that they still receive faith through the
mediation of the Church, but this mediation is partially frustrated
in regard to them. The mediation of the Church extends beyond its
visible boundaries as a society. It does so because the different
dissident bodies retain in varying degrees elements that belong to
the Church. Some of her possessions exist outside as well as inside
her unity. All recognize that in relation to the sacrament of
baptism. Baptism as a sacrament belongs to the Church; it is hers
even when administered outside her unity, and it attaches to her
anyone who receives it. There are other elements, similarly part of
her divine inheritance, which are found not only within her visible
unity but also outside of it. Among these elements are those that
minister to faith.

What are the means through which our separated brethren hear
the Gospel? Above all comes the Bible, the inspired Word of God,
the very centre of all the teaching of the Church. A number of
Catholic theologians, returning to the older tradition, even see the
Bible as containing the whole of Christian revelation. Then there
is preaching based on the Bible. This may draw as well on the past
tradition of the Church and the past declarations of her teaching
authority, though the extent to which this is so will vary considerably in the different Christian bodies. Indeed, the present teaching
of the Church may be said to have its influence on some who,
while rejecting her full claims, allow themselves to be guided by
her faith through the writings of her theologians or the decisions of
her magisterium. Through all this the Church is able to fulfil
partially her role as the *ministra fidei* and to place before dissident Christians the message of Christ. They do not recognize it as
coming from her. They may be illogical, for example, in accepting
the Bible, which is the Church's book, and rejecting the Church,
but the important point here is that they have the Bible. Thus,
owing to the Church and in various ways, they are confronted in

part with the revelation of Christ. They have not its fullness, and what they have is accompanied with error, but there is a sufficient presentation for an act of faith.

Such a presentation of the Christian message carries with it sufficient though diminished signs of its credibility. There are the signs inherent in the doctrine itself and those connected with its fruitfulness in those who live by it. This fruitfulness results in the fact that, although the notes of the Church can be found all together and in their fullness only in the Catholic Church, some degree of them may be present in a dissident communion. It may not be possible to discern the total revelation of Christ apart from the true Church, but any reasonable theology of faith must admit the credibility present in a lesser presentation of the Christian message.

If the object of faith is there, the interior grace of faith is not lacking. Most will have received the virtue of faith by their baptism in childhood, and all the further graces necessary will be given by God. All such graces are given by God in relationship with the Church, and they attach the person to the Church. Any culpable refusal of the Church is, then, a refusal of these graces and a rejection of God. But where there is sincerity, a dissident Christian is given that interior grace which enables him to recognize the Word of God in the divine message put before him and to give to it the assent of faith. Despite the mutilated state of the message and the errors with which it is mingled in the person's mind, there takes place the personal encounter of faith. God using as the instrument of his communication the truth that is there and illuminating it with his grace. With the surrender to God, there is *divine* faith; where there is a surrender to Christ as God and Saviour there is *Christian* faith.

Several problems come to mind at once. How far has the principle of private judgement destroyed the motive of faith among Protestants? How can there be a true faith where the person's professed creed is full of error? What is the role in faith of the dissident Churches as Churches?

Faith exists only when the mind bows down before the authority of God. We speak rightly of the obedience of faith. It is a free assent and an assent made in darkness. This assent is not unreasonable, because the mind is shown the credibility of the message; it sees that it is worthy of belief, sees, in fact, that it has a duty to accept it as from God. In faith, however, we do not assent to the message because we see its inner truth or because we like it or because it fits in with our personal ideas or because we regard it as socially or ethically helpful; we assent to it simply because it is the Word of God, and we do so in an act that is a surrender of our minds to God as Truth. Faith is a personal decision, but it is not a private choice of creed. The principle of choosing for oneself and insisting on an autonomy of personal judgement is inimical to faith and ultimately destructive of it. Is the attitude of Anglicans and Protestants dominated by such a principle?

The answer, I think, must be No. The mass of devout Anglicans and Protestants do not arrogate to themselves a freedom of choice before the Word of God but recognize the duty of submission. The basic attitude essential to faith is there and is manifested in their lives and in their writings. What obscures its presence, particularly to the eyes of many Catholics, and what in reality endangers it, is the absence of any clear rule of faith. We must not, however, in this matter confuse the motive and the rule of faith. That we must surrender our minds unconditionally to the Word of God in faith would be granted readily by our separated brethren. They think of this more easily in a personal form as a surrender to God or to Christ. That does not make their submission less authentic—far from it! But what is the Word of God and how are we to determine the content of the divine message? Here confusion reigns.

The devout Protestant reading his Bible and convinced that God speaks to each man individually in its pages is often filled with a deep submissiveness to the Word of God, nor is he entirely wrong about the action of God in the Scriptures. He has a real faith. What he lacks is the recognition of the corporate rule of faith established by Christ. Catholics have as their rule of faith the faith and teaching of a Church indefectibly one and infallible. This is a rule of faith admirably adapted by its corporate and hierarchical character to strengthen and secure the basic attitude of faith, an attitude of surrender and obedience. In contrast, we all know the inadequate substitutes for this rule among dissident Christians: the appeal to the Bible privately interpreted, to the Church of the Fathers, to sound scholarship, to the consent of undivided Christendom and so on. This inadequacy has deplorable consequences for the object of faith and leads to the multiplication of errors, but it can still leave intact the basic attitude of obedience to the Word of God. There will then still be an act of faith motivated by God's Truth.

Nevertheless, the absence of a clear rule of faith is a danger not only for the object of faith but also for its motive. The spirit and principle of free enquiry does not seem to have been specifically Protestant in origin. The following remark of the Protestant pastor Max Thurian is interesting, not only as asserting this, but also as a testimony to the modern Protestant attitude on the matter. He writes: "The doctrine of free examination has never been received in orthodox Protestantism and does not derive its foundation from the Reformers of the sixteenth century; it has had some fortune in the liberal theologies of the nineteenth century. The doctrine has bit by bit destroyed the true spirit of Protestantism."[2] The outlook in question originated, it seems, in the humanist Renaissance and the related cultural movements. However, as part of the cultural background of the time, it was bound to influence and to some extent coalesce with the Reformation break with authority. At any rate, all know the ravages it eventually caused, from the eighteenth century onwards, in the heyday of rationalism and liberal Protestantism, and, although there has been a strong and healthy reaction, the spirit is by no means dead.

Now, it would be quite wrong to declare sweepingly that liberalism in religion destroyed faith in all who were infected by it. Few men are entirely consistent; most are influenced by principles to which they do not allow full play, and the grace of God is never lacking. But what can be asserted is that the mentality engendered in religion by rationalism and liberalism, with its antidogmatic prejudices, its arrogant claim to autonomy of reason, its rejection of the supernatural and its rebellion against all authority, is diametrically opposed to faith. Newman continually insisted on this. The Church has never underestimated the value of reason, even where revealed truth is concerned, and she has frequently stressed the complete compatibility between reason and faith. None the less it remains true that faith requires us to sacrifice the autonomy of our reason, and the sacrifice is mortifying because of the darkness of faith. Faith is a surrender of mind that calls for humility

2 Quoted in Baum, *op. cit.*, p. 150, n. 90.

and obedience, and fallen man does not always find this easy. To go beyond the sphere where reason can exult in its own light is hard to pride.

Catholics find this so. But Catholics are protected and helped in this matter by their rule of faith. We live the life of faith in union with the faith of the Church and subject to the authority of her hierarchy. The corporate, authoritative and clear character of this rule of faith provides a context and a discipline to our faith that strengthen its basic surrender. Our faith is in an environment where it can grow steadily greater in respect of its motive: that is, we can become increasingly surrendered to God, with the submission of faith more deeply rooted in our souls. It is the absence of a clear and adequate rule of faith that leaves dissident Christians exposed to tendencies that, in themselves, are destructive of faith. When there is no corporate rule of faith—and what does Anglican comprehensiveness mean but that?—when the decision about the revealed character of different truths is left to a personal judgement, when the ultimate appeal is to human learning, so that scholars rather than the simple inherit the kingdom of heaven, the mind is ill-prepared for a surrender that sometimes goes against its personal preferences or is inimical to its cherished ideas, or, at the very least, goes beyond what we can judge for ourselves. The very principles which are opposed to faith are brought in alongside of it, in order to do service as the rule of faith. The sincere Christian life of so many shows that the danger to faith is often overcome by the grace of God. All the same, an important difference in situation between the faith of Catholics and that of dissident Christians is that the latter is continually threatened by forces that attack it in what it is by its very essence, a homage motivated simply by the unseen Truth of God.

But granted that, despite all, the motive of faith in sincere Christians outside the Church remains intact, what about the numerous errors in what they believe? How can there be a true faith where the creed professed is full of errors? It is useful here to recall a few principles. The virtue of faith, the theologians tell us, is infallible wherever it is found. What they mean is that the virtue of faith draws us only to what is truly divine revelation, and that there cannot be an act of faith having error as its object. But because faith is infallible, it does not follow that each believer is infallible. The subject who possesses faith is not infallible, because he possesses faith only imperfectly and is not completely submissive to its influence. Faith does not lay full hold on his mind and he is but partially subject to its promptings. Other forces co-exist with faith in his mind and hamper and obscure its workings. Were a man completely possessed by faith and entirely subject to it, then it would give him a perfect discernment in matters of belief, but that is an ideal that is not realized.

As it is, our imperfect faith can and does co-exist with errors. What is the result? A mental state or conviction where erroneous opinion and true belief come together in the mind in an organic unity. In a way the believer himself cannot analyse, there is mixed up in his mind an object to which he is drawn by faith under the light of divine grace and various erroneous opinions which he holds for a variety of reasons. (We are leaving out of account here the clumsiness in conceptual formulation or verbal expression which may sometimes be found, owing to lack of training or even to the newness of a problem. Such clumsiness need not imply any intellectual error in the mind, whatever the appearances to the contrary.) The presence of error may be found in a Catholic believer —in fact, it is often found. An ordinary Catholic may have, intermingled with his understanding of Catholic doctrine owing to bad instruction, a number of false ideas. A theologian may be mistaken in holding a doctrine as of faith when it is not, or denying it when it is. No inculpable error of this kind destroys faith, though it does lessen the purity with which the object of faith is grasped. And we must not dismiss as of no significance the possession of a reasonably correct and full knowledge of the object of faith.

While all this is true, any genuine faith must, in a certain sense, be total in its grasp of revealed truth. The believer must accept, at least implicitly, all that God has revealed. The motive of faith demands this. The reason for our faith is the authority of God; our act of faith is a surrender to God as Truth. Were we to refuse to accept something which God has revealed, we should show that we had not so surrendered our minds. It would prove that what we did accept was not accepted in homage to God as Truth but for some other motive. Faith, then, necessarily includes a willingness to accept everything that God has revealed; it therefore implicitly embraces the totality of divine revelation. To deny culpably but one article of faith is to destroy faith completely and to render impossible any true faith in the rest of revelation. But the denial of revealed truth may be inculpable; in that case faith remains. Then is found the paradoxical situation of a man implicitly believing what he explicitly denies. This would be a plain absurdity were the motive of our assent to the truths of faith our perception of their inner truth. But our motive is the authority of God, a motive extrinsic to the truths of faith, which leaves their inner truth unseen and in obscurity. It is possible for such a motive to cover implicitly matters that we do not yet know explicitly or which we, not knowing them to be revealed, deny on other grounds.

Even for a Catholic, then, his true faith may not coincide with the creed or list of truths in which he professes belief. The Catholic Church is infallible, and the Catholic in his act of Catholic faith implicitly accepts all the Church teaches. The creeds of the Church, which the Catholic thus makes his own, are free from error. But if we asked an individual Catholic to sit down and write what he believed, his statement of his faith might well contain some surprising omissions and some remarkable errors. His creed, in the sense of his personal knowledge of the object of faith, is by no means always perfect. This indicates that there is, in fact, no particular difficulty in admitting that in the sincere non-Catholic a true divine faith co-exists with a professed creed that is riddled with errors. The same principles apply, although the errors and omissions are usually more numerous and more damaging. His faith is implicitly total, though his knowledge of its object is lamentably deficient and mingled with errors.

However, in a very important respect, he is situated differently from the Catholic. A Catholic is in a position which makes possible a steady and secure development of his faith and a purification of his mind from error. He believes in visible union with the one and infallible Church and in subjection to the divine rule of faith. He only has to unite himself closely to the life of the Church and draw as fully as he can on her life and teaching, for his faith to grow and become ever more explicit, with a corresponding enrichment of his spiritual life, and for the errors due to his ignorance to be gradually rectified. We need not deny that such growth and purification has its own problems and is not always smooth, but the setting and means are there for normal development. On the other hand, the Christian separated from the Church receives his faith set in a framework of error and with no regular means of rectifying this. The dissident body from which he receives his faith owes its existence to error as well as to the truth it retains; it purveys error in the same way as it purveys truth. Error will be mingled with the truth in what surrounds the individual Christian and in what is given to him to nourish his Christian life. As he tries sincerely to live that Christian life, the grace of faith will exert its influence and power, but it will be hampered by the force of the errors in the dissident creeds, which will war against it and tend to destroy it. His faith can in fact only fully develop by breaking free of the environment which he has been taught to regard as inseparable from it. In the mental struggle that often ensues, the normal external aids established by God are to a great extent lacking. His providence will not fail the sincere believer in his anomalous situation, but that situation is, all the same, anomalous and dangerous. It explains the dialectic of truth and error that marks the life of dissident Christians.

A Christian outside the unity of the Church receives his faith through his membership of some dissident Christian communion. Has, then, a dissident Church a part in mediating Christian faith? A simple Yes or No is not enough here. To determine theologically the exact status of the separated Christian Churches is a difficult problem, still under discussion. Clearly these are not members or branches of the Catholic Church. To hold otherwise would be to deny that the Catholic Church is the one true Church, preserving an unbroken unity. On the other hand, they are clearly societies possessing a certain historical and sociological identity. Are they, as societies, simply human in nature? In other words, is there outside the Catholic Church only a multitude of individual Christians, with nothing supernatural of an ecclesiastical nature? The existence of the Orthodox Churches, with all that there is of value in their institutions, tradition and liturgy, forbids us to answer in the affirmative. But in what sense can we admit the existence of other genuinely Christian Churches?

We have seen that elements belonging to the Church, things which are part of her divine heritage, can continue to exist outside

her unity. Such elements are not merely elements that concern
the individual Christian as an individual. They are elements which
bring Christians together and contribute to the work of building
the Church. The dissident Church unites in its structure as an
historical society two different kinds of components. There are
heretical and schismatic components, to which it owes its existence
as a group outside the unity of the true Church. There are the
Christian components, such as baptism, the Bible, sometimes
apostolic succession, various Christian traditions, customs and institutions, which give to these societies a partially Christian structure as societies. Something of the reality of a Christian Church
is found in them. The proportion of Christian components in their
structure will vary enormously from one dissident group to another.
The Orthodox Churches seem to have practically everything that
forms a local Church, while lacking that which integrates a local
Church into the unity of the one, universal Church. That is why
Rome always refers to the dissident Eastern bodies as Churches,
while it avoids the term in speaking of the Protestant bodies. A
significant official usage, though it is not intended to prevent us,
in ordinary usage, using the term "Church" in a looser way. In
both cases, however, we are confronted, not simply with a mass
of individual Christians, but with groups that are partially Christian and supernatural in their structure and significance.

It is not surprising, then, to find that these Christian bodies do
fulfil the task of making the revelation of Christ present in the
world and bringing the truth of Christ to men. It is true that their
role in this respect is ambivalent. They propagate their errors
as well as the truth. That does not prevent their work achieving
a sufficient presentation of the Gospel to give rise, under the grace
of God, to a truly divine and Christian faith in their members
and in those whom they convert. The resulting problem of the
co-existence of error with faith has already been examined. This
function of ministering to Christian faith belongs to them, not by
that which separates them from the Catholic Church, but by that
which they still retain of her heritage. In the ultimate analysis, it
is still the Catholic Church that is mediating the faith to those
who receive it through the dissident bodies. She is doing so
through elements that have never ceased to belong to her and

that she can still claim as her own, but which are existing and continuing to bear fruit outside her visible unity as a society.

A consequence is that our attitude to the dissident Christian communions cannot be a simple one. Careful discernment is called for. We cannot dismiss in a single judgement their life and activity. It is quite unsound to rejoice in their decline or to lament their progress as if it were simply the progress or decline of error. When their progress is the progress of the Christian values they retain, it is in effect the progress of the Catholic Church. Everything that they have of Christian value and truth must be counted among the possessions of the Catholic Church, despite the anomalous condition of its existence. We must therefore rejoice in any progress in the separated Churches that marks an advance in what is truly Christian, while we must deplore anything that indicates a further encroachment of error. We must do what we can to preserve what they have that comes from Christ and through his Church, and help them to disentangle it from error. A simply negative approach is as much a betrayal of what we believe and hold dear as is a simply positive approach.

From the dissident Churches we must turn again to their individual members and discuss the implications of their conversion to the Catholic Church. What, theologically speaking, is the nature of such a conversion? A matter of terminology must first be dealt with. For the Scholastics the term "heretic" always meant someone who was culpable in his denial of the faith; a heretic was one who was pertinacious, or sinfully obstinate, in his rejection of revealed doctrine. To speak of a heretic in good faith would have seemed as odd to them as, for example, to speak of a murderer in good faith seems to us. Likewise, "heresy" properly designated a sin, not a mere error in doctrine, however serious. The same applied to the terms "schism" and "schismatic." A later terminology has, however, abstracted the element of guilt from these terms and given them a wider application. "Heresy" can mean simply a doctrine opposed to a dogma of faith and a "heretic" one who holds such a doctrine, whether in good faith or bad faith. Hence, there can be innocent heretics as well as sinful heretics. Both terminologies are reflected in the *Code of Canon Law,* but it is interesting to notice that in the papal documents examined by Fr. Baum the older usage is followed. The documents do not speak of heretical and schismatic Churches or communities but of dissident Churches or communities; they never speak of heretics in good faith but of dissidents or separated brethren.[3]

If we follow the older terminology, sincere non-Catholic Christians are not heretics or schismatics, whereas in the newer usage they are heretics or schismatics in good faith. The first usage seems preferable, if only to avoid arousing unnecessary resentment through the ambiguity of the terms and the infamy they implied in the past. We may speak then of dissident Christians. Dissidents in bad faith are heretics or schismatics; dissidents in good faith can be called more warmly our separated brethren. But what is more important than the terms used is the different nature of conversion in the case of these two different kinds of dissident Christians.

The heretic by his guilty rejection of revealed truth has lost his faith. He no longer has any Christian faith. If he still holds some Christian truths and is a heretic not an apostate, he does not hold them by supernatural faith. His conversion is a return to faith, which must be achieved by a repentance for his sin of heresy. Such repentance involves an abjuration of his heretical opinions. All repentance includes a detestation of the sin committed, and detestation for the sin of heresy means the abjuration of the heretical errors which the heretic has been guilty of holding. In his repentance the heretic receives once more the gift of faith. Such a conversion may be a return to the Catholic Church; it may, however, be a conversion to the Christian faith in some separated Church, where the presentation of the Christian faith on which it is based still remains imperfect.

The conversion to the Catholic Church of a dissident in good faith means something different. What is involved can best be described as a growth in Christian faith, leading to a crisis of faith and resulting in a return to the Church. It is a growth or an unfolding of faith. Such converts do not receive in their conversion the interior gift of faith; they already have it. Their conversion manifests an increase in the faith they possess. The increase is made notable by their new acceptance from the Church of the full content of Christian revelation, which they had until now

---

[3] *Op. cit.,* p. 143, n. i, and p. 68. For a full discussion of this question of terminology, see Charles Journet, *L'Église du Verbe Incarné,* II (Paris, 1951), pp. 708–18.

known only in a mutilated form. Such an enrichment in the object of their faith will lead, if they co-operate with God's grace, to great progress in their life of faith and a consequent increase in the virtue of faith itself. Their faith also changes its situation by their reunion with the Church and submission to the divine rule of faith. But more of that in a moment. The point here is that their conversion is not a return to faith, using "faith" to mean the interior gift of divine faith, although it can be called a return to *the* faith, meaning by this the integral object of faith given by the teaching of the Church.

Such a conversion is usually the culmination of a long process of growth in faith. The growth will have had both a positive and a negative aspect. Positively, there must be an ever greater hold on the Christian truths already possessed; an increasing influence of these in the life of the person. Negatively, the influence of the errors in which the truths are enmeshed must weaken, and then eventually the errors are left aside. They are aside; it is not a question of abjuration of them, because they have never been pertinaciously held. (We are concerned here with the interior nature of conversion, not with the requirements of the external forum, determined by the canonists on different criteria.) A sincere Christian coming to the truth does not have to repent of his errors, because he has never guiltily held them. He simply gives them up when confronted with the truth. It is similar to the way a theological student, studying the treatise on grace and finding that he has held semi-Pelagian views, begins to make his own the authentic Catholic teaching. The difference between the two cases will lie in the greater psychological difficulty and the consequent mental struggle of the convert, but such a struggle need not imply the least disloyalty to faith nor any guilty countenancing of error. If there has been some fault, say negligence, short of a sinful denial of revealed truth, the convert must repent accordingly; such a repentance is still different in nature from an abjuration of heresy.

No attempt is being made here to simplify the incredible complexities of conversion as it actually occurs. The purpose is simply to indicate a few theological principles governing the matter. The growth referred to may be realized in an endless variety of ways. Sometimes it will be almost exclusively positive; the convert's faith has been perhaps of the vaguest kind and he simply advances steadily in his knowledge of Christian revelation, after he has made contact with the Catholic Church. For others, the negative side will be acutely marked, and they will come to the Church only after much searching and mental anguish. But in all cases, conversion must be said to involve a crisis of faith, however little or great be the spiritual disturbance caused by this. And for this reason. Every conversion must be a personal decision, and in the choice which confronts the person the very existence of his faith is at stake. Faced with conversion, the person now sees his duty of accepting Catholic teaching as the revealed truth of God. He knows that he must assent to it as the Word of God and now realizes that the motive of his faith covers the Catholic claims. His faith remains a free assent; he can give it or refuse it. If he refuses, he destroys entirely the Christian faith he already possesses. Faith must be total; a refusal of one revealed truth is enough to extinguish it completely. The person has failed in the crisis and is now a heretic. On the other hand, if the person gives his assent, his faith is not only preserved but considerably strengthened. The resolution of the crisis then brings him into the unity of the Church. This changes the situation of his faith. It no longer exists in the anomalous and dangerous situation described above, but is now placed in the environment connatural to it, with the rule of faith and the other normal means established by God for its protection and development. He has not lost what he possessed but gained what he lacked. He had belonged to the Church in an initial and incomplete way; now he enjoys full membership.

While we must rejoice at the conversion to the Catholic Church of any of our separated brethren, it would be wrong to limit the task of the Church in regard to dissident Christians to one of convert-making. Our belief in the Catholic Church undoubtedly requires us to hold that the reunion of Christendom will mean the return of all Christians to the unity of the Catholic Church as the one, true Church of Christ. Our ultimate aim is and must be the return of all to the Church of Rome. Likewise, it is true that the absolute and revealed character of the Catholic claims means that, once recognized by a person, they imperiously demand the assent of his faith and reconciliation with the Church. Yet, unshakable as they are, these principles need supplementing when we try to determine our approach to the present complicated situation.

What are the facts? Millions of Christians are separated from the unity of the Church. They receive their Christian faith and live their Christian lives through the activity of the dissident Christian communions and in the setting of their institutions and traditions. This will continue, perhaps for a very long time, until—only God knows when and how—the reunion of Christendom is achieved. This is the situation that has called forth the ecumenical activity of the Church. What is mean by ecumenical activity? It is not the same as missionary activity properly so called. The missions of the Church are directed to those who have not yet received the preaching of the Gospel and who, though they may have through the grace of God an implicit supernatural faith, have not a faith based on the presentation of the Christian message. In contrast to this, the ecumenical action of the Church is addressed to those who have already heard the Gospel and have a Christian faith, but who have yet to be brought into the unity of the Church of Christ. The distinction helps us to see the special character and needs of ecumenical work.

What must characterize ecumenical activity is the recognition of Christian faith and life in those to whom it is directed. An objective assessment of the task it faces must include an acknowledgment of the Christian elements present in the dissident communities. That determines its immediate aim, which must be to foster and encourage all that is true and valuable in the separated Churches and to assist in eliminating the errors. This is a wider task than that of making converts. Those to whom God gives the grace of conversion are to be helped and welcomed by us. Their return is often a providential aid to the Church in her ecumenical activity. But over-eagerness to make converts must never lead us to despise or to trample upon anything that is truly Christian in the separated Churches. The Christian elements they retain belong to the Church, and it is our duty to cherish them. Apart from this, healing is always achieved by the strengthening of life; our separated brethren will be brought to the fullness of the truth by the growth of the life they possess and not by its decay. And when the fruits of their Christian life and traditions are brought eventually within the unity of the Church, her life will be enriched.

We know well enough that the Church, in her unbroken unity and indefectibility, has lost nothing essential by the damage inflicted by heresy and schism, but this does not exclude the fact that the return of all Christian gifts, now found in a state of separation, will be a real benefit to her life. Part of our task is to see that these gifts do not meanwhile perish.

The missionary work of the Church requires a sympathy, knowledge and appreciation of all that is sound in the customs and traditions of the peoples to whom it brings the Gospel. What sympathy, knowledge and appreciation are needed when confronted with the fruits of Christian faith in our separated brethren! The fact that these are marred with the fruits of error does not mean that we can be content with an attitude of opposition. What is called for is a work of delicate discernment, which will enable us to encourage what is true and combat what is false. The task demands an enlightened Christian charity. How far are we fulfilling it?

CHAPTER VI

THE CHURCH AND UNITY

What is the relation of the Church to unity of faith. Are we to conceive the unity of the Church as resulting from doctrinal unity or as prior to it? Are all Catholics agreed in doctrine because the Church is one, or is the Church one because all agree in holding the same doctrine? This is not a minor issue but a basic one. What is at stake is the necessary function of the Church as a visible community in mediating Christian faith. It is only in and through the Church as the visible community which stems from Christ and is animated by his Spirit that the faith of the Christian can exist in its fullness. It is the community in its wholeness and in its unity that ensures the integral possession and transmission of the Christian message. Our doctrinal unity exists because the Church is one, not vice-versa. The integral unity of faith presupposes the unity of the Church.

Most non-Catholics, I think it safe to say, hold the diametrically opposite view. This view has been put very forcibly by E. L. Mascall in *The Recovery of Unity: A Theological Approach*.[1] For the sake of both clarity and convenience, I shall refer to the general non-Catholic position in terms of Dr. Mascall's presentation of it.

Thus, at the very beginning of his book, Dr. Mascall expresses his conviction that the fundamental problem of Christian unity is a theological one. Taken in its immediate context, this statement has an acceptable meaning that a Catholic must heartily endorse; namely, it rejects the purely pragmatic approach of those who wish to get together without delay and bypass the theological

[1] New York and London, Longmans, 1959.

issues. Rightly such an approach is declared impossible. We are divided in doctrine and no genuine Christian unity can be other than doctrinal. Questions of doctrine are unavoidable, and there must be discussion of these on the deepest level if Christians are to be united once more. In that sense Christian unity is fundamentally a theological problem.

But Dr. Mascall, I think, means more by this than a Catholic would. For him we must and can achieve doctrinal unity by theological discussions. We must thrash out our differences, discuss theological questions as profoundly as we can, overcome the uncriticized assumptions that burden us from the past, and we shall achieve a unity of doctrine that will prepare the way for ecclesiastical unity. "Before we can achieve ecclesiastical unity we must achieve theological unity, and before we can achieve theological unity we must drastically examine our theology." At first sight nothing could seem more plausible, but it assumes that through a sound theology we shall be able to rebuild the unity of the Church. It is this claim to create the visible unity of the Church of Christ, the Messianic community on earth, that a Catholic cannot accept.

This refusal is familiar. What follows from it? That Christians have not to harmonize their faith by theological discussions and then establish themselves as a community of believers, but to receive the one faith in and through the visible unity of the community established by Christ. It is even true to say that the key division between Christians is not their doctrinal differences but the division of association. It is the division of association, the break with the Church, that gives a doctrinal difference its power to destroy unity of faith. Without such a break with the Church, a doctrinal difference or error is never a heresy. The basic question always remains this: have we to set about creating an association of believers by harmonizing their beliefs or does a Christ-given community already exist in order to mediate its corporate faith to men?

It would be possible to make much of the great difficulty of achieving a sufficient theological unity and of the extreme precariousness of it if ever achieved. Theologians have argued some points for centuries without coming near to resolving their differences. Is there any reason to suppose that the many doctrinal differences underlying the divisions of Christendom will ever be overcome simply by theological discussions? And suppose unity were achieved, what would prevent it being lost again after a short duration? It might indeed be retorted that such remarks show an undue pessimism about theological progress and neglect the role of the Holy Spirit, who is surely working to bring about the union of Christians. Certainly, no one would wish to give the impression of undervaluing the immense contribution that can be made by eirenic theological discussions. But can the unity of the Church be made dependent on theology? Is not rather theology dependent on the unity of the Church? To ask this is to see the objection to Dr. Mascall's approach.

Community of faith means more than similarity in faith. When Christ established the Church he set up a community with a corporate faith. It is in and through the corporate existence and life of that community that the Christian faith is continued and brought to men. Unity of faith demands the visible unity of the Church as a community. Outside of that, there will be but a similarity of belief, partially and precariously achieved from time to time. The weakness of the Anglo-Catholic position is that it cannot do justice to the role of the Church in the economy of faith. In the last analysis the Anglo-Catholic cannot avoid a Protestant ecclesiology. He believes that the Church is in some sense visibly one and that this unity comes from Christ, but he has, as he can, to reconcile this belief with an acceptance of the fact of a divided Church. This antinomy in his position prevents the proper appreciation of the visible unity of the Church as the means of ensuring unity of faith among Christians. This function of the Church is slurred over by remarks about the excessive stress placed by Catholics on the juridical aspect of the Church or by the emotive use of words such as "organization." But this is to cloud the issue. Even before jurisdiction or the magisterium is mentioned the unsoundness of the Anglican view becomes apparent. Anglicans cannot maintain the unity of the Church in the obvious sense of one undivided community. There is in fact no unity of association in the Church as they recognize it. They must hold that there are several Christian communities, communities severed from each other, with no unity of association between them. How, then, can there be a corporate faith? How can the

Church as a visible community mediate one faith to its members?

What is being upheld here is this. It was not the intention of
Christ that we possess the faith as isolated individuals or in
separate groups but as members of one community. Unity of faith
does not mean simply that we all have a similar faith and believe
the same truths; our faith is a corporate or communal faith. It is
derived from and dependent upon our membership of a community. The faith of the community is the rule of faith for the
individual believer; the faith of each Christian must be measured
against the faith of the Church. The fullness of Christ's message
is possessed and preserved, not by the individual as such, however learned, but by the Church as a community. The individual
Christian must purify and perfect his faith by thinking with the
Church. How topsy-turvy to put doctrinal unity first and see it as
a means towards ecclesiastical unity! Yet, what else can be done,
if there is not a sufficiently clear and consistent conception of the
visible unity of the Church to leave it at all effective in ensuring
a unity of faith?

When Dr. Mascall examines the distortions and mistaken assumptions that he considers as common to the theological thinking of all the Christian traditions, what is lacking in his analysis?
It is the recognition that there is in the visible Church an unfailing corporate faith which must be the rule of belief for each Christian. How can one maintain that all Christian groups are equally
in a doctrinal morass, from which all must try to emerge by
theological discussion, without equivalently denying this truth:
that Christ left one visible community, promising indefectibility
to its corporate faith and doing so precisely because in this way
the fullness of his revelation would remain present to each age
and be mediated to all men? Admittedly, fashionable intellectual
trends can obscure even Christian truth in the minds of men, but
are we in the last resort dependent on the sagacity and learning
of theologians for our discernment of the true teaching of Christ?

There is a distinction, and it is a very traditional one, between
inadequate theology within the Church and the aberrant thought
of those who refuse to think with the Church. There has been and
is much wrong thinking within the Church, and the nominalist
theology of the late Middle Ages is a conspicuous example, but
what makes a heresy is the will to continue in one's own thought

even in opposition to the faith of the Church. Although in a given age certain Christian truths may be generally neglected and obscured in the minds of the majority of the faithful, and theologians may distort what they are endeavouring to expound, what is truly the universal faith of the Church, what is genuinely the corporate belief of its members, always remains the integral and uncontaminated teaching of Christ. That is what is demanded by a Catholic view of the Church.

The same defect in Dr. Mascall's thinking reappears when he criticizes the Catholic attitude to the magisterium. He sees that the practical attitude of the Catholic believer to the teaching of the Church cannot be explained merely in terms of the juridical binding force of individual decrees, but he does not seem to perceive the basis of the more generous docility of the Catholic. That basis is the conviction that the corporate faith of the Church is of unfailing truth.

The fullness of the Christian revelation is preserved and transmitted in the corporate faith of the Church. The Christian does not live his life of faith as an isolated individual. He has his faith as a member incorporated into the Church of Christ. To the extent that the individual unites himself to the communal faith he cannot go astray, and in union with that faith lies the source of any genuine renewal and advance of his own faith. If that is so, is it surprising that both the ordinary faithful and theologians in the Catholic Church feel impelled to think with the Church and to treasure every sign of its corporate faith, even when the magisterium has not been led to issue any infallible decree? *Sentire cum Ecclesia:* that is the law of Catholic thinking. The duty of the Catholic in this respect does not cease when he has measured the precise degree of assent demanded by a particular decree. No ordinary believer has the right to impose his insights on others, and hence it is always necessary to determine the exact juridical force attached by authority to particular decisions; but the primary concern of the Catholic is the wider one of uniting himself as closely as possible to the faith of the Church. He is well aware that the different means and signs for declaring and discerning this corporate faith vary in their force. But he is guided here not merely by external decrees but also by the Holy Spirit, and his basic conviction is that there is but one corporate faith in the one

Church of Christ and that this faith is always the truth of Christ in its undiminished integrity. /

In parenthesis, we may note that many Anglicans might well say that they admit a general Catholic consciousness or a possession of Catholic truth by Christendom as a whole. Their view, however, must remain radically defective, because they are unable to maintain the existence of a genuine visible community. Consequently, any talk of a general Catholic faith disappears into vagueness. There cannot be a corporate faith and a corporate testimony to that faith where there is not one undivided community. A Christian cannot live his faith in union with the Church and conform his faith to that of the Church if the Church is broken up into a number of separate communities; even less so when these proclaim different doctrines. A living unity of faith demands that the Church be united as one community.

What, then, is the root issue between Dr. Mascall and ourselves? It is not, as he thinks, a particular interpretation of the magisterium. That question comes in the second place; that is, after one has recognized the oneness and indefectibility of the Church of Christ and proceeds then to investigate its structure and its organs. The fundamental issue is the ever-enduring presence of the integral revelation of Christ in the faith of a visible community that stems from him and is still united to him in the Holy Spirit. Is there a visible community in which men are associated together in the profession of one faith and which is so united to Christ that the corporate profession of faith always and without fail preserves and transmits the fullness of his message? That there is such a community is the Catholic contention. It is the Church, the Messianic community, the new People of God. Such a belief is incompatible with the idea of restoring the doctrinal unity of Christ's Church by theological discussion as a means towards the later establishment of ecclesiastical unity.

The same point may be made in another way. What is genuine teaching of Christ? It is the present belief and teaching of the Church is the Catholic reply. That question is a theological problem, replies Dr. Mascall; the genuine Christian tradition must be disentangled from the distortions it has suffered in the traditions of the different Christian denominations; at best our task of disengagement can have but a relative success, but the situation is at present more hopeful than before, because our theology has become much sounder; in a sound theology lies also the way to the recovery of Christian unity. Surely, what is at stake here is the conception of the Church of Christ and of its function in bringing faith to men.

After criticism, the task of a more positive analysis must not be shirked. What, then, is the role of the Church in the faith of its members? The Church with its authority is not the motive of our faith. Let that be clear. Faith is a theological virtue, and that means it enables us to encounter God. God alone is the motive of faith; we believe because in our act of faith we rest upon God as Truth. Whichever of the many explanations of faith is preferred, it is beyond doubt that nothing less than the uncreated Truth of God, present in some way to the mind, moves us when we assent to the divine message. That is the nature of an act of divine faith. It remains essentially the same when it is mediated by the Church and is called divine and Catholic faith. Why, then, does the Church intervene?

To answer this it is first necessary to see the way God offers himself to the mind in faith. The Christian message comes from outside the person in the form of an external testimony, marked with the signs of its divine origin. There is indeed an action of God on the mind, enlightening it so that it recognizes in the external testimony the presence and voice of God. Nevertheless, it is only in and through the external testimony that God makes himself known to the person and solicits his act of faith. The structure of signs through which the message is externally presented is used by God as the place and means of his self-disclosure. Now, the role of the Church is to provide a permanent and general testimony to the revelation of God in Christ. This testimony of the Church, it is important to note, is not a substitute for the divine disclosure itself—our faith remains divine and involves a personal encounter with God; but the teaching of the Church is where God presents himself to the mind and calls for its faith. In brief, the testimony of the Church is the condition of our motive of faith. It is that in and through which God offers himself to us for our acceptance.

This role of the Church as the general and permanent witness of the divine revelation simply continues the role of Christ. When

God became man, he became present to men in Christ in such a way that the thought and teaching of the man Jesus was the thought and teaching of God. To believe Christ was to believe God. In his human nature, he was the instrument of divine revelation. To mould one's thought on him was to mould one's thought on the thought of God. The Church, the Body of Christ, has to fulfil a similar function. The Church continues Christ as the general witness to the Christian revelation. To conform one's thought to the thought and testimony of the Church is to conform one's thought to God. Not that the Church is now in the place of God, but that God is present in the Church, making himself known through the Church, using the Church as the instrument by means of which he offers himself in the same revelation he made in Christ.

Christ left his followers visibly associated together. They continued to live a corporate life, possessing and developing their own institutions in accordance with the teaching he had given them. They were a society, a Church, forming in their association the new People of God. Christ had promised to be with them, he had sent them his Spirit, he had sanctioned beforehand as his own the teaching and authority of this Church. As Paul saw, the Church was the Body of Christ. Its unity transcended that of all merely human groups. All its members were united through baptism and the Eucharist with the risen body of Christ, the source from which salvation flows to men. The effects of these sacraments might be impeded in individual men, but the existence of the Church as a corporate entity was assured. How could it fail? This Church in what it is and believes and teaches is the permanent embodiment of the Christian revelation. This Church is Christ present to each age in what he was and what he taught.

This community, enjoying an unbroken life in Christ through the Spirit, possesses the truth of Christ. The Church preserves through the centuries the Christian revelation in its fullness. The revelation it has now is one and the same with the revelation that was given in its entirety already in the apostolic age; and it remains unchanged. Age differs from age in its understanding and appreciation of the riches of this revelation, and since there is an unbroken continuity in the Church there is a doctrinal progress as successive generations display its contents and develop their implications. But no new object is ever added by God to this deposit of truth given once for all in Christ. That does not mean, however, that revelation ceases to be a present reality and becomes a mere historical tradition. We do not encounter the saving Word of God only indirectly by trying to bridge the gap of long centuries of history. That Word is present to us here and now. God is present in that deposit of truth in the Church to make it his living message. When the teaching of Christ is handed on by the testimony of the Church, God is there in that testimony and makes it his own. He uses the witness of the Church as the means whereby he offers each man his message of salvation, together with his truth to motivate the acceptance.

The role of the Church in possessing and bearing testimony to the revelation of Christ cannot be limited to the magisterium and its activity. There is no need to repeat here the Catholic teaching on the magisterium. Like all communities, the community of Christ has its structure. Scripture and tradition show us what that structure is. Christ established a hierarchical society. In the service of the community, the apostles and their successors were given a power and an authority not possessed by the other members. To affirm the existence of a magisterium in the Church is to affirm that the bishops alone in the community have the function of proclaiming officially the message of Christ and of authoritatively deciding what its content is. Expositions of this doctrine are readily available. What is more to the point here is to stress that the function of the magisterium, its teaching and juridical authority, cannot be properly understood unless attention is first given to that general task of testifying to its faith which belongs to the entire Church as the visible community of Christ. The magisterium undoubtedly has the principal place in the Church when this is considered under that aspect by which it is the permanent witness in the world to the teaching of Christ. This follows from the structure Christ gave to his Church. But the principal part is not the whole, and it is the failure to put the magisterium in its setting that leads to such frequent misunderstanding of the Catholic position.

There has been in recent Catholic theology, chiefly under the influence of Dieckmann and Billot, a tendency to identify tradition with the magisterium. This is regrettable, because the older approach, represented notably by Scheeben, which gave a wider

meaning to tradition, is far sounder. It is perhaps necessary to recall here that tradition for Catholic theology is not merely an
historical memory helped by documents. No doubt, tradition in
the Church always refers to the past because what is handed
down from generation to generation is ever the same revelation,
preserved by the Holy Spirit intact and without addition. And such
continuity means that documents which give evidence of the past
faith and teaching of the Church always retain their value and
remain part of the Christian faith. But tradition is primarily
something of the present. In its first sense it is the actual witness
of the Church to the revelation of Christ present within it. The
Truth of Christ is handed on by the testimony of the Church. This
tradition preserves and perpetuates the faith of the Church;
through it the individual members can grow in faith according to
their union with the Church; by it the message of Christ is transmitted to all men. In so far as tradition implies an official and
authentic proclamation of Christian doctrine and an authoritative
judgement concerning it, it belongs exclusively to the magisterium
in the Church. Nevertheless, despite the outstanding importance
of this organ of tradition, it has not the only part to play. All
Christians in varying ways bear witness to the faith of the
Church, and the tradition of the Church includes this witness.
The fact that the members of the Church are dependent upon the
magisterium in matters of faith does not mean that their function
is restricted to a passive reception of the teaching of the hierarchy.
The Holy Spirit dwells within the members of the Church. Their
faith is a personal reality. By living a life of faith, they can pass
on the faith to some, help the faith of others and by the insights
granted to them enrich the life of faith within the Church. The
hierarchy of the Church has from Christ the commission to teach
and the authority to judge in all doctrinal matters, but its existence
and its function are meaningful only within a community of which
the corporate faith and life were intended by God to be the permanent presence and revelation of Christ in each age.

The same communal setting must be kept in mind if one is to
understand the teaching on the infallibility of the magisterium. The
best approach to this question is through the infallibility in believing that belongs to the Church. On the one hand, the infallibility in teaching presupposes this infallible faith and, on the

other hand, it is directed towards it as a means of ensuring it. What, then, comes first is the truth that the Church of Christ must be indefectible in its faith. Whatever may be the lapses of individual members, the Church as a whole, the Church as the visible community of Christ, cannot fail in its faith. If it did, how could we regard it as the Body of Christ and the Messianic community? The promises of God would indeed have been made void. Basic in the Catholic conception of the Church must be its indefectible faith. How, then, does God secure this infallibility of belief? In the first place by the Spirit of God dwelling within the Church and its members. The Spirit must come first, and it is an undue limitation of the action of the Spirit within the Church to describe the infallibility of belief as a passive infallibility in relation to the magisterium. Nevertheless, by reason of the structure Christ gave to his Church, the infallibility promised to the magisterium, to the universal episcopate as a body and to the pope in his personal office as the Vicar of Christ, is of outstanding importance in keeping intact the faith of the Church. There is no need to analyse here the Catholic teaching on the infallibility of the magisterium. The purpose of these remarks is to show the close relation between the activity of the magisterium and the corporate faith and witness of the Church—a theme to which we shall return in the next chapter and in Chapter XVI.

It has just been said that under one aspect the infallible teaching of the Church presupposes the infallible faith of the Church. The magisterium exists in order to teach and interpret the faith held by the Church. How could it do otherwise than presuppose that faith? It receives no new revelation; the doctrine it must proclaim and judge is the one deposit of faith unceasingly possessed by the Church. The holders of the magisterium must find out that faith by reflexion and investigation. That is patent from the manner in which any papal or conciliar decree is prepared. But here an error lurks that must be avoided. It is fear of it that leads Catholics to separate unduly the magisterium from the corporate faith and witness of the Church. Let us exorcise that fear. What has been said does not mean that the decrees of the magisterium are dependent on the consent of the Church. The judgements of the teaching authority are immediately binding in their several degrees of force; they do not wait upon the approval of the

Church. The pope and the bishops do not derive their authority
from below as representatives of the Church but from above as
representatives of Christ. Their power comes from on high; it
does not arise from the members of the Church. What remains
true is that it is given by Christ in an organic relationship with
the Church and its faith. What the bishops receive is the authority,
divinely guaranteed as infallible under certain conditions, to express the faith that has existed within the Church since the apostolic age and will continue to do so unchanged until the end of
time. To make the statements of the magisterium subject to the
judgement of the faithful would not be a simple affirmation of its
organic connexion with the Church; it would be to deny the
existence in any real sense of that magisterium.

Shall we put it in this way? The faith of the Church is permanent. It is handed down by an unbroken tradition, in which the
authoritative teaching of the magisterium has the principal but not
the only place. Again and again in the course of time the question
must arise: what is the faith of the Church? A dispute has started,
a new problem has been posed, and an answer is demanded concerning the meaning of Christian revelation. How is that question
answered? Catholic belief in the hierarchy and the papacy means
that, according to the structure of the Church as established by
Christ, such questions are answered finally, not by any vote of the
members of the Church, whether of the learned or of the holy or
of all, but authoritatively by the decision of the apostolic hierarchy;
and further, that in the episcopal body the pope's decision is essential and self-sufficient. To hold this is not to isolate the hierarchy from the Church; it is simply to believe in the promise of
Christ that its definitive decision will always be in conformity
with the truth of Christ; that is, in accord with the perennial faith
of the Church. The magisterium is not made a source of fresh
truth, acting without any dependence on the mind of the Church,
but a means, infallibly guaranteed by God and hence of unquestionable authority, whereby the faith of the Church is expressed.

The drift of these remarks may be shown more clearly by considering the personal position of the pope as a Christian believer
and member of the Church. Dr. Mascall makes this objection to
Catholic doctrine:

The Papal theory in fact divides the members of the Church into two entirely distinct classes: one which is continually bound by duty of unquestioning obedience, and one which is subject to no earthly control. The fact that the latter consists of only one member does not alter the fact of this dichotomy; it makes the Pope's membership of the Church different in kind from that of every other member. It makes him alone among Christians incapable of the supreme act of ecclesiastical loyalty, namely of willing submission to the Roman Pontiff, for no man can make an act of submission to himself.[2]

This is a caricature. Take first the pope's act of faith. As an act of divine and Catholic faith, it does not differ from the act of faith of the ordinary Catholic. His faith is mediated, like ours, by the living testimony of the Church. The pope must humbly and docilely believe, as we believe, what he discerns to be the faith of the Church. He knows that he is divinely guided in his teaching office, but does that mean that his act of faith is independent of the Church? No; accepting Christ's Church to be indefectible in its faith, he conforms his faith to that faith. In the very exercise of his teaching office he endeavours to discern and present that faith. Those efforts, he realizes, have a divine guarantee attached to their results, but that does not take away the duty of making them. And we, on our part, know that God does not allow any short-comings in the occupant of the Holy See to interfere with the truth of what he definitively imposes on the belief of the Church. The faith of every Christian, pope as well as peasant, finds its measure in that deposit of truth unfailingly possessed by the Church and manifested in the unbroken continuity of its life and teaching as the community of Christ.

The pope's supreme jurisdiction otherwise than in matters of doctrine is not part of the theme selected for consideration here. It must be enough to point out that all jurisdiction in the Church is closely connected with its faith. It reflects the faith of the Church; it is the guiding of the members of the Church according to the teaching of the faith and to the ends placed before them by faith. The pope has his teaching and governing authority in order to make clear what is involved in the faith of the Church and to apply this to the circumstances of each time. It must be said again

[2] *Ibid.*

that the hierarchy and the pope do not derive their authority from below as the representatives of the Church in any democratic sense but from Christ as his representatives; and in this respect there is no authority on earth higher than the pope. But the divine assistance is promised for the government as well as for the teaching of the Church, and this ensures that the human element in the hierarchy is never allowed to injure in any essential way the structure and the mission of the Church. What must always be remembered in considering the Catholic claims for the hierarchy and the papacy is that the promise of unfailing divine assistance is an assurance of the permanent organic oneness of these with the Church. The promise removes and does not bring any threat of isolation from the Church. If, then, one must speak of a "supreme act of ecclesiastical loyalty," this is undoubtedly the act of submission to the Church as the Body of Christ, and this is found in the pope as well as in all the other members of the Church. But clearly the expression of that loyalty to the Church and the duties it involves will be determined by each person's place in that organically structured community which is the Body of Christ.

To bring now these lengthy remarks to a conclusion. It may be freely admitted that Catholic theologians in their anxiety to defend the truth concerning the magisterium have often neglected to treat the other aspects that make clear its organic relation to the Church. But that relationship has always been a part of Catholic doctrine. It is found in the repeated denial that the magisterium receives any new revelation. Again and again it has been stressed that the function of the magisterium is to preserve and transmit the one revelation of Christ, the unchanging deposit of faith. That deposit of faith for Catholics does not belong simply to the past but is a permanent living reality in the Church. The corporate universal faith of the Church is at all times integral and indefectible. And, although this may seem paradoxical to Protestants, it is precisely all this that has been brought into relief by the definition of the Assumption of our Lady, with its reliance on the actual faith of the Church.

The defect in Dr. Mascall's account is of a different order of seriousness. What he fails to give us is the Church as a visible community. The attempt to drive a wedge between the sacramental and the administrative (does not tradition reckon with the pos-

sibility of a schismatic bishop?) and the endeavour to soften the
impact of a divided Church on earth by an appeal to a hierarchy
in heaven do not obscure the fact that he is compelled to deny
the existence of a visible association of men with a corporate faith
and a corporate life which has enjoyed an indefectible continuity
as the Church of Christ and serves as the unfailing embodiment
and presence of his revelation in the world. What is at stake, I
repeat, is not a particular interpretation of the magisterium or the
papacy, but the very nature of the Church.

CHAPTER VII

THE LIVING WORD

There is today a spiritual renewal in the Church. This shows itself in many ways. No need now to tell people about the liturgical movement—that wave of desire and effort, due to the pull of the Spirit, carrying Christians forward to a deeper sacramental life and a more intelligent and fruitful share in the worship of the Church. Closely allied, though not confined, to it is a new recognition of the place of the Bible in the life of the Church.

Catholics are learning once again to go to the Bible to nourish their faith by assimilating the Word of God present there. Modern biblical scholarship, after many difficulties and deviations, has led now to a new understanding of the Bible. There has been a rediscovery of its key doctrinal themes and its unity, and this has brought its perennial value and relevance into sharp relief. The central place of the Bible down the ages in the teaching and theology, in the liturgy and spirituality of the Church is now no longer notionally accepted as a puzzling feature but seen as a meaningful fact; and Catholics are beginning to draw the obvious conclusions from this for their own personal thought and piety.

Meanwhile, and partly owing to these trends, dogmatic theology has made notable progress in its reflexion on the Church. The present renewal of ecclesiology is of basic significance. Consider its importance for the liturgical revival. It has given that insight into the corporate nature of the Christian life which alone makes possible a true understanding of corporate worship. The biblical movement also is benefiting from its findings. This is principally through the better conception that has been achieved of the meaning of tradition and its relation to the Bible.

The liturgy, the Bible, tradition and the Church: there is a deep unity underlying all these varying signs of renewed life. The purpose of this chapter is to discuss one point where all these trends converge. All are leading to a fresh appreciation of how the Word of God lives on in the Church.

This study must begin with some reflexions on the relation between the Bible and tradition. All know that they are two channels through which revelation reaches us. It is less easy to determine what precisely that implies.

How has the revelation of Christ come down to us? In this way. From the beginning the good news has been preached orally to men. Christ left his followers gathered together in one community, the Messianic community, the Church. This community has a definite structure. In it the apostles, and later their successors, have the commission and the task of proclaiming authoritatively the message of Christ and judging what is its content; at the same time, all the members of the Church are called upon to know and live their faith and to bear witness to it before the world.

This Church has enjoyed, and will enjoy till the end of time, an unbroken continuity and an indefectibility of its life and faith. That means that the message of Christ has been handed down through the ages and is given to us today in the teaching and corporate witness of the Church. The Church is the permanent embodiment of the revelation of Christ.

This oral transmission or tradition has left behind it in the course of centuries much documentary evidence of its past existence and activity, and this constitutes part of our inheritance; but essentially this treasury of revelation, tradition, consists in the ever-living and never-failing teaching and witness of the Church of Christ.

The apostolic age, however, left us as its legacy a documentary record of a unique kind, the New Testament. From the outset, the Church had incorporated into its teaching the inspired writings of the Old Testament as a divine record of the preparation for Christ and a permanently valid account of God's intervention in history for the salvation of men. The writings of the apostolic age were seen to be similar in nature and to form part of the written Word of God. They completed the Scriptures by giving us the revelation of Christ in the very thought-forms and expressions of Christ himself and of his apostles.

The Bible, then, with tradition conveys to us the truth of Christ. Each in its own way is a place from which we take the good news of Christ. But how are they related?

Should we conceive them as two separate reservoirs, each containing only part of the revelation of Christ but giving if taken together the sum-total of Christian truth? According to this conception, Scripture is incomplete and gives only part of revealed truth, and the purpose of tradition is to complete its contents and make known to us that part of revelation not contained in Scripture.

This is the wrong way to think of the relation between the two; it does not do justice either to the role of tradition or to the place of the Bible in the Church. Nor is this view of the matter in any way imposed on Catholics by the Council of Trent.

Here we must be deeply grateful to Professor Geiselmann of Tübingen for the light he has thrown on this question. In an interesting essay,[1] he traces the origin of what can be called the *partim-partim* opinion and finds it in the controversial theology that immediately preceded Trent.

Though new, this opinion influenced the first draft of the Tridentine decree on Scripture and tradition, which stated that the truth of the Gospel "partim contineri in libris scriptis partim sine scripto traditionibus" (is contained *partly* in written books, *partly* in unwritten traditions). This text was opposed at the Council by those who maintained the plenitude of Scripture. The decree was redrafted, so that the final text runs: "contineri in libris scriptis et sine scripto traditionibus" (in written books and in unwritten traditions). This vaguer phrase leaves the question open and decides

---

[1] "Das Konzil von Trient über das Verhältnis der Heiligen Schrift und der nicht geschriebenen Traditionen," in *Die mündliche Überlieferung. Beiträge zum Begriff der Tradition,* hrsg. von Michael Schmaus (München, 1957). Cf. also "Scripture and Tradition in Catholic Theology" by the same author, in *Theology Digest* (Spring, 1958), pp. 73–8, and "Scripture, Tradition, and the Church," in *Christianity Divided,* ed. Daniel J. Callahan, Heiko A. Oberman and Daniel J. O'Hanlon, S.J. (New York, Sheed and Ward, 1961).

nothing about the way Scripture and tradition are related. Despite Professor Geiselmann's opinion to the contrary, it may be doubted whether the opposition to the *partim-partim* formula caused the change to be made in the decree. Intent on excluding the Protestant negation of tradition, the Fathers of the Council were not directly concerned with our present question and were probably unaware of the full implications of their choice. The fact, however, remains that they were finally content with the vaguer statement, and it is the text that they actually chose that is authoritative. This says nothing that imposes belief in the incompleteness of Scripture. In other words, a Catholic is free to hold that the whole of revelation is contained in the Scriptures, provided the existence of tradition is recognized. This view, affirming the plenitude of Scripture, is more in accord with the traditional attitude of the Church and the teaching of the Fathers and medieval writers, whereas the other is a product of Reformation controversy.[2]

Unfortunately, after Trent the opinion, which the Council had refrained from consecrating in its final text, succeeded in imposing itself on theology as the one interpretation of Trent. Professor Geiselmann traces the stages by which this misunderstanding has been slowly overcome.

It was seen without great difficulty that tradition could not be limited to supplying what Scripture had omitted. Wider and richer notions of tradition have long been put forward, though not without certain deficiencies. The idea that Scripture is incomplete in content has been less easily relinquished. At last, its rejection can be found in Kuhn, the disciple of Möhler. This Tübingen theologian thus completed the work his master had done for the renewal of the concept of tradition and finally shook off the shackles of that inadequate account of Scripture, tradition and their relationship imposed by the post-Tridentine controversial theology.

Kuhn belongs to the nineteenth century. Despite his work, it is only now under the influence of the researches of Professor Geiselmann that theologians are in any numbers returning resolutely to

[2] Professor Geiselmann's interpretation of Trent has been attacked by some, notably by Fr. Lennerz. For a balanced assessment of the matter, see Yves M. J. Congar, O.P., *La Tradition et les traditions* (Paris, 1960), 207–18, where full bibliographical details are given. Professor Geiselmann's work remains substantially intact.

the older and deeper understanding of the relation between Scripture and tradition.[3]

Seen in the light of this new yet old understanding, what is the Bible and what is its role as a channel of revelation?

The Bible can be described as the inspired record of revelation, coming from the time when the revelation was being given. Revelation was closed with the apostolic age; after that period there has been no fresh revelation and nothing is ever added to the deposit of revealed truth. Before this, throughout the Old Testament time and up to the end of the apostolic era, a gradual revelation of God and his plan of salvation for man took place. The final disclosure came in Christ and in the revealed understanding given to the apostles of the event of Christ and of his teaching. The Bible records the story of that progressive revelation as it took place: both its history and its growing content. It gives us the Word of God clothed or rather incarnate in the human events, thought, language and modes of expression which God chose for his self-disclosure.

Now, if we examine the manner of God's revelation more closely, we find that he made his revelation in the setting of a community. No doubt, he raised up leaders and bearers of his message to the people and these men became the immediate recipients of his communications. Nevertheless, it is right to say that God revealed himself in the life and history of the People of Israel. He intervened in that history and guided it towards his purpose; the very sins of the People served to make known the action of God. Not merely the events of Israel's history, but also its beliefs and customs were under the divine directing influence and formed the vehicle of God's revelation.

It is this centuries-long process of divine revelation that is recapitulated for us in the writings of the Old Testament. These

---

[3] In another chapter in this volume, "The Starting-Point of Mariology," I describe how the great Mariologist, Fr. Dillenschneider, and the well-known theologian, Mgr. Journet, have unequivocally adopted this point of view in dealing with what would at first seem the most difficult doctrine for its application, the doctrine on Mary. The foundation for all subsequent Marian development is the revealed deposit as found in Scripture. An appeal to oral tradition as providing additional revealed data not contained in Scripture is rejected.

form the residue left by the life of this chosen nation. From the human point of view they are but the residue of its literature, but faith tells us that this portion is the inspired record of it all.

When God revealed himself in Israel it was for the sake of mankind. That is why he moved men by his Spirit to write down the history and customs, the beliefs and aspirations in which his revelation was enshrined. Those who did so were often the great men he had raised up as leaders or prophets, but many others played their part. The Sacred Books were designed as an expression of the community, and many in the community contributed to their formation. God saw to it that they expressed Israel adequately.

Obviously, in many ways the divinely guided life of the community overflowed what could be set down in writing, but the divine inspiration was there to see that there was summed up for all future ages all that he had done and said in that People and the way he had done and said it.

The way he had done and said it is important. We must not neglect the human element in the history of Israel and in the writings it left; for this was the vehicle of the divine communication. And it is only the Bible that enables us to make contact with the human mentality and mode of expression in which God uttered and embodied his message.

The history and faith of Israel were brought to their fulfilment in Christ. Christ, in what he did and in what he preached, was the definitive revelation of God to man. That revelation was deposited in a community: this time, the Church, which is the new Israel formed from the faithful remnant of the old and enriched by the influx of the Gentiles. This community was directed by those who had listened to the teaching of Christ and were the eyewitnesses of his resurrection, and in the apostolic period new revelation still came from the Spirit to clarify and confirm what Christ had done and said. The writings of the apostles and their disciples re-create for us the Church of apostolic times.

What the New Testament gives us is the deposit of faith in the state in which it existed in the apostolic age; it puts us in touch with the message of Christ such as it fell from his lips and was understood and expressed in the Church of the apostles. No doubt, from the human point of view the writings of the New Testament are occasional writings and but the residue left behind by a life and beliefs of overflowing richness, but under divine inspiration they are a summary or crystallization of the faith of the apostolic age which represents its integral and authentic truth.

Any set of writings is more limited in its power of expression than the many manifestations of its corporate faith found in the actual pulsating life of a living community. This shows at once that the continuing life of the community remains the necessary context in which the Bible must be understood. But it also allows us to understand how the Fathers and medieval writers, while maintaining that all the truths necessary for salvation were to be found in Scripture—in other words, while maintaining the material sufficiency or plenitude in content of Scripture—yet held that there were apostolic traditions not recorded in the Bible. When we examine their references to these unwritten traditions, we find that these writers had in mind various disciplinary and liturgical customs and practices. Mistaken as the Fathers sometimes were in identifying particular practices as apostolic, they were rightly convinced that basically the organization of the Church's liturgy and discipline came from the apostles. Hence a prescription or custom going back to time immemorial might well claim an apostolic origin, even if not mentioned in Scripture. But the existence of such unrecorded traditions or usages is no reason for supposing that anything essential has been omitted in the biblical presentation of the Christian message. The Fathers would have rejected the idea that we are given in the Scriptures but an incomplete, partial picture of the belief of the apostolic community. The Christian message as a body of revealed truths about the new relation between God and man in Christ is given totally in the Bible. Tradition does not add another part to the message; it gives the same message in another manner that complements that of the Bible. After all, we must remember that the New Testament is our only means of contact with the teaching of Christ and the apostles according to the form, prior to development, in which it was historically given. Apostolic traditions in no way recorded in Scripture are confined to various liturgical and disciplinary usages, arising from the apostolic organization of the churches.

The Scriptures, then, enjoy a plenitude in the sense that they give expressly all the basic truths and facts from which everything in Christian teaching can be drawn. The entire body of revealed truth is contained either explicitly or implicitly within their pages. That does not mean that everything can be *proved* from Scripture. Very often all that the Bible offers us is a hint: it merely points a direction which has led to the realization of some new aspect of revelation, or it forms but the starting-point of a development. But what it does give us is an inspired résumé of the deposit of faith in its apostolic and original state.

The indispensable role of the Bible should now be clear. If we want to get into contact with the life and thought of the People of Israel as these were historically realized and developed, we have to go to the Old Testament. If we want to get into contact with the teaching of Christ in the thought-forms and expressions in which he gave it, we have to go to the New Testament. There too we have to go if we want to see the Christian message expressed in the concepts, images and words used by the apostles.

The message of Christ has, indeed, come down to us by an unbroken tradition in the Church. Take away the Bible and we should still have in the present teaching of the Church the authentic and identical revelation of Christ. But in the course of centuries it has undergone development. The same revelation has been expressed in different ways. The Church has used other than scriptural concepts to clarify certain aspects against error or to penetrate more closely into its meaning.

That development has not corrupted or added to the deposit of faith, but it has changed the thought-forms and language in which it is expressed. The *Quicumque,* the "Athanasian Creed," expresses the scriptural doctrine of the Trinity but not in the way Scripture expresses it.

Now, God wished the Church to keep revelation in the actual form in which it was originally given at the centre of its life and in the midst of its developing understanding and formulation of the revealed truths. That is why he gave the Church the Bible. Just as the Word of God in person became incarnate in a human nature of a particular race and constitution, so also the Word of God given as his message through the ages was made incarnate in the thoughts and expressions of a given mentality. The message of

God remains wedded in a special way to those thoughts and expressions preserved for us in the Bible.

Hence the Bible is the permanent starting-point to which the Church must always refer and the perennial centre around which her teaching must always revolve.

That explains the part played by the Bible in the life of the Church and of every Christian. That explains too its inexhaustible richness; it is God's own expression of his revelation.

Tradition places it alongside the Eucharist. The Bible and the Eucharist are the two great means of nourishing the Christian life. In the Eucharist, the Christian unites himself to the body of Christ and feeds his love; in the Bible, the Christian unites himself to the thought of Christ and feeds his faith. The Church as a wise mother gives her children both in the liturgy.[4]

But before the liturgy is considered, what has been said about tradition must be further clarified. The Bible originated in the life of a community. Israel with its living tradition and the Church with its living tradition came before the written Scriptures, which crystallized those traditions in the form in which they existed when the period of revelation was still open. This was the period of *traditio constitutiva*—tradition which was a process of revelation and which gradually built up or constituted the deposit of faith.

The living tradition of the Church continues still and provides now the necessary context for the Bible. This is now *traditio continuativa et explicativa,* which adds no new revelation but which must remain permanently subordinate to the unchanging deposit of faith, taking this as its objective standard. It is this continuing tradition that interprets the Bible. The Bible does not stand on its own and was never intended to do so. It was given to be embedded in the life of a community. The living teaching and witness of the Church alone give the Bible its full intelligibility. It is tradition that draws out all the implications of the biblical revelation so that its riches are gradually displayed ever more fully. Tradition alone can provide the authorized interpretation of

[4] An excellent introduction to the Bible, which treats with remarkable insight its place in the Church and in the life of each Christian, is Dom Celestin Charlier's *The Christian Approach to the Bible,* trans. by Hubert J. Richards and Brendan Peters (Westminster, Newman, 1958).

Scripture. Scripture depends on tradition if it is to fulfil its function in the Church.

But what exactly is tradition? The actual witness of the Church to the revelation of Christ, received from the apostles, which remains present within it as the community of Christ. It is a mistake to think of tradition as principally something of the past and consider it merely from the point of view of history. Christian tradition always includes a reference to the past, since it is the one immutable revelation that has been handed down to each age of the Church from the apostles. Since the Church is indefectible in its faith, the corporate faith of the Church in any period of the past is identical with the faith of the Church today. Hence the evidence of the past teaching and faith of the Church always retains its value and remains part of our heritage. Nevertheless, in its primary sense tradition is something of the present; it is the corporate witness of the Church to that faith which is unfailingly possessed within it. That witness is the means that transmits or hands on the faith so as to preserve and increase it in the members of the Church and proclaim it to those outside the Church.

In the corporate witness of the Church to the faith, the hierarchy has the principal place, since it alone has the commission to teach the Christian message officially and to judge its meaning authoritatively. The community of Christ is a structured community with a hierarchy and papacy; the corporate witness to the faith is structured in a similar way.

All the same, it is a mistake to limit tradition to the official and authoritative teaching of the magisterium. It is the Church as the Body of Christ, a community made one by the Spirit, which possesses the truth of Christ, and gives testimony to it. All Christians possess the faith as a personal reality and are under the movement of the Spirit present in the members of the Church. They bear witness to the faith in their lives as Christians, and by their reflexion and spiritual insight they enrich the life of faith within the Church and contribute to the development of its understanding of revelation—needless to say, under the guidance of the magisterium. Theologians have recently been paying special attention to the sense of faith in the members of the Church: that supernatural insight into the object of faith, which has played such an important part in the unfolding of the truths concerning Mary.[5]

Can we pause now to gather together what has been said so far? God gave his revelation to a community and preserves and transmits it within a community. Tradition is the expression of the life and thought of the community. For long centuries God used the tradition of the People of Israel and then its continuation in the Church of the apostolic period as the vehicle of a progressive revelation. He made himself known through leaders, prophets, Christ and the apostles, who were the immediate bearers of his revelation, and through the events in which they were involved. These communications became part of the deposit of truth forming the faith of the community and were manifested in its tradition. Then at the close of the apostolic age revelation was completed. Nothing new was to be added but the integral revelation was to be passed down from age to age in the tradition of the Church.

Since revelation, however, was given to men not as dead formularies but as living truth, development was inevitable and willed by God. He gave the Church a magisterium to proclaim authoritatively the revelation and to judge questions that arose when this revelation passed into the consciousness of each age and was meditated upon by generations of many different mentalities. In that way, the revelation of Christ is preserved intact in the corporate faith and witness of the Church.

But although God wished men of all cultures and mentalities to assimilate and express his revelation, he wished them to do so by drawing on the inspired record of that revelation, which expressed it in the form in which it was originally presented to mankind. Hence he left the Bible at the centre of the Church's doctrinal life.

The Christian, therefore, first receives his faith from the Church as the living embodiment in the world of the Word of God. His faith then grows and develops by his union with the corporate

[5] See, in particular, *Le sens de la foi et le progrès dogmatique du mystère marial*, by Clement Dillenschneider, C.SS.R. (Rome, 1954). This significant study is dealt with at considerable length in Chapter XVI of the present volume.

faith and witness of the Church and under the guidance of the magisterium. Finally, pre-eminent among the means given him by the Church to nourish his faith is the inspired Word of God in the Bible.

This at once brings us to the liturgy, where we see realized these various factors. Once more the liturgy stands forth as the life of the Church at its essential core and in its highest manifestation.

The liturgical assembly gives us the community. We are indeed the Church when dispersed from each other in our daily occupations, but when we come together in the Sunday assembly the Church is given its visible expression as a community. Our Eucharistic gathering is the realization, the symbol and the cause of our union together in Christ. Then, in and through the assembly, each one is united to the corporate faith and witness of the Church; all and each are strengthened by the testimony given by all and each when gathered in Christ around the altar.

The part played by the liturgy in the tradition of the community has always been of outstanding significance; it is a privileged place for the expression of its corporate faith. An important role must be assigned to the liturgy of Israel and of the Church in the formation of the Bible, and it remains a factor of some moment in the development of doctrine.

Here, too, we see the magisterium at work; for all is under its guidance. Although it is the element of worship, not that of teaching, which is uppermost in the liturgy, yet the doctrinal aspect remains of very great consequence. The liturgy is rightly considered the most important organ of the ordinary magisterium of the Church.

And in the liturgical assembly, in which we see in miniature the life of the Christ, what part does the Bible hold?

The mere material place occupied by the Bible in the liturgy is remarkable. Even more striking is the way the Church uses the Bible in the Eucharistic assembly.

The first part of the Mass, the service of the Word, consists principally in the presentation of the Bible to the congregation by selected readings, interspersed with chants that use the words of the Bible. The living voice of the Church in the person of the priest comes as an exposition of the Bible and an application of it to the actual circumstances of the community. The people are thereby given first the Word of God in Scripture, in order to prepare them to receive the Word of God in the Eucharist.

The second part of the Mass also is biblical, though in a different way. The Eucharistic Prayer, full of biblical quotations and allusions, expresses the doctrine of oblation and communion not in the form of scientific theology but along biblical lines; and indeed it is only in the light of the biblical tradition and doctrinal themes, which the Eucharist brings to fulfilment, that what is done and said can be rightly grasped. And the same observation applies equally to the other parts of the liturgy and their manner of doctrinal expression.[6]

Since the Church offers us the Bible in the liturgy, the liturgy shows us how the Church understands the Bible. We do not indeed look to the liturgy—or for that matter to the Fathers—for the detailed exegesis of individual texts. We should not be afraid to make our own the contribution brought by modern biblical scholarship, and especially the light it has thrown on the initial meaning of the texts taken in their immediate context. What we do find in the liturgy and in the Fathers is a grasp of the profound meaning of Scripture and a deep insight into its unity and basic doctrinal themes. The advances made recently in biblical theology have confirmed the soundness of the liturgical interpretation of the Bible.

In brief: through the liturgy we are united to the living tradition of the Church and inserted into its corporate faith and witness; in the liturgy we are shown how to read and interpret the Bible, since there it is put before us by the Church to be the food of our faith. No cause for surprise, then, to learn that it is the liturgical movement that is leading Catholics to rediscover the Bible and to deepen their sense of the Church and of tradition.

All that has been said has shown how the Word of God is present in the Church: incarnate in its corporate faith and witness;

---

[6] Cf. "La Bible et la liturgie" by L. Bouyer, in *Initiation biblique* (Tournai, 1954), pp. 1011–20; and then for a comprehensive survey of the whole question of the Bible and the liturgy by various authors the volume giving the papers read at the Congress at Strasbourg in 1957, *Parole de Dieu et liturgie,* Lex Orandi 25 (Paris, 1958).

preserved and transmitted by its living tradition; set down in writing in an inspired record of the original revelation; and preached and presented in a special way in the liturgical assembly, which is a privileged manifestation of the life of the Church.

Yet, still not a half of the wonder of the Word has been told. The Word of God in the Church does not merely recount for us the past; it is a power for the present. It is with us not only as a message but as an effectual and saving Act. The liturgy does not simply sing the mighty deeds of God in the past but accomplishes them again amongst us in the sacraments. There is a continuity, worth our meditation, binding together the preaching of the Gospel, the reading of the Bible and the administration and reception of the sacraments.

But this requires another chapter to explain.[7] Let me at least recall by way of conclusion one sense in which the Word of God present in the Church is a living Word: it is a message addressed to each of us here and now by the living God himself. Faith is always a personal encounter with God. The teaching and witness of the Church are not substitutes for God's disclosure of himself to each of those whom he calls to faith. In and through the external testimony, which from without offers to men the Christian message, God makes himself present to the mind as the motive of faith. In the preaching of the Church, in the Bible read in and with the Church, in the liturgy as the expression of corporate faith, the Spirit of God is there. The Spirit is there to enlighten the mind to perceive in the external signs the presence of God the First Truth calling to man to give the humble and saving obedience of faith. The Word of God is in the Spirit a living Word.

[7] The reader is referred back to "The Theology of Preaching" in this present volume (Chapter IV), where this continuity is dealt with at some length.

CHAPTER VIII

CAN UNBELIEVERS BE SAVED?

Can unbelievers be saved? Not if they remain unbelievers. This answer shows that there are two problems involved in the question: first, what are the requirements for salvation? second, how does God see to it that all men are in a position to fulfil these requirements? The first problem is the easier, since it concerns principles that are easily determined. The second is more difficult, because it must take account of the concrete situations in which men find themselves, and so there is scope for various hypotheses.

What, then, are the requirements for salvation? All are fulfilled if the person loves God with a love of charity, and without such love, no salvation is possible. We are talking of adults, namely, those with the use of reason and free will and capable of a personal decision. The love necessary must be the love of charity. The person may not be able to give a name to this love or be aware reflexively of its distinctive elements, but he must possess it. We may turn, then, to theology for an analysis of it, while recognizing that the possession of it and the ability to analyse it are two different things.

The love of charity is a supernatural love of God. This statement does more than declare that grace is needed for it. It means that this love must be based, not on a natural knowledge of God such as is acquired by reason and developed in philosophy, but on a special self-disclosure of God given by revelation and accepted by faith. Charity cannot exist without faith, and faith is man's response to a revelation from God. A man must encounter God revealing himself to him as his last end and calling him to a destiny that lies beyond his powers as man and the demands of his nature. In the present order man has a supernatural destiny and no other. To be saved, an adult must direct himself towards it by a personal decision. He can do so only if he meets God in a divine revelation. Faith is the basic acceptance of such a revelation; charity is the effectual movement of man's will towards God as accepted in revelation.

The love of charity is a love of God above all things. An initial movement towards God, such as even a sinner may possess, is not enough. Our love must be an effectual love. We must prefer God to all else; his will must be the supreme norm of our conduct. We do not love God if we refuse to do his will in a serious matter.

We need not worry further about the motive of charity. Of its nature charity is a love of God for his own sake. Unless it includes an unselfish, disinterested love, it is not charity. But the desire of God as our supreme happiness, a self-interested love of God as our Good, is also part of charity, as we may affirm with St. Thomas and against Scotus. If this desire leads us to prefer God above all things, then it carries with it necessarily the presence of some degree of unselfish love. In other words, it is already charity, even if desire or love of God as our own Supreme Good rather than unselfish love or love of God as Good in himself is uppermost on the psychological level. As charity grows, its character as a disinterested love of God for his own sake becomes more prominent, but provided we effectually appreciate God as our Supreme Good and act accordingly, our love fulfils the minimum requirements of charity. When we dispose ourselves for contrition, we might well remember that the test of charity is the effectual placing of God above all things, not the attainment—often only apparent—of disinterested purity in our motive.

If a person has such charity, he will be saved; without it, he will be damned. Obviously, if a person loves God in this way, he will go on to fulfil God's will so far as he knows it. For some, this will mean a full sacramental life under the guidance of the Church. Others will have only the dim guidance of a badly formed conscience. We need not ask how far conscience can become deformed. The point relevant here is that the love of charity includes every essential requirement, provided ignorance excuses us from a more complete fulfilment of God's plan. Thus, baptism is necessary for salvation, but a person who does not know about baptism can be saved by baptism of desire. Now, baptism of desire is not the same as desire for baptism; it means, in fact, an act of charity. A person who has never heard of baptism but who loves God has baptism of desire, because of his general acceptance of God's will. A person who knows all about baptism and intends to receive it but who does not yet love God has not baptism of desire and would not reach salvation in that state. Again, no one can be saved without being in some way united to the Church. But an act of charity gives a sufficient link with the Church if no other is possible. Baptism of desire and membership of the Church by desire are statements of the objective implications of charity rather than additional subjective requirements. Further, a person who has sinned mortally must turn away from his sin in detestation and turn towards God in repentance. But contrition is simply the love of God as found in a sinner conscious of his sin.

We can sum up the matter in this way. Man's destiny is a new personal relation with God which goes beyond what human nature can achieve by itself. Man must accept this self-relevation of God by faith and move towards God with an effectual love. Such an encounter with God finds its normal development in a conscious adherence to the Christian relevation in the Church of Christ. But even in its minimal form, it must be such that a man takes a personal decision about his supernatural destiny.

That brings us now to the second and more difficult problem: how does each man get the opportunity of fulfilling these requirements? It is an unquestionable part of Catholic teaching that each adult is given such an opportunity. Our task is to try and see how, in order to clarify and explain the doctrine. The crux of the difficulty is the possibility of faith. Once we have seen how a person reaches faith, it is easy enough to grasp how grace leads him to embrace God with love. But faith presupposes revelation, and multitudes seem to be cut off from any contact with divine revelation. There is the problem.

We need not delay here over those who are in touch with the historical Judaeo-Christian revelation in some way or another. Their knowledge of this revelation may be very imperfect; the true faith it makes possible may be intermingled in their minds with various errors in a confusion that they themselves cannot disentangle; but we can suppose without difficulty that, despite all the imperfections and errors, their minds are confronted with the minimum essential object of faith, namely, God and his call of man to a higher destiny and life. Once this message has been offered by outward testimony, the grace of God, working from within, enlightens the mind so that a person perceives that it is worthy of belief and can accept it by faith. To explain this process in detail would take us again into the theology of faith. It must be enough here to remark that if the message about man's destiny reaches man in at least its essential minimum content, we can apply the theological principles about faith in a straightforward fashion and understand how grace leads a person to faith and charity. The inaccurately named problem of the salvation of un-believers is really the problem of those who remain unevangelized, that is, those who do not hear the message of the Gospel, even in a fragmentary way. How can they believe if the Gospel message is never presented to them? We think at first of the millions of pagans in remote lands, but the same question arises over individuals living in a Christian country who, owing to obstacles created by upbringing and environment, never meet the Gospel message in a way that demands their personal attention. They too must be counted among the unevangelized.

The supposition that God intervenes in an extraordinary way and puts the object of faith in the minds of the unevangelized by an immediate revelation is unsatisfactory. It was all right to hold this when people thought that such a revelation would be needed only rarely. There was a time when theologians supposed that the whole world had heard the Gospel and were worried only about isolated cases. Since the discovery, at the end of the Middle Ages, of the true extent of the world and the fact that millions re-main still unevangelized, the hypothesis has become unlikely. The extraordinary acts of God are reserved for extraordinary occasions. Moreover, the supposition lacks any basis in experience. Again, the idea that the primitive revelation made to Adam has been handed down to all subsequent generations is far-fetched. No recognizable message could have survived a transmission of half a million or so years without a miracle, for which there is no evidence. We must approach the problem differently. The solution lies in the facts of man's moral life in this fallen world. An embryonic faith becomes possible through man's moral experience.

Man's moral state after the Fall is one of helplessness if he is left to his own forces. Not of complete helplessness, because fallen man can still do actions that are morally good, even without grace. But a stable moral life, just on the natural level, is impossible; for man needs grace to avoid sin for any length of time. And so, man's present state leads him to recognize his moral weakness and blindness and draws him to seek light from the beginning of his moral life. But it does not draw man to a merely natural moral ideal. The light it gives and the desires it arouses move man to an ideal of virtue which transcends the ethical and is actually the supernatural, Christian ideal. What comes before him as good and obligatory is a life higher than nature could reach, though he does not recognize it as such. A confident surrender to light and strength coming from above and directing his life, a love on his part that must embrace all men, a renunciation of earthly satisfactions: these and similar elements make up an ideal that transcends what a philosopher would deduce from human nature. Imperfectly as all this may be perceived, the weight of his moral helplessness and the positive work of grace succeed in presenting man with an ideal for his life which is supernatural. And this ideal points to God. God can be recognized as the origin and end of this transcendent moral order. To recognize God in this way is to make an act of faith.

To understand the point a little better, we must recall that faith presupposes a twofold revelation. What is ordinarily called revelation means the presentation of the object and motive of faith by means of outward signs. More simply, the Gospel is preached as a message from God. But by itself this is not enough for faith. There must be an inner enlightenment due to God's grace, which enables a person to interpret the signs and discern in the message the marks it bears of its divine origin. Across the structure of preaching and outward signs, God calls man by his grace to that personal encounter which is the act of faith. When a man responds by faith to God, present in the message and drawing him by grace, he makes contact with God as the motive of his faith, although God remains unseen and hidden in darkness. Now, in the embryonic faith just described, God uses as signs through which he presents himself as the object and motive of faith, not the signs of an historical revelation, but the signs which arise in man in the course of his struggle with the help of grace to lead a moral life in the present world. It is in this way, and not by an immediate revelation putting an explicit message before his mind, that man is presented with his supernatural destiny and with God as its origin and end. This presentation is accompanied by the inner enlightenment or grace of faith which makes it possible for man to embrace this destiny and God its author in an act of faith.

Since this process is at work in all unevangelized men, it need not take place exclusively on an individual plane. A person called to faith will meet others who have benefited from God's action and who by their influence will serve to some extent as witnesses of the call of God. Certain features of the higher moral ideal, such as confident surrender to divine help and a need for redemption, may be embodied in social and religious institutions or expressed in myths and rites. The faith reached is but an implicit faith, since it rests on no clear and explicit message from God. It can be and is intermingled with many errors and deformities in religious matters. But even Christian faith does not always escape these, and their existence should not lead us to deny the authentic if embryonic faith that can be present in their midst.

What is essential in this minimum of faith is the vital movement of mind and will to the Spiritual Reality which is God calling the person to union with himself. Several theologians have remarked how such a movement may be found in a man who is a professed atheist and who denies God on the level of his conceptual thinking. Such a man is only apparently an atheist. He has a wrong idea of God and denies what he represents to himself as God. But on a deeper level of affirmation, he accepts the reality of God, even though he knows that reality under a different name or is unable to form an adequate conceptual representation of what he affirms. Faith may co-exist with confused thinking.

Reflexion on the universal possibility of faith helps us to see how God offers salvation to all men. It should not make us forget that only in the Church of Christ can faith achieve its normal development. Faith found in the unevangelized is a mutilated faith and such believers are cripples in the life of faith. Here we confront a mystery—God distributes his graces unequally. Christians owe thanks to God for their privileged position, and they have a serious apostolic responsibility. The purpose of missionary work is not simply to establish the Church but to give other men the opportunity of that full life of faith of which they are deprived. If God has seen to it that in any event each man has the opportunity of reaching salvation, he has made those whom he has freely chosen as Christians responsible for bringing the full fruits of Christ's redemption to the rest of mankind.

CHAPTER IX

THE CHRISTIAN MYSTERY
AND THE TRINITY

The difficulty of a subject like the Christian mystery is to know where to begin. "What is the Christian mystery?" is a question as wide as, "What is Christianity?" Clearly, what is wanted is a presentation of the basic theme that gives meaning and unity to the Christian religion. What lies at the heart of the Christian message? So often the Christian religion is made to seem a collection of heterogeneous doctrines and a list of commands and prohibitions, together with a decorative but highly complicated ceremonial. What is the point of it all? In a sense there is and can be only one answer to this, but this answer can be presented in different ways. Every presentation must deal with the area of our faith that can be roughly indicated by the three words: grace, Christ, the Trinity; but what has to emerge is the inner unity and basic significance of these doctrines—they are sometimes reduced to a series of disconnected theses. The presentation of the Christian mystery offered here is a personal one. This chapter does not aim at giving an exposition of the theology of mysteries, associated with Odo Casel. Indeed, the conception of the liturgy as a mystery is not its direct concern; the purpose in view is the more general one of giving a synthesis of the three doctrines mentioned. The chosen angle of approach is from the doctrine of the Trinity, and what I am going to try to do is to show the importance of this doctrine for our understanding of the Christian mystery. My hope is that this will provide some of the doctrinal insights necessary for an understanding of the liturgy and, in particular, for an appreciation of liturgical prayer.

The Christian mystery may be described as the self-gift of God made to men through Christ and in the Spirit. God gives us himself. This point is basic: without it all the rest is unintelligible. The plan of God in its ultimate purpose is not to give men created gifts, however wonderful, but to give men himself. God wants to communicate his own divine reality to men; he offers them a share in his own divine life and happiness; men are invited to possess God. Here we meet the difference between the order of nature and the order of grace: in the order of nature God gives what is distinct from himself, namely the creature's own being and the created gifts that accompany it, whereas in the order of grace what God gives is himself.

Fully to appreciate this point—and it is a vital one—we need to alter the current conception of the state of grace. Most people when asked what the state of grace meant would reply by saying the possession of sanctifying grace. They would not mention the indwelling of the Trinity, except perhaps as an afterthought or when questioned further. But what comes first in the state of grace is not sanctifying grace but the indwelling in us of the three divine persons. It is this indwelling, called sometimes by theologians uncreated grace, that constitutes the primary element in the state of grace. This state is the state in which we possess God and share his life, and the indwelling is God as possessed, or God as present in us, joined to us and drawing us into his life.

It is even true to say that created grace, as sanctifying grace is called, is intelligible only when related to uncreated grace. This is because in itself it is simply the link that makes the indwelling possible, the bond that establishes the presence of God, the impress, if you like, made on us as the divine reality shapes us to itself. Or put it in this way: when two things are united, one at least must change; otherwise, there would be no difference between union and separation, and it would be meaningless to talk of union. But we are united to God. God cannot change; therefore we must change. Sanctifying grace is the change in us that establishes our union with God. That makes it essential to the state of grace. All the same, what comes first is the self-gift of God. The fact that God wants to give us himself, to communicate to us his own reality, is the only reason for all the other gifts of grace, the created gifts necessary for him to achieve this self-communication.

God, then, gives us himself. Why? Because God loves us. But we exist only because God loves us. God's love is the creative source to which we owe everything. That means there is no cause of this love. The only explanation is that it is like God to have such love. As St. John put it, "God is love" (1 John 4.16).

The love that is God must be completely free in regard to creatures, since there is nothing in creatures that demands that they should exist rather than not. Even more strikingly gratuitous is the love by which God gives men, not only their existence, but also himself in friendship. It is this gratuitous and utterly selfless love, hidden from all eternity in the depths of God, which is the Christian mystery at its ultimate level. God's love comes first. Everything in the Christian revelation goes back to an effectual plan of love, an eternal resolve of God to give us himself. And this love is simply the inmost depths of God, his inner nature, considered as the well-spring from which flow the wonders of creation and of grace.

The word "love," so debased in modern usage, is hardly capable of bearing this weight of meaning, and so many writers prefer to use *agape,* which is the Greek word used in the New Testament for this divine characteristic.

This eternal agape or divine love is, I said, the Christian mystery at its deepest level. Though the point is now widely known, it is perhaps wise to pause here to explain that the word "mystery" is being used in a fuller sense than that customary up to recent years. For a long time a mystery meant simply a mysterious truth beyond our reason; the word was used exclusively of doctrines. The same is true of the word "revelation"; it was taken to mean a list of statements coming to us on the authority of God. Now, there is a revealed body of doctrine, which contains mysterious truths beyond our reason: Christianity is essentially a dogmatic religion which imposes authoritative teaching on our minds. But God has made himself known to men, not only in words, but also in deeds. God has revealed himself by giving himself. He has not remained at a distance and communicated with man merely by authorizing doctrinal statements. He has made himself present in such a way that man can encounter him and enter into personal communication with him. Revelation, then, is twofold: there is revelation as a reality as well as revelation as words. Revelation as a reality is the very reality of God's love coming into this world and reaching out to us; it is the reality of God's self-gift. The function of the revelatory words is to tell us of the existence of the reality and interpret its meaning for us. But the Christian revelation is the Christian mystery. "Revelation" and "mystery" are two words to express the same reality, namely the eternal love of God who gives himself to men. "Revelation" directly expresses the communication or giving and implies the hidden transcendence of the divine love; "mystery" directly expresses the hidden transcendence and implies the communication or giving. But since they mean the same, it follows that just as revelation understood as the divine reality is basic and revelation as words is a message that points to this reality, so likewise the term "mystery" means in the first place the divine reality as communicated to men, and then, in relation to this, the doctrinal statement that expresses it.

When we take the word "mystery" in this full sense, the statement that the Christian mystery at its deepest level is God himself becomes obvious. Obvious, but worth pondering. I have heard it said that the greatest benefit brought by the liturgical revival has been the deepening of our understanding of God, the new awareness it has given us of the mystery of God. Ultimately, the mystery is God. We are led into the hidden depths of God, who is holy and utterly other, inaccessible in his inner life to man as man. The term "mystery" reminds us of the holiness of God— holiness in the Bible is not just one divine quality among many; it is *the* divine characteristic, the godhood or complete otherness of God. But however remote God as God is from man as man, the staggering truth is that God wants to draw near and offers man a personal communion of friendship with himself. This God of holiness is a God of love. The inner depths of the divine being are a well-spring: if they are holiness, they are also agape or love, the source of an outpouring or self-giving that reaches a point that seems folly. Yes, indeed; the eternal agape or divine love is the mystery at its deepest point.

But the God of love is a Trinity. This truth is central in the Christian faith, though one would not think so from the place it has in the life and prayer of many Christians. People who are honest will sometimes ask why the Trinity was revealed, since it does not seem to have any relevance to their Christian life. Are not many Christians, who indeed confess the Trinity in an orthodox way, merely monotheists in their spiritual experience? Suppose for a moment that the doctrine of the Trinity were excluded as untrue, how much spiritual writing could remain unchanged or survive with a few unimportant corrections! Even the Incarnation is understood simply as God becoming man, without any particular significance being attached to the fact that it is God the Son who became man. Yet, no account of the Christian mystery or of the life of grace is even remotely adequate unless it is Trinitarian; and the doctrine of the Trinity must be woven into it, not just stuck on afterwards. Nor can we understand the liturgy without an appreciation of this doctrine, because liturgical worship is Trinitarian in structure.

The doctrine of the Trinity tells us that there is a self-giving within the Godhead itself. God is love, and when we asked why God wills to give us himself, we could answer only that God is like that. Now we see that God is so like that, that an inner self-giving constitutes the very nature of God and the outward communication of himself is but the external continuation and re-flexion of an eternal, inward and necessary self-communication. The mystery of the divine agape is in the first place the mystery of the Trinity.

God the Father is without origin and the ultimate personal source of the inner life of the Godhead. He gives himself by generating the Son; and the giving is so perfect that Father and Son are identical in what they are, being distinct only by the relation they have to each other—a mutual relation that alone distinguishes them as persons. The Father's generation of the Son is an act of knowledge, and so the Son is the Image or perfect expression of the Father and his love. Father and Son together as one breathe forth the Spirit. Again a perfect giving, and the Spirit is identical in nature with Father and Son, distinct from them only as the term of their giving. The breathing forth of the Spirit is an act of love, and the Spirit proceeds from Father and Son as the immanent impulse or momentum of their love. Since everything the Son has comes from the Father, it is the Father who gives it to the Son that he breathes forth the Spirit, and the Son is the source of the Spirit only because he has received this from the Father. On the other hand, if the Father enjoys the society of the Spirit, this is only through the Son, since the procession of the Spirit presupposes two persons. So, the Spirit is their mutual gift, a pledge and expression of their love. The Spirit is there as a bond of love between the Father and Son, a bond which seals the love of the Godhead and closes the inner flow of divine life.

Thus, God the Father, without origin, is the starting-point of the divine life and love; God the Son is the Image or perfect expression of that life and love; God the Holy Spirit is the Gift that completes the self-giving which is the divine life: three living and loving persons, who invite us to share their life and enter into personal communion with them.

But when the divine life is communicated to men, it remains the life of a Trinity. The life of grace is Trinitarian. Grace, then, establishes us in a personal relationship with each of the persons of the Trinity; we are related to each person as distinct, entering into a personal communion with him.

This has been denied by many theologians, because they fear it contradicts the unity of the Godhead. They maintain that grace relates us to God only in his unity; we have no real relation to the persons as distinct. As one theologian put it, we are sons of the divine essence, not of God the Father. Any difference of role given to the persons in our Christian life is to be explained by appropriation—that usage of speech by which we refer to one person what is really common to all three, in order to help ourselves to think of the divine persons and their respective places in the inner life of the Trinity. Any relations with the persons as distinct, they say, are merely in our thought and affection; they are not objective relations found in the structure of grace.

Such a theology is increasingly seen as quite inadequate to account for the biblical, traditional and liturgical ways of expressing the role of the divine persons in our Christian life. It makes it very difficult to give any convincing plea for the importance of the Trinity in the Christian revelation.

The fear of derogating from the unity of God by allowing distinct relations with each of the divine persons can be shown to be unfounded if we recall what has been said about the state of grace. Since the three persons are one in all that they are and distinct only by their mutual relations, it is undeniable that all created effects, whether in nature or of grace, are produced by them as one. That by which they cause created effects is identical in all three. Therefore grace as a created effect is produced by the three persons as one. Now, if created grace came first, and all that could be said about grace was that it is a wonderful effect produced in our souls by God, then grace would relate us to God only as one; there could be no question of any relations with the persons as distinct. But grace is in fact more than the production of a created effect. First and foremost it is God giving us himself. We are joined to God as he is in himself. Uncreated grace or the indwelling of the Trinity is the principal element in the state of grace. In other words, God becomes present to us in his intimate reality; besides the causality (efficient causality) by which some effect is produced, there is another causality (call it what you will) by which the reality of God is given to us. Joined to God as he is in himself, we encounter the three persons, we are joined to each of them in a real relationship. Or preferably, we have a triune relation to a triune God;—God is Three in One, so our relation to God by grace is a three-in-one relation, reaching the persons as distinct persons but one in nature. Such a relation does not offend against the unity of God any more than does the relation which the human nature of Christ has with God the Son alone.

But here what is more important than the theological arguments is to determine more closely what our relations with the divine persons are. To do so will give us a much deeper insight into the structure of the Christian mystery as realized both in history and in our own lives. There is a twofold movement of the divine agape, or love: it comes to us from the Father through Christ and in the Holy Spirit; and then, present and active in us by the gift of the Spirit, it draws us back through Christ to the Father. The Christian mystery is dynamically Trinitarian, both on the side of God in his saving love and on the side of man in his return to God. (By "dynamically Trinitarian" I mean that the persons have distinct roles, so that in the plan of salvation and in our Christian life the three persons have a part that corresponds to their place in the inner life of the Godhead.)

The starting-point in the outgoing movement of divine love is the love by which the Father loves us. This eternal love is indeed common to all the three persons, because it is identical with the divine nature. But the Son and the Holy Spirit have it from the Father, since they proceed from him and have the divine nature from him. Hence it is the Father's love in a special way: he is the ultimate personal source from whom it comes. When we are given a share in the life of God, we owe it in a special way to the Father. He alone is our Father, since to be a father is to be the ultimate personal source of life. The special relation that grace give us to the first person is a relation of sons to him as our Father. When Christian prayer addresses God as Father, it is directed to the first person of the Trinity; the title of Father is reserved to him. Such prayer expresses perfectly our relation to God the Father. It is a pity that more people are not aware of the meaning of such prayer. They regard prayers such as the *Our Father* as being directed vaguely to God rather than to God the Father, and the result is a great loss in personal communion with him who is our Father.

The mention of prayer to God the Father already indicates that, just as the outgoing movement of the divine love springs from him, so also the movement of return in our response and worship goes back to him. We must now add that liturgical worship in its basic form is directed to God the Father. The structure of the Mass is that of a sacrifice offered to God the Father, to whom the Eucharistic Prayer is addressed. The other Mass prayers—the Collects, Secrets and Postcommunions—are likewise addressed to God the Father, except for a number of more recent prayers addressed to Christ, which are out of keeping with the genius of the Roman rite. Though, as we shall see, other forms of prayer are necessary, the basic form, which expresses most completely our relation by grace to the Trinity, is prayer addressed to God the Father.

But the love of the Father comes to us through the Son. The Son, who is the Image in the life of the Trinity, is the exemplar or model of our life of grace. We enter the life of the Trinity by becoming sons in the Son. We are called to share the relation of the Son to the Father: that is our place in the life of the three persons. There is reproduced in us the relation which the Son has to the Father. We receive the divine life as it is found in the Son; hence we are joined to the Son as sons with him and heirs with him, sharing his sonship.

That is why it was the second person who became incarnate and why the incarnate Son is our mediator with the Father. God the Father sent his Son into this world. This sending was simply the generation of the Son as prolonged into this world; it extended into the created order the procession of the Son. This means that it continued the Father's act of self-giving by which he generated the Son. And so the sending by the Father imparted divine sonship to a human nature. It did so in a unique way; for the human nature was made a human nature belonging to God the Son and existing in him as his human nature. God the Son began to exist as man, and the man Jesus was God the Son himself. A man existed who was in person the only-begotten eternal Son of God. This imparting of divine sonship to a human nature in the incarnation was intended as the basis for the further communication of sonship to the rest of mankind—a communication that makes men adopted sons sharing, though in a lesser way, the sonship of Christ. Christ became the foundation of the structure into which men are to be built and in which they are to share the divine life. Every communication of the divine life comes through Christ, and we must be incorporated into Christ, because the life that we receive is a share in the life of Christ, a participation in his sonship.

The relation of Christ as man to the Father is the reproduction in a human nature of the relation of the Son to the Father. The mystery of Christ is the mystery of his sonship as unfolded in a human nature and lived in a human life in the conditions of this sinful world needing redemption. When we contemplate the events of Christ, and above all his death and resurrection, we are looking at what divine sonship means and demands in this present order. That is the sonship which we share, and share under similar conditions; so the mystery of Christ must be reproduced in us when we become one with him.

We return, then, to the Father with Christ, and our prayer and worship should be directed through Christ to the Father. At its deepest level, Christian prayer is not prayer *to* Christ but the prayer *of* Christ. Just as the sacrifice of the Mass is the sacrifice of Christ, the sacrifice which Christ offered to the Father and into which we now enter, so our Christian prayer and worship in general is basically the prayer of Christ in which we now have a part as one with Christ; it is his prayer extended to us, his Body. We pray to the Father through and with Christ.

Certainly, from the beginning Christians have also prayed to Christ, and worship of Christ is a permanent element in the liturgy. This is because the relation with Christ which makes us one with him is not an impersonal but a personal union. For this reason, the theme of the Body of Christ, which tends to make our union with Christ seem impersonal, needs complementing with the theme of Christ as spouse. We are called to a nuptial union with Christ, and there is little need to display the depths of love and tenderness, of friendship and reverent familiarity, which this should mean to a Christian. There is ample room and a compelling necessity in our lives for prayer to Christ. Nevertheless, our union with Christ is meant to bring us into the loving surrender of Christ as man to the Father and into the relation he has as Son in the inner life of the Godhead. Prayer to Christ should pass over into a prayer through Christ to the Father: the prayer to Christ is meant to lead to the prayer of Christ.

When we go to the Father through Christ, we do so in the Holy Spirit. Our relation to the Spirit is that of possessing him as the Gift given to us by Father and Son as a pledge of their love. Since the Father and Son love themselves and us in one and the same act of love and of this love the Spirit is the fruit, we can say that it is in loving us that the Father and Son breathe forth the Spirit, who therefore comes to us as a Gift of their love. Or to put it in a better way: the Father loves us through the Son, and, in his love for the Son and for us in the Son, breathes forth the Spirit which pledges that love. The Spirit is the bond of love joining us to the Father and Son, and it is the function of the Spirit to unite us to Christ and to join us through our union with Christ to the Father. The Spirit, who is in Christ, comes forth from Christ into us, in order to incorporate us into Christ. Joined to Christ by the Spirit, we go in the Spirit through Christ to the Father.

The Holy Spirit dwells within us as the principle of our return to the Father, as the source of our prayer and worship. The term of the life of the Trinity, the Spirit, is, as it were, our point of entry into that life. The Spirit comes to us as the first Gift, and by the Spirit we are incorporated into Christ and become sons in the Son, so that united to Christ in the Spirit, we go through and with Christ to the Father and rest there in an eternal exchange of love. Here some texts of St. Paul take on their full meaning: "God has sent out the Spirit of his Son into your hearts, crying out in us, Abba, Father" (Gal. 4.6, KV); "Those who follow the leading of God's Spirit are all God's sons; the spirit you have now received is not, as of old, a spirit of slavery, to govern you by fear; it is the spirit of adoption, which makes us cry out, Abba, Father. The Spirit himself thus assures our spirit, that we are children of God; and if we are his children, then we are his heirs too; heirs of God, sharing the inheritance of Christ" (Rom. 8.14–17, KV). So Christian prayer is prayer *in* the Spirit. The Spirit is the source within us from which our prayer wells up. "When we do not know what prayer to offer, to pray as we ought," St. Paul writes, "the Spirit himself intercedes for us, with groans beyond all utterance" (Rom. 8.26, KV). True, our relation with the Spirit is a personal one, and we can address him personally in prayer and worship. We do so chiefly by asking him to come, so that in him we might love and worship. But Christian prayer is prayer in the Spirit rather than prayer to the Spirit.

Such, then, is the movement of the divine life as it flows forth from the Godhead and brings men into itself: it comes from the Father through Christ in the Spirit and, taking men with it, it goes by the Spirit through Christ to the Father. This gives us what may be called the inner structure of the Christian mystery, which is also the inner structure of our Christian life. It is essentially Trinitarian.

What we have been considering is the self-giving of God. Within the Godhead itself, this self-giving is the mystery of the Trinity; and, for that reason, when the self-giving reaches out to man, it remains a Trinitarian process. But what has not yet received sufficient attention here is that the self-gift of God to man takes place in history. The same process that is the Christian life in each individual is, in its corporate universality and full duration, the history of salvation, embracing the Old Testament preparation, the once-for-all work of Christ and the life of the Church with its liturgy. Indeed, it takes place in the individual only in so far as he is inserted into the history of salvation.

God, then, gives himself to man in this historical order. The gift comes to us as we exist in this visible world of flesh and blood. God reaches down to us and gives us himself by visible actions, and it is through such actions that the reality of the divine life enters this world and becomes present to us. And our response, our movement of return to God, is also expressed in a visible way; we embody it in our lives as lived in this material world. The mystery of God's self-gift and man's response is embodied in the visible actions, earthly forms, symbols and events of this world.

That the mystery is brought to us in this way is most suitable, because it is in accord with our human nature. Only in this way could the mystery embrace fully what we are and the lives we lead as men. The fact that the mystery is thus realized is expressed by saying that the mystery is sacramental. Recent theology uses the word "sacrament" in a wider sense than has been customary for centuries. It is not an arbitrary procedure to do this, but a return to an earlier usage; and it helps us to place the seven rites called sacraments in a wider context. "Sacramental," then, is used to describe the reality of the divine life or love as present visibly in this world, as embodied in the visible actions, events and things of this historical order. The love of God makes contact with men in visible signs and the response of men makes contact with God in visible signs: our personal communion with God is lived in the visible activity of human existence in this world. Any embodiment of the reality of the divine saving love in historical events or earthly forms is called a sacrament, though there is an order among the various sacraments.

The mystery, which is the divine agape or self-giving of God, was inserted into this world as a historical process. Redemptive history, as it may be called, is made up of a series of historical events and visible actions each having a transcendent significance, each containing within itself the action of God and, consequently, in some way altering the relation between God and man. Behind redemptive history lies the Trinitarian life of God, manifesting and communicating itself. A word, taken from St. Paul and much used by the Greek Fathers to describe this working out of the divine design in history, is "economy"; it is a Greek word meaning arrangement or dispensation. The economy of salvation is the mystery in history, the unfolding or dispensation of the mystery in time.

The background of the economy of salvation and of the realization in the present order of God's self-gift to man is the fact of sin. Man refused God's initial offer and separated himself from God by sin. He fell into a state marked by sin. Sinful man was cut off from God and entrapped in a world of suffering, corruption and death. The grip of sin and its effects on the whole of his existence made a slavery for him. Moreover, his world became a world in which the powers of darkness held sway. But God did not allow his rejection by man to frustrate his purpose: in his love he decided to save men. His self-giving love became a redemptive love. The purpose of God was still to give man a share in his own life, but the gift now came to sinful man as a gift of salvation.

The first period in the history of salvation was a time of preparation. The gift of salvation was not fully given then, and anything that was given was only an anticipation and preparation of what was to come in Christ. It is impossible to describe here in detail the characteristics of this first period, which laid down the pattern for the divine intervention in history and remains important for our understanding of the meaning of Christ and his work. Notice, however, that the God of the Old Testament is God the Father. True, he was not yet clearly recognized in his personality as Father; it was not known that he was constituted as a person by his relation to a Son. But the men of the Old Testament looked to God as to a person who was without origin and who was the ultimate personal source of life and salvation. In that sense the Old Testament was the revelation of God the Father, and the New Testament could reveal the Trinity by the announcement that the God of Abraham had a Son. For the same reason, the name "God" stands in the New Testament for God the Father. So, the Old Testament makes known God the Father and his saving power and teaches men to look to him as to the source of the salvation to come. There we find too the idea of a special relation with God, of a personal communion with him; and the pattern for God's self-giving is also sketched.

But the centre of redemptive history is Jesus Christ. With him came the definitive intervention of God in history. The action by which the Father saved us took place in Christ; the imparting of the divine reality to men was achieved in and through Christ; Christ in what he was, in what he did, in what was realized in him was full expression and complete communication of the divine love. Hence the mystery of the divine agape will always be for us the mystery of Christ. The rest of the history of salvation, or the time of the Church, does not add anything to what was given in Christ, but simply diffuses and makes present in different times and places the salvation accomplished in him; it gives men the opportunity of joining themselves to Christ and entering into the mystery as realized in him.

When in the incarnation the Father sent his Son into this world as man, he established, as we have seen, the foundation of the new order in which men were to be sons of God. Christ was his only-begotten Son made man, and men were to be made Sons of the Father by becoming one with Christ and sharing his sonship. But the Father's self-gift made in Christ by which men were regenerated as his sons was brought about in a particular fashion, because it had to come to men as a gift of salvation, enslaved as they were in sin. We must see how the mystery of Christ was actually unfolded, with its climax in a death and resurrection.

As it took place in this present order, the incarnation involved the acceptance by Christ of a certain distance from his Father. By becoming man, the Son entered the world of sin and death. He could not be touched by the moral guilt of sin, but he took upon himself the conditions of our sinful existence. He came in the likeness of sinful flesh; he became subject to suffering and death; he was made lower than the angels. The Spirit, which he possessed from the beginning, did not fully penetrate his created nature. Christ did not enjoy in his human nature all the privileges that were implied in his sonship. His sonship was not immediately realized in full. Christ as man renounced the glory that was his due and accepted a solidarity with the sinful human race.

Now, what took place in Christ, the events of Christ, can be grouped under the idea of a *transitus*. (The word simply means a *passing* from one order to another.) But how was it achieved? Christ was embraced by the Father and brought through death to the resurrection. God the Father intervened with an act of saving love, which transformed the manhood of Christ, rescued him from this world of sin and death, penetrated him completely with the

Spirit and exalted him as Son. The paschal mystery is the supreme expression of the love of the Father for the Son, a love which was pledged in the gift of the Spirit. By the *transitus,* Christ as man was fully established as Son, and when the relation between the Father and Son was thus fully displayed, the Spirit was sent to complete the progressive revelation of the Trinity and its insertion into history.

On the part of Christ himself, the paschal mystery was a reaching out to the Father and an expression of filial love. Christ as man was free, and the redemptive process was achieved only through the loving obedience with which he freely responded as man to the divine will. There was in Christ a human love for the Father that was the counterpart and reflection of his divine love as Son. This unswerving and unchanging love as man for the Father was the underlying force governing the life of Christ and giving it unity; it lay behind all that Christ did and penetrated it with its influence. His life, death and resurrection form the history of the loving obedience with which as Son he accepted the abasement of a redemptive incarnation and made his way back to the Father along the path appointed by his Father's will. His death was the lowest point in his obedient self-abasement and the culminating expression of his love. In an act of sacrificial oblation he gave himself into the hands of his Father, and so merited his resurrection and the gift of the Spirit.[1]

The paschal mystery, then, is an expression in history of the love of the Father for the Son and of the love of the Son for the Father, with the pledge of their mutual love in the gift of the Spirit. Since this expression took place in a struggle against sin and death, it took the form of a *transitus* in which the incarnate Son passed from darkness to light, from a death to life, from slavery to freedom; or, in other words, it was a new exodus, involving the defeat and destruction of the powers of darkness.

But God the Son became incarnate for our salvation; and the coming of Christ and his life, death and resurrection are inexplicable except in relation to our salvation. How, then, does what was done in Christ affect us? In this way: what was done in Christ is an efficacious sign through which God brings about in

[1] We shall examine the central significance of the paschal mystery in greater detail in Chapter XIX, "The Resurrection and the Atonement."

us the same transition from death to life and establishes us as his sons. The mystery of Christ is the visible embodiment of the mystery of God's self-giving. That visible embodiment was set up by God as a permanent sacrament or effectual sign in which he offers sonship to men. We must see the mystery of Christ as a sacrament through which we receive salvation.

In Christ is expressed the divine love and will to save. But notice that this human expression of the divine saving love is not a single, static sign but a history. The entire history of Christ from beginning to end forms a dramatic, effectual sign or sacrament in which God's saving purpose is set forth and through which his self-giving comes to men. This sign is Trinitarian in structure in that it manifests the different roles of the three persons in the divine self-giving. Every event of Christ's life and work forms part of the sign, since every event manifests some facet of the divine saving love. The sign was completed and given permanence in the risen Christ, who is penetrated with the Spirit and reigns in glory as Son at the right hand of the Father. It is efficacious as a sign, so that every event in the historical work of Christ shares the efficacy that belongs to the entire mystery of Christ as the effectual sign or sacrament of the divine agape. Thus, Christ in what he is and in the events of his historical work is the Great Sacrament, and every communication of divine life is due to the causal influence of this Great Sacrament.

But how does this Great Sacrament act upon us? How does its efficacy reach us? How are we brought into contact with it? By the liturgy. The liturgy is a subordinate sacramental expression of the mystery. The mystery, it may be recalled, is ultimately the eternal love and inner life of God, from which comes the self-gift of God to man. The mystery of Christ is the second level of the mystery, since it is the primordial expression of that divine love and life; it embodies the definitive act by which God gives himself to men, so that any communication of divine life to us is due to it as cause. But we must somehow make contact with the mystery of Christ. We do this in the liturgy, which symbolizes the mystery of Christ and brings it present. The liturgy, then, may be seen as a third level of the mystery; it is the mystery of Christ made present so that we can share in it and come under its influence.

The liturgy as sacramental is subordinate in two ways to the mystery of Christ, which I have called the Great Sacrament. First, as an expression of the mystery. The mystery of Christ embodied the divine love in historical events that took place once for all and formed the basic and definitive expression in history and for all time, the mystery of God's self-gift. The liturgy is a symbolic representation and memorial of these once-for-all events in ritual gestures and words that are constantly repeated. Secondly, the liturgy is subordinate in its efficacy. It has but a limited and derived efficacy: limited, because it conveys to a limited number of persons in a given time and place the universal and enduring efficacy of the mystery of Christ; derived, because all the efficacy it has comes from the mystery of Christ which it makes present.

How and in what sense the liturgy makes present for us the mystery of Christ are questions that will be taken up in a later chapter, "The Mass as the Assembly of Christians." Nevertheless, this treatment of the Christian mystery would be defective unless it made quite clear the point that through the liturgy the mystery of Christ must be reproduced in us and in our lives. That the mystery must be realized in the life of each Christian was the theme of the first part of the chapter, which dealt with our relations to the three persons of the Trinity, but what must be reiterated here is that the events of Christ show us the implications of divine sonship in this present order. When the love of the Father reaches us, it must bring about in us a *transitus,* a passing from death to life, from the order of this world to the order of the resurrection; and our loving response must take the form of a suffering love and find expression in a sacrificial oblation. If we are to be sons in the Son, we must share the death and resurrection of Christ; we must share his sufferings if we wish to share his glory; and there must be imparted to us the gift of the Spirit he received at his resurrection and glorification. In other words, what happened in Christ must now happen in the members of his Body. Since it can happen in the members only under the influence of what happened in Christ himself, their *transitus* is a participation in his own; the mystery of Christ is extended to them, is continued in them. That is the meaning and function of the liturgy.

Unfathomable in its depths of meaning and various in its manifestations, the Christian mystery is essentially one. It is the divine agape, according to which self-giving is the inmost nature of the Godhead. Contemplated within the inner life of God, it is that procession of the Son from the Father and of the Holy Spirit from the Father through the Son which we call the mystery of the Trinity. The same divine love reaches out into creation and calls man to enter the life of the Trinity. The self-gift of God to man becomes the mystery of Christ when inserted into the flow of human history. In its central act it is the paschal mystery or *transitus;* in its full dimensions it becomes the entire history of salvation, which is being continued in the Church and will end in the Second Coming. In the individual this same mystery is the Christian life; in its corporate fullness it is the life of the Church as the Mystical Body of Christ. In its ultimate fulfilment it is beatitude and final glorification. And the structure of this mystery is always the same: from the Father through the Son and in the Spirit, and by the Spirit through the Son to the Father. Hence in the liturgy we pray to the Father through our Lord Jesus Christ in the unity of the Holy Spirit.

CHAPTER X

WHAT IS ORIGINAL SIN?

God called our first parents to a personal union with himself that went beyond what belonged to them as human beings. He created them as friends, gave them a share in his own life—something they could not have claimed as necessary for an adequate human existence. It was a free gift, over and above the gift of creation. We call it the gift of original justice. Essentially it was the same as the grace we now receive, but when given to the first, innocent couple, it brought complete harmony to the various faculties and tendencies of our complex human nature. God added the assurance that men would be preserved from all suffering and harm, even death, if they remained faithful to him. And he placed them in an environment suitable for such an untroubled existence. The earthly paradise of Genesis is a simple, pictorial description of all this. The first man and woman may well have been of a more primitive physical type than are modern men, but that does not exclude the full harmony of a nature under complete control or the possession of the gift of divine friendship.

God did not give men immediately the fullness of this higher state. Its fullness would have been the vision of himself face to face, with all the happiness that brings. Had he given them this, they would have infallibly responded with love and been incapable of holding back. Such a necessary love would not have done violence to man's nature; for God is the fulfilment of all man's desires and not an alien force. But no creature can resist the unveiled loveliness of God, and there would have been no freedom of choice, no possibility of a refusal. That means that eternal life would have been less perfect, because it would not have implied the free response of man. Man would have had no opportunity of offering God a free homage and love or of meriting his eternal life as a reward.

This would not have fitted into the general scheme of creation. We notice how creatures are made in such a way that they reach their full perfection only by their own activity. God had a similar plan for man. He created him in such a way that he had to move towards his destiny by his own intelligent and free activity. That is what we mean by a period of trial—not an arbitrary test by God, but the opportunity for man to accept his destiny freely before the splendour and beauty of God saturated his soul. God wanted his eternal communion with man to be rooted in a free response.

And so, exalted as the state of our first parents was, they lived in the darkness of faith. They had first to believe, without seeing, that their final happiness lay in surrendering themselves to the mysterious call of God. However intimate their communion with God, it was a union in faith, not in vision. Gradually, we may suppose, the intimacy would have increased until it opened out almost spontaneously into the beatific vision and final happiness. But if the opportunity of accepting freely God's friendship was a great honour given to man, it involved the possibility of man's refusal. And man did in fact refuse. At the origin of human history is the negative response of man to God, a response that destroyed man's first state.

There are two points in the Catholic doctrine of original sin. First, there was a primitive sin, a sin of Adam the first man, which brought about the downfall of the human race from the privileged state in which it had been created. Second, all men inherit by descent from Adam, not merely death and bodily sufferings, but also in itself, the death of the soul, so that we are all born sinners. The first point is taught already in the Book of Genesis; the second emerged clearly only in the teaching of St. Paul.

Whatever part we allow to imagery and symbol in the biblical account of man's fall, we must recognize the clear intention of the author to teach that the present condition of mankind, with the suffering and wretchedness it involves, is due to a primitive sin. God did not create man in his present state; the reason for the

universal disorder is a sin at the origin of the human race. That
is the bearing of the narrative. It teaches the fact of Adam's sin as
the explanation of the present situation of mankind.

But can we be more precise about the nature of that sin? As
with all sin, the important element in the sin of Adam was not
the external action but the inner, spiritual attitude. At first sight,
it seems strange that Adam sinned at all. He was in a privileged
state where it was easy to preserve his friendship with God. Even
a sinner is seeking some apparent good. What could Adam have
wanted to make him rebel against God? The clue to the answer
is the supernatural character of man's vocation. It goes beyond
man's natural powers. Adam was called to a life and destiny
where his own natural forces were helpless by themselves. This
higher vocation demanded a greater recognition of God's transcendence and a greater acknowledgement of dependence and limitation than would have been required by mere creaturehood. Adam
had to surrender something of his autonomy and self-sufficiency.
This autonomy would have been severely limited in any event by
his position as a creature. But had man been left to an ordinary
human existence, he would have been guided by the light of his
own mind, and he would have judged the good of his moral
actions by his unaided reason. In a supernatural state, that is
impossible. Since God did not give man immediately the fullness
of his new life, man had to allow himself to be guided in faith towards a destiny he could not clearly envisage. And, in order to
reach it, he had to agree to use various means he was unable to
evaluate for himself but had to accept on trust from God. He
was drawn by a hidden God towards a mysterious destiny which
lay beyond the furthest point where human reason can see and
judge for itself. He was commanded to follow a course of action
the usefulness of which was a matter of faith, not of rational appraisal. Had he submitted, his surrender would have brought him
to a direct union with God which, while surpassing, would have
completely fulfilled his nature. How true it is in general that an
openness of self, a surrender of self to others, is the only way to
the realization of self! It is even more true in our relationship
with God. But we can see how man might have preferred, as he
did in fact prefer, the illusion of his own autonomy to acceptance
of the call of God.

The sinful attitude of Adam is finely analysed in the Book of Genesis. Man wanted to be like God. Not that he pretended that he could possess the omniscience or omnipotence of God. But he wanted to decide for himself what was good and evil. He claimed a moral autonomy; that was the knowledge of good and evil which tempted him. He wished to judge for himself what was good and make his way towards his destiny by his own forces and with his own reason. This was pride—the rejection of the sovereignty of God and of his plan for man. This pride was expressed in some disobedient refusal. We have seen that it was part of man's condition to have to accept on trust from God the necessity of certain means required to prepare him for his destiny. He would not always have been able to see their value. The purpose of various commands and prohibitions was not immediately clear. He should have trusted God and accepted with love the means God had freely chosen to draw him closer to himself. He did not, and sinned by a disobedient refusal motivated by pride.

The traditional explanation of Adam's sin is firmly based on the text of Genesis even if this is interpreted symbolically, as it is today. The account gives a penetrating analysis of temptation and sin. But does the author give us any information about the external action in which Adam's sinful attitude was embodied? No. The author did not know, any more than we do, exactly what occurred. The concrete details are symbols. Guided by revelation, the writer teaches the fact of Adam's sin, its spiritual significance and its universal consequences. He had no historical knowledge in the ordinary sense about the events of the Garden of Eden. He cast his teaching in the imagery of his cultural environment. How are we to interpret the symbols? Beyond what I have already said, scholars are not agreed. The investigation of the detailed meaning of the symbolism will throw light on the message about human life and sin which the author addressed to his contemporaries. It will not yield any further information about the way in which Adam sinned. That much is clear from the nature of the narrative.

Thus, a view of increasing popularity gives the symbols a sexual meaning. Not in the sense that the first sin was the use of sex. Besides being ridiculous, such an interpretation would be against the clear tenor of the narrative. The second account of creation, which includes the story of the Fall, is an account of the origin of the sexes more than a simple account of the origin of man. The purpose of the narrative is to show the relationship of the sexes as God intended it, and the normal union of the sexes is presented as the divine plan. But the author has in mind the Canaanite cults, which so often seduced the Israelites. These involved the worship of the sexual principle, the free gratification of the sexual passions and the degradation of woman by exclusive stress on her sexual function. What the author is saying is that this is not what God had intended. In the beginning it was not so. It is a debasement due to sin. He shows the relation between man and woman as God had created them and contrasts with it the degradation, the perversion, brought about by man's sin and manifested in the Canaanite cults. He is not teaching that the primitive sin was this sin of deifying sex. But, in teaching that the universal disorder in the world is due to a primitive sin, he does so with the use of symbols that indicate the worst disorder present in his contemporary world. His condemnation is relevant even today, which is also an age of sexual licence in which sex is glorified. But it is not relevant to the question of the nature of the first sin.

By his sin Adam lost God's friendship, with its accompanying gifts, not for himself alone but for all mankind. We must remember that his friendship with God was a higher personal union coming not from his nature as man but from a special gift. It was a free gift given to men in the way God freely decided. He chose to give it to the first man as a gift attached to human nature, so that other men would receive it in virtue of their descent by generation from Adam. Not that physical generation can be the direct cause of a spiritual gift, any more than it is the direct cause of the spiritual soul. But just as the normal law of human generation demands the creation of the soul in the course of bodily conception, so it would have demanded the bestowal of original justice. Just as the soul belongs to the body and is given when the body comes into existence, so original justice was bound up with human nature and would have been given according to a normal law when each human nature came into existence. That was God's plan, a plan in keeping with man's social nature and the unity of the human race. But the plan required for its working that original justice should not be lost by any link in the chain of human parents. The loss of it by Adam, the first link, the father of the human race, deprived all men of it. Original sin is essentially the lack of original justice. Its transmission to all Adam's children is the perversion of the divine plan for the transmission of original justice.

We may ask, in passing, about the sin of Eve. According to the common teaching, Adam's sin alone was the original sin in the sense of the sin that caused the downfall of the human race and deprived future generations of grace. Whatever the woman might have done affected only herself, except in so far as she influenced the actions of the man. This teaching was bound up in medieval theology with an antiquated physiology, according to which only the man and his seed had an active part in the generation of a child. This is untrue, and the medieval argument falls to the ground. Nevertheless, the place of man as the head of the woman in the partnership of the sexes makes it still reasonable to hold that it was the action of the man that had the decisive role in determining the fate of mankind.

As children of Adam, men are cut off from God and in absolute need of redemption. Catholic doctrine is not content with saying that they inherit the effects of Adam's sin; it says that they inherit the sin itself. This is strange. What does it mean? It does not mean that men are held responsible for the personal sin of Adam. They are not, and no argument could make that anything but unjust. But what they were deprived of by Adam's sin affected their moral status before God. Suppose a diseased child is born of syphilitic parents whose disease has been contracted by sin. The child suffers from the effects of sin; it inherits the effects of sin. But its own moral status before God is untouched; in no way does it inherit sin itself. Now, this is not an adequate parallel to original sin. We do suffer from the effects of Adam's sin, but, more than that, our own moral status before God is affected. We are put in a state of sin, not by our own act but by the act of our first parent.[1]

This is due to the nature of the gift lost by Adam. The gift of grace given to Adam was not an added titbit given to sweeten

---

[1] The next chapter, "The Two Adams," will deal with the difficulties encountered by the human mind regarding the doctrine of original sin.

man's life; it was a gift that determined man's destiny. God could have created man for an ordinary human existence, but he did not. He created him with the sole destiny of being a son of God. Without grace, man is cut off from the purpose for which God made him. He is unable to make a single move towards the final end which should govern all his moral activity as a responsible person. To be cut off from one's ultimate end is to be in a state of sin. It is what is meant by a state of serious sin. Original sin in us is a state of sin without a personal act of sin; a state of sin caused by the act of another. That makes it different from an actual sin. The word "sin" is not used with the same meaning in both cases. The actual sin of Adam is not imputed to us. But a state is induced in us that deserves the name of sin because it separates us from our ultimate end. Our moral status is destroyed, because we are unable to live according to our moral destiny. We are not the cause of this, and so we should not have been punished positively for it, but we should still have been lost in the sense of being barred from our ultimate end.

But worse than that. The separation from his ultimate end would have upset man's moral life even on the natural level. It is the choice of his final end that gives direction and equilibrium to a man's moral life. With such a choice impossible, man would have been in a state of confusion and weakness. Fallen man cannot avoid sin for long. If left without grace, each man would have added personal sin to original sin with little delay. It is not that man's very nature is corrupt; it is not. It is simply that he is unable to cope with a universe geared to a supernatural purpose. He is unequipped by nature to deal with it. The scheme of the universe planned by God demanded grace in man; bereft of grace, man would have floundered in it helplessly. He could not have survived morally. A man can live naked in the tropics without difficulty; put him naked in the Arctic and he will soon die. Had the universe been designed for man to live merely on the human level, he would have lived a moral life without undue difficulty. Unclothed with grace, he cannot survive in this universe designed for a higher purpose. And so, the children of Adam would not merely have been deprived of their destiny by original sin but also have fallen into a state of positive enmity with God by personal sin.

The sin of Adam marked the end of the first state of mankind. It was succeeded immediately by a new scheme of things, the economy of redemption. God had not been taken by surprise or forced to change his plan. He permitted original sin only because he had decided to remedy it by the wonderful gift of salvation. But redemption does not make original sin a merely theoretical matter. God did not will to remove its consequences at a stroke. Although enough grace was always available to each man, the plan of redemption was unfolded only gradually. Long centuries passed before Christ came, centuries which saw but a restricted flow of grace. Even now, after the coming of Christ and the outpouring of the Spirit, we still await the full fruits of Christ's victory. God has allowed a certain latitude to sin, so that history is a long struggle between good and evil. The effects of sin are used by God in the process of salvation; and the passion of Christ shows us the manner of our redemption. Man is given an opportunity to expiate his sins and prove his fidelity. He is taught humility and a sense of his own weakness; he becomes aware of the malice of sin and the depths of God's justice and love. We cannot understand the present world and the plan of salvation without the doctrine of original sin. That is why the Church insists upon it. It was, in fact, the New Testament revelation of the meaning of Christ's salvation that first brought the full realization of the significance of Adam's sin, and when that realization grows dim, man becomes a mystery to himself.

Many people today, for example, just do not know what to think about man and his future. Should we be optimists or pessimists? Much in the present situation seems to justify hopes of great progress, while much again provokes a feeling of despair. Men have never seen before such a rapid advance as we are now making in the sphere of material and scientific achievement. A change is coming about in our everyday lives that could gradually free us from the worst burdens of bodily existence and open to us unparalleled opportunities for spiritual betterment. But is material progress in fact enlarging our spiritual existence? It is a commonplace to observe that moral progress is lagging behind. Some would go further and say that never before has man's spiritual stature been so low or human nature shown itself so untamed and bestial. "Since about 1930," wrote George Orwell in *Critical*

Essays (1946), "the world has given no reason for optimism whatever. Nothing is in sight except a welter of lies, hatred, cruelty and ignorance." We may think the outburst exaggerated, but few would dismiss it as entirely groundless.

What is the Christian attitude to all this? The Christian view about human achievement and social progress is closely linked to the doctrine of original sin. It is most relevant to the question to know that each of us comes into this world alienated from God by sin; not indeed by a personal act of sin, but by a state of sin brought about in us by the rebellion of Adam from whom we descend. This doctrine is undeniably difficult for our minds, but it can be confirmed by reflexion on the actual state of this world; and then it does not stand alone but gets its true significance in the context of the redeeming love of God. Here, I am going to take the fact of original sin for granted. My present interest is the implications of it. What does the fallen state of man imply? What are the repercussions of a racial sin on man's make-up and potentialities?

But first, what is the gist of the doctrine? By original sin man is deprived of sanctifying grace and, with this, of the other free gifts conferred on Adam. Presupposed to the teaching on the Fall is the truth that Adam was not created by God simply as a man. He was raised to a higher level of existence and given a share in the life of God by grace. He received also other gifts intended to bring his natural powers into full harmony with this high status. The fall of Adam was not, then, the fall of a mere man; it was the fall of a freely favoured creature from a superhuman and divine level. All these gifts, known collectively as original justice, were made dependent on the free response of man to God. When Adam rebelled he lost them; and, in doing so, he deprived us of our inheritance. God had attached these gifts to human nature itself; they were to be handed on with that nature in generation. But Adam now had only an impoverished nature to give his children. And not only an impoverished but a tainted nature, because it left man incapable of reaching the one destiny willed for him by God.

This, then, was the tragic ending to a vocation of great promise. But need we be so very worried about man's condition? After all, these gifts were uncalled-for; they were not needed for man to live

an ordinary human life. God could—it is Catholic teaching—have
created man without them, and have destined him for an ordinary
human existence and happiness. Should not reflexion on this make
us optimistic about fallen man? Man by the Fall, shall we say,
has returned to the state in which he would have been had God
never raised him above the human level. True, his state is sinful in the sense that he is cut off from the end for which God
made him, but otherwise all is well. His condition on the human
level is quite sound; he has all his human resources, and the possibility of an ordinary human existence with its progress and happiness lies open before him. Some theologians have given the
impression that such is in reality the condition of fallen man.
Tradition, however, seems to take a gloomier view. A truer and
more firmly founded way of understanding mankind's disaster is,
we find, far less optimistic.

Fallen man is stripped of the gifts with which God clothed his
nature; but that is not all. He is wounded in his natural resources.
His potentialities even as man are diminished. His moral vision
and his moral power are seriously affected. Man in his fallen
state, says St. Thomas and the central line of theological thought,
cannot love God above all things. It is not a question here of the
supernatural love of charity, which is clearly impossible to a
man without grace, but of that adherence to God that belongs
to the moral order of nature. Now, such a love is at the root of
man's moral life. It is the choice of God, the Supreme and Absolute Good, as supreme that gives the human will that basic
direction which guides aright its other choices and gives firmness
and stability to the moral life. Unable to achieve such an act,
man remains in a state of disequilibrium, easily led to pursue
some particular good in a disordered and sinful way. Not all that
he does is evil; he can do actions that are good. But without
much delay he will fall into personal sin and add a state of personal rebellion to his inherited estrangement from God. Fallen
man cannot avoid sin for long; he cannot keep for any length
of time the moral obligations even of the natural law. So, it is
not the supernatural alone that is closed to him. He is incapable
in his weakness of living a life in accord with the standards
embedded in his nature, conformity to which is necessary for a
life lived on a reasonable human level. He is not, it is true, en-

tirely immersed in evil and can do on occasion what is good, but perseverance is beyond him and the choice of the Supreme Good as his ultimate end is something above his strength. In the disorder of his activities and the uncertainty of his random moral achievements, fallen man drops below the human level.

This seems a startling conclusion. Does it mean that human nature has been corrupted in its constitutive principles? In other words, has man been deprived of his freedom or mutilated in his faculties? If so, man would no longer be man but some monstrous result of an essential decay. No; that must be rejected. Besides being philosophically untenable, it is heresy—the heresy of the Reformers and the Jansenists. Man remains man; his nature complete. Even without sin, the imperfect make of man would have left him subject to concupiscence, suffering and death. Man's moral impotence does not come from any intrinsic corruption in what makes him man, but from his concrete situation in this present universe. The point is that he does not exist in some hypothetical order of nature pure and simple but in this present universe, which is governed by the Fall and redemption. Devastating though the results may be, the helplessness of fallen man is simply his inability to cope with a universe such as this.

We do not know what the condition of a universe without grace would have been. But man would have found it an easier universe, one within the range of his natural resources. God would have given man all the help he needed to achieve a stable moral life and to reach a natural happiness in him. The present order is not geared to such a purpose, and consequently it forms a terrible environment for man unequipped by grace to meet its demands. Even after the Fall, God does not intend man for a natural end, so he does not help him towards one. It is redemption that he offers him. Moreover, God has permitted in this world as a result of sin a fierce struggle between Good and Evil, and Evil is allowed a sway difficult to conceive as permissible in a universe left at the natural level. As things are, man cannot survive the encounter if he refuses to welcome grace. A life of natural moral goodness is but a mirage. Man is offered help by God, but it is not to build a natural human order; it is a redemption, a restoration of man to the supernatural order—and that only through the suffering of the Cross.

The whole world, John tells us, is in the power of the Evil One. This world has Satan as its Prince (cf. 1 John 5.19 and John 16.11). We must never forget that sin placed mankind under the slavery of Satan; men became his captives. Our struggle to do good and to follow Christ is a struggle with powers that are more than human. "You must wear all the weapons in God's armoury," writes St. Paul, "if you would find strength to resist the cunning of the devil. It is not against flesh and blood that we enter the lists; we have to do with princedoms and powers, with those who have mastery of the world in these dark days, with malign influences in an order higher than ours" (Eph. 6.11–12, KV). It is a disastrous mistake to underestimate the force of evil in this present order. This world, in fact, fell into the grip of the Evil One. After the account of the Fall, there is given at once the story of Cain and Abel, and the sacred writer intended by this to show how sin immediately began to spread. What else, in fact, is biblical history but the drama of the long struggle between good and evil? The forces of evil were let loose by man's sin; man, though intact in his essential make-up, had been wrenched spiritually and psychologically by the calamitous change in his condition; he became their easy prey.

But redemption, it might be argued, came to man's rescue. Certainly; from the very beginning Christ's redemption was operative. It offered already to Adam grace for eternal salvation, and it has been generally held that Adam himself was actually saved. Grace has always been available. Then in the fullness of time Christ came down into this world. He overcame this world and the powers of this world. By his death and resurrection he gained the victory. Evil has been defeated, and the risen Christ rules in triumph. He is now gathering his chosen ones to himself, and the day will come when his kingdom will be gloriously manifested and the universe will be transformed and made new. Any consideration of sin must be balanced by the thought of the overwhelming victory of Christ. Nevertheless, the actual scheme of redemption as willed by God makes a study of the Fall far from theoretical. What has been said about fallen man is not mere unrealized hypothesis. In God's plan redemption is achieved by a struggle with the power of evil. The consequences of original sin are not removed at a stroke; they are used by God in the process of salvation. Man is thus given an opportunity to expiate his sins; he learns humility; he becomes aware of the malice of sin and glimpses something of the mysterious depths of God's justice and love. Mankind had to wait many long centuries for the coming of Christ, during which, if grace was sufficient for individual salvation, it was not abundant. And we are still waiting now for the full fruits of Christ's victory. The cockle is still growing with the wheat, and men flourish who refuse the grace of Christ. This remains a fallen universe, and it requires the Fall to explain its present state. All the same, if sin is still rampant, the power of the redemption is with us; grace is offered to all, and the just can expect the final glorious vindication of the Good with secure confidence.

We are now in a position to answer the question with which we began. There can be no lasting human achievement without grace. To hope to establish with human knowledge and by human resources a new order on earth is a tragic illusion. A Christian has his own attitude to this world. He is neither an optimist nor a pessimist. He is not an optimist, because he does not think it is easy to put this world right. This fallen world can only be righted by the Cross and the saving power of Christ. Nor, again, does he look for the definitive victory in this present order. Christianity is a religion of the Resurrection; the final order, the restoration of all things, will be brought by the Second Coming of Christ and the resurrection of mankind. But the Christian is not a pessimist. This world is not regarded as without hope. Christ has won the victory. He has risen, and the power of his resurrection is already working in the world. Every activity of ours in Christ, every initiative that springs from faith and charity, has saving power. And, although we cannot measure its progress, the kingdom of God is making its way in this world; for Christ is carrying out his plan. There is here and now in this world a radiant influence of Christ's power, and the Christian life should exert its beneficent effect throughout the entire range of human enterprise. And it is the whole of human existence that is capable of redemption. All that is good in human achievement will be taken up into the final order and receive there its full meaning and complete perfection. The order of redemption presupposes and, by remedying man's sin, preserves intact the order of creation. But we must wait in patience a little while for the victory and not be surprised at the continual upsurge of evil. It is the time of our sharing in the Cross of Christ, for we must learn not to trust in our own power. It is only through the Cross that fallen man can share the resurrection.

CHAPTER XI

THE TWO ADAMS

Confronted with the doctrine of original sin, our human minds protest. Or perhaps in complacency we do not realize the full force of this mystery. Some aspects of it are not too difficult. However deep our regret at the initial calamity of the human race, the simple assertion that by the sin of Adam mankind lost a certain number of free gifts is intelligible enough. Again, although we wistfully look back on Paradise, a humble awareness of our bodily natures and of their material composition leads us to accept with resignation the pain and the disease, the suffering and the death, which are the present lot of men. The struggle of flesh and spirit within ourselves is more serious in character, and this drag on our spiritual activity with the frequent degradation of our higher selves it brings is apt to make us question the wisdom and goodness of God; or, at least, it causes us bewilderment at the apparent lopsidedness of the divine plan. But there is more than all this. We do not merely inherit these consequences of Adam's sin, we inherit that sin. We are born not only in a state of impoverishment but in a state of guilt; we come into the world estranged from God by sin. Such is the dogma of original sin as defined in the Council of Trent: there is handed down from Adam to all his natural descendants, except Mary, a sin, a true sin, not simply the penalties of sin.

At once the mind jibs. How can we be blamed for what we did not do? Who can be culpable for what was not within his choice? Can sin be inherited? Let us beware here of turning the mystery, which this truth is, into absurdity, which it is not. God does not hold us responsible for Adam's personal sin. He does not in any way pretend that we committed it. Original sin does not make us culpable before God of any act of sin. The act of sin involved in this issue was committed by Adam alone; we inherit the state of sin resulting from that act.

It is impossible to understand the meaning of this without widening the perspective. The determining factor in the moral order is the ultimate destiny of man. It is that which is the primordial principle of a moral life. What is in accord with that destiny is good and what goes against that destiny is moral evil or sin. To be on the way to one's destiny, to possess the rectitude that places one's condition and activity in its direction, is to be in a state of righteousness before God; to be out of harmony with one's destiny, to lack such a rectitude and such a direction, to be turned towards another end, is to be in a state of sin before God. In the present order the destiny of man is the share in the divine life and happiness given by the beatific vision. That is man's sole destiny—there is no other—and it is a destiny beyond his reach for which he requires with an absolute necessity the grace of God. For man, then, to be without grace is not simply the lack of an adornment; it is the privation of an essential moral factor, so that the absence of grace is by that very fact a state of sin—a state in which man is without the basic moral rectitude which orders him to his ultimate destiny and thereby makes a virtuous life possible.

To return now to Adam. Sin and grace are incompatible. By his rebellion against God, Adam lost his endowment of grace; he was left in a state of aversion from God. Without grace, in a state of sin, he was helpless before the demands of a virtuous life. Deprived of grace, he found his one and only destiny absolutely beyond his grasp. Still, it was his own choice; the cause of his pitiful state was his own personal act. But why did this state of sin stretch out its tentacles and embrace us too? It did so because God had decreed that the grace necessary to put us on a level with our destiny should reach us through our descent from Adam. Adam's loss in that way became our own. Grace had been given at the origin of the human race to be handed down with human nature itself to all men. The rebellion of our first parents deprived the entire human race at its source of the grace essential to it for its moral destiny. All men are born without grace; by that fact all are born in a state of sin. In truth, this is not the positive aversion from God that results from a personal individual sin; but it remains an absence of righteousness in regard to human destiny that is a moral evil or sin. Man is found helpless before his destiny and before the demands of a true moral life.

The mind remains disquieted. The mystery of original sin is the mystery of our solidarity in grace with Adam, and, in the last analysis, that solidarity is due to a free decree of God. We are indeed one with Adam by natural descent, but that is not enough to explain our oneness with him in the bestowal of grace. However fitting this might be, God could have decreed it otherwise. In actual fact God willed that grace should reach man through his natural descent; he established thereby a solidarity in grace between us and Adam. What causes disquiet is that he did this with the knowledge that Adam would sin, and thus by divine permission the entire human race was plunged by the act of one man into the state of sin and left helpless before its destiny. There lies the mystery of original sin.

Now, God did not make known to us this sombre truth until after the coming of Christ. Its first revelation is to be found in St. Paul in a passage concerned with the salvation brought by Jesus Christ. Certainly, the Book of Genesis had described the original disaster, presenting it as the reason for the existing wretched condition of mankind. Again, the subsequent ravages made by sin amongst men had been frequently bewailed in the Scriptures. None the less it remains true that not until Paul do we find a clear statement that we inherit from Adam sin itself, and not merely the penalties and consequences of sin. In the fifth chapter of his Epistle to the Romans Paul makes an antithesis between Christ and Adam in order to drive home the truth of our salvation in Christ. And it is in this perspective, that of Christ's redemptive work, that the meaning of the Fall is first made plain. The ruin brought about by the first Adam was understood in its full extent only in the light of its undoing by the second Adam, Jesus Christ. Here are the words of St. Paul: "So, then, as through one offence condemnation came to all men, so also through a single justifying act there cometh to all men lifegiving justification. As through the disobedience of the one man the many were constituted sinners, so also through the obedience

of the one the many shall be constituted just . . . where sin hath
been multiplied, grace hath abounded yet more, that, as sin
hath reigned in death, so also grace may reign through justness
unto life everlasting through Jesus Christ our Lord" (Rom. 5.18–
21. Westminster Version).[1]

There is a telling significance in the manner of this divine
revelation of original sin. It shows us where we must seek the
solution to the troubling enigma that this doctrine offers to our
human minds, namely in Christ the Redeemer. Adam's sin was
indeed a fact of human free will; for God's positive will cannot
bear even indirectly on moral evil. It took place, however, under
the permission and all-embracing providence of God, and God
knew all that it involved. He allowed it in spite of its disastrous
effects because he willed to make it the occasion of a communication of his goodness, an outpouring of his gifts, far surpassing all
that had gone before. Think for a moment what the mystery of
Christ means. God the Son made man: a union between God and
a created human nature, between the Infinite and the finite, so
close that a man, one of our own race, can say, I am God. God
the Son made man for us: the Only-Begotten of the Father becomes one with sinful humanity; he shares our life with its limitations and our sufferings, and then he offers himself as our redemptive sacrifice on the Cross. Jesus Christ, our Head, our
Priest, our King: it is he who dominates the providential plan of
God. It is to him that Christian writers of all ages point when
they wish to reconcile the permission of original sin with the
wisdom and goodness of Almighty God. In doing so, they are
but formulating in measured terms what the Church proclaims in
the paschal shout of joy: *O certe necessarium Adae peccatum,
quod Christi morte deletum est! O felix culpa, quae talem ac tan-
tum meruit habere Redemptorem!* "O truly needful sin of Adam,
which was blotted out by the death of Christ! O happy fault, that
merited so great a Redeemer!" And St. Francis de Sales com-
ments: "Ruin brought us profit, since in effect human nature has
received more graces by its Saviour redeeming, than ever it would
have received by Adam's innocence, if he had persevered therein."[2]

[1] New York, Longmans, 1933.
[2] *Treatise on the Love of God,* 2.5. Translated by the Rev. Henry Bene-
dict Mackey, O.S.B.

There is a parallelism in contrast between the dogma of original sin and the dogma of the redemption. The former tells us of a first Adam, the head of the human race, and of our oneness with him—a oneness that led to sin and death; the latter of a second Adam, the new head of mankind, and of our oneness with him—a oneness that leads to grace and eternal life.

The first Adam as he left the hands of God was himself a mystery, with a life that lies outside our natural understanding. Placed in the state of original justice, endowed with grace and other gifts, he enjoyed a life and happiness that went far beyond the requirements of a mere human existence and raised him to a share in the very life of God. Then as an extension of this, as its complement, there is the mystery of our solidarity with him—a solidarity that became through Adam's rebellion a sharing not in life but in sin and death.

The second Adam is himself a mystery, but in an incomparably greater way than the first. The personal mystery of the second Adam is the wonderful fact of the incarnation with all the consequences that flow from this, such as the infinite dignity and value of every action of Christ. Further, the mystery of Christ includes all his saving work, culminating in his death and resurrection. Then as a continuation of this mystery, as its complement in the decree of God, there is the mystery of our solidarity with Christ, whereby we are made sharers in what we achieved and in his life and grace. Like our oneness with Adam, our oneness with Christ depends in the last analysis on the free ordinance of God, and in that gratuitous decree lies the core of the mystery of our redemption. God willed that our salvation should depend on the life and sacrifice of Jesus Christ, a new head of the human race in whom mankind was to be reassembled. By his providence he made this possible and he put this plan into effect. As he had linked us to the first Adam, so now he bound us to the second Adam, and in Christ and only in Christ is salvation to be found. "Neither is there salvation in any other. For there is no other name under heaven given to men, whereby we must be saved" (Acts 4.12). Such is the inescapable law of our salvation.

The mystery of the redemption has not yet been completed; the unfolding of God's plan of salvation is still taking place in our midst today. God shows a delicate respect towards man as a

person, and he does not will to save him without his personal acceptance and co-operation. For that reason, our oneness with
Christ is realized in two distinct stages. At the origin of all the
rest is that radical solidarity, decreed by God, which makes the
life and sacrifice of Christ the principle and source of salvation
for the entire human race. In virtue of this, Christ's death and
resurrection were achieved for us; Christ went before us as our
Leader, making it possible for us to follow him in the same path
through the redemptive power of what he had done. But it still
remains for us to follow him. In this phase comes the second level
of solidarity—that effectual incorporation of each of us personally
and of all of us collectively in Christ Jesus whereby what was
done in Christ is done also in us, so that we actually share his
life. This is the oneness with Christ realized in the Church
through the sacraments, so that the Church is the issue of the
redemption, the new Assembly of God, the new People and
the new Mankind with the second Adam as its head.

For those who see with the eyes of faith, the course of human
history presents a meaning unsuspected by the men of this world.
Its centre is Jesus Christ. All that went before prepared for his
coming, and the important events of history took place in an insignificant little people whose religious development was in the
purpose of God served by the rise and fall of great empires. After
Christ, the true significance of history is found in the progressive
gathering of the new People of God, the gradual incorporation of
men who accept his grace into their new Head, the second Adam.
When this task is completed according to the mysterious design
of God, Jesus Christ will return in glory to take full and visible
possession of his People. All will then be brought to its achievement. Such is the magnificent vision of St. Paul: "For as in Adam
all die, so in Christ all shall be made to live. But each of his own
order: Christ the first fruits, then they that are Christ's shall rise,
at his coming; then shall be the end, when he shall surrender the
kingdom to God the Father, when he shall have brought to
naught all other rule and all other authority and power. . . .
And when all things shall be subject to him, then shall the Son
himself be subject to the Father who subjected all things to him
that God may be all in all" (1 Cor. 15.22–8. Westminster
Version).

CHAPTER XII

THE PLACE OF CHRIST

At the centre of our religion, then, is Jesus Christ. He is that centre itself, and he is so in every way in which that can be understood. Our Christian religion is not in the first place the acceptance of a creed and the following of a moral code. In its innermost essence it is a commitment to a Person. Being a Christian means surrender to Christ. It means to say yes to him and to do so unreservedly. Unreservedly, because Christ demands an absolute, a total commitment. We must give our all; our self-surrender must be complete. To hold something back is to be a Christian by that much the less. So, at the heart of our Christian life there is this personal relationship with Christ in which we give ourselves over to him in obedient love. Christian tradition, following the Bible, has not been afraid to compare it to the marriage union.

All this is disturbing to the modern Anglo-Saxon. He dislikes an absolute commitment and prefers to remain detached, to keep his independence. It would be easier if Christianity were only a creed. Then it would be possible to select certain points and leave aside others. A moral code also could be adapted to the times. In other words, a creed and a moral code could be admired and partly accepted without any loss of personal autonomy. They would be subjected to his scrutiny, and man himself would remain intact in his self-sufficiency. But surrender to a person who demands all is a different matter. There is not the same room for compromise. We are asked for a plain yes or no. A person stands before us who wants our undivided love and tells us that in it alone is to be found salvation. We find ourselves obliged to admit or refuse dependence. Many would like to think that the offer had

never been made; some are angry and bitter at the thought that
it has been made. Sinful man shrinks from the absolute, even
when it comes as love.

And who makes the demand? A first-century Jew. It is easy
enough to praise his work, to speak highly of his wonderful
teaching. Though even here, more often than not, there are un-
spoken qualifications. After all, we know so much more than the
first century about the world and man. However much we discipline our thoughts, we find it hard not to regard any past age
as backward in comparison to our own. It is difficult to allow
that a man of the first century, however great, has said the last
word on all that matters. But the demand to surrender ourselves
to him as a person has even more alarming implications. It implies that he is alive and present, that we can come into contact
with him. The crucifixion must have been a beginning not an
end. And Christian faith knows only one answer to the question
about the nature of that beginning: it was a bodily resurrection.
The men of Athens laughed yesterday; the men of London or New
York laugh today. Christians continue to confess that Jesus is the
Lord. They believe that God raised the man Jesus from the dead
and made him the ever-living and ever-active Lord who rules the
Church and the world. They believe that they meet him now in
faith and worship. It sounds harsh to say it, but a man who follows Christ as a great figure of the past, as the greatest religious
teacher in history, is not yet a Christian. Nor will it do to try to
evade the part about a bodily resurrection; for it is in the core of
the Christian message.

But who is Jesus? Can any man, however exalted, command the
complete obedience of my mind and will? He was certainly a
man. We know when and where he lived. We know the main facts
of his life. We have seen the belief of Christians in his resurrection.
But unless we dismiss his claim as a blasphemous absurdity, we
cannot stop there. We are confronted with the mystery of this
person, this man, who demands all. Bewildered, we are led
further. This man was God. This man *is* God. The first Christians gave the attributes of Yahweh to the Lord Jesus. This was
the way they understood the revelation of Christ given to them
by his resurrection. They were then able to see the bearing of what
Christ had said about himself during his lifetime. They came to a

realization of that unique relationship which he had as Son to his Father. The Christian faith remains the same. At its centre is a personal encounter, a total commitment to a living man who is God.

Our surrender to Christ is achieved by faith; it is faith. All faith is a response to a revelation of God. And Christ is the centre of our religion in as much as he is the complete revelation of God to man. He is this not simply by what he said but much more by what he was and what he did. Let us go back a little. The plan of God for man is to raise him, with his consent, above the level of merely human existence and introduce him into the divine sphere with a share in the distinctively divine life and activity. It is a plan that takes account of man's sin and the *impasse* in which it has placed him and includes the remedy for his situation. Such a plan requires a special self-disclosure on the part of God, and this self-disclosure we call revelation. We have just seen that this is given in Christ. Christ is not merely its completion; he is its totality. The partial revelations that went before were a preparation for Christ, the first glimmerings of the light of Christ. He came as the fullness of revelation. What had been said and done were seen now as foreshadowings of what he said and did. Placed at the centre he had cast light before him as he now casts light on all future ages. He is the very Word of God—the complete disclosure of God to man.

We are inclined to identify divine revelation with a series of statements that bear the stamp of divine authorship. Revelation includes such statements. Through the prophets and other inspired writers, through Christ and the apostles, there has come down to us a body of teaching, of words, which constitute a divine message, interpreting for us with divine authority the purpose and acts of God. But the message points to a series of interventions by God in history, and these interventions must be counted as important constituents in God's self-disclosure. There are revelatory acts as well as words, and God has made himself known to men by acting in the course of human history.

The Christian religion is an historical religion in a special sense. We believe that there is a line of events in history which have transcendent significance. These events are unimportant when judged by the ordinary criteria of historical enquiry; it is faith which sees their real meaning and groups them together in a unity. We call this line of events the history of salvation. It is history of a particular kind, redemptive history, because it is the divine redemptive plan being unfolded in history through the special action of God. Each event has the ordinary unrepeatable, transitory character of an historical occurrence, but each includes a divine action that gives it a transcendent significance. The call of Abraham, the rescue of the Israelites from Egypt, the covenant of Sinai were such events. This series of events, this redemptive history, has a decisive, determining influence on the rest of human history. What decides the final outcome of history, what determines the destiny of the world and mankind, is not the happenings studied by historians but a number of apparently heterogeneous and insignificant occurrences in which faith sees the acts by which God brings about our salvation. Christ is at the centre of redemptive history and, therefore, at the centre of all history. The incarnation, life, death and resurrection of Christ form the definitive intervention of God. In him all was accomplished. What went before was a preparation for his work; what comes after is its widening application. And what took place in Christ is the determining factor that controls the entire course of human history from its beginning to its end.

We should not underestimate the difficulty this faith presents to an unbeliever. He is often ready to acknowledge the permanent, we can say transcendent, power of ideas. Love, the brotherhood of man, justice, mercy: these and other ideas he may see and admire in the life and teaching of Christ and acknowledge that they have acted as a leaven in all subsequent history. But the Christian faith says more than this. It says that certain events which occurred in Palestine some two thousand years ago were decisive in themselves and have determined the whole course of history from its remote beginning to its unforeseen end. This presupposes more than the providence of God guiding the natural workings of his universe. It presupposes that God has raised human history to a higher level and arranged it in a new pattern, a pattern inaccessible to the investigations of reason, and that God has brought about this new pattern, not from afar, but by entering human history, acting inside it and ordering it from within. The incarnation means that the history of mankind is in fact the history of God. When we are confronted with the man Jesus, we are before a mystery. We cannot fathom the meaning of his life and work, despite its human character, because it is the human life and work of God. It is the same when we are faced with the problem of human history, its meaning and development. We are before a mystery. Christ is the centre of history and the centre which determines the pattern of the whole. Human history is only the wider aspect of the incarnation; it belongs to the God made man.

There is only one plan governing this universe, and it is the plan which finds its centre and meaning in Christ. We cannot, then, leave out of account God's work of creation when we are considering the primacy of Christ. Creation does not represent a separate plan of God, different from the one that culminated in Christ. It is rather the basis of the latter. Christ is the purpose which explains creation. Everything in this universe is directed to him and placed under him. The very beginnings of the workings of material forces were intended to lead to him, and the final state of the universe will be its transformation effected by the power of his resurrection.

We are not forgetting the fact of sin. Sin is a contravention of God's will and, consequently, it is an element of disruption. We know that a disruptive disaster of this kind occurred at the beginning of human history and changed its course. But we cannot suppose that this was unforeseen by God. It was present to him when he chose to create this universe and not some other. Adam did not take God by surprise and make him hastily alter his plans. However contrary to God's will, no sin can prevent what God intended to achieve when he decided to create. He can allow for it and bring it under his over-all purpose. His original creative intention remains valid. God chose this particular order, with the sin it includes, because he wanted the Christ we know. He wanted, not the incarnation as it might have been realized in some other possible scheme of things, but the incarnation as we know it. He chose Christ the Saviour, who was the Suffering Servant before he was glorified as Lord. The choice of Jesus Christ as Saviour, this will of God to communicate himself to us in this supreme way, explains all the rest. Christ is the key element in God's plan. He came first in the divine intention. He is the centre of the created universe. The primacy over all creatures belongs to him. It is in him and through him that creation will achieve the purpose for which it was made.

We are treading here on difficult ground. There is a long-standing dispute between two Catholic schools, Thomist and Scotist, on the primacy of Christ. We can ignore that here. It is not likely to trouble the ordinary reader, and nowadays defenders of opposing views are often closer than it appears at first sight. What is more likely to cause concern today is the geocentric character of this claim for Christ. It implies that something which happened on this planet was of universal significance and that man in Christ is the centre of the universe. Can such a claim survive the exploding of the old geocentric physics? Is it compatible with the knowledge we now have of the vastness of this universe and the complete insignificance of our planet in the physical cosmos? Everyone now knows about space and has some acquaintance with what science is saying about it. This makes our talk about the primacy of Christ seem strangely incongruous.

The mere size of the universe and the physical insignificance of our planet are not really a serious objection. Size is no criterion for determining rank in an intelligible order, and the sense of the puny stature of man in the face of the great forces of the cosmos is an old one; it can be found in the Psalmist. Nor can we say that the incarnation is made less intelligible by the discovery that man is comparatively weaker and smaller than was previously suspected. The distance between man and God is infinite, and the divine condescension involved in the incarnation is not significantly increased by diminishing further man's littleness. The universal primacy of Christ rests on the truth that the man Jesus is God. This places him above the highest of the angels; it is certainly enough to make him surpass the material universe, however vast.

The problem is more complicated if we suppose the existence of intelligent life in material beings elsewhere in this universe. It is unlikley that there is such life on the other planets of our solar system, but the immense size of the universe and the enormous number of heavenly bodies now known to exist make it mathematically probable that there are many other planetary systems similar to our own. It is similarly probable that in some of these the conditions for life are verified. We may then take a further step in the same reasoning and say that in some places the development of living beings has reached the stage when intelligent life has emerged. The numbers involved are so great that if the laws of probability are applied to this question the conclusion is that man is not unique and that there are many other instances of such intelligent life in the physical universe.

Such a conclusion need not bring us into conflict with the doctrine of creation. We may hold fast to the need for a creative act of God in each fresh instance of intelligent life without denying that this life emerges in accordance with laws observable by scientists. We do in fact do this when it is a question of the origin of the individual human being. Nor is there any doctrinal reason why we should deny that the statistical method with its laws of probability expresses a true insight into the processes which govern this universe. Moreover, the mere existence of other intelligent creatures causes no difficulty. Catholic thought has always held the existence of innumerable hosts of angels or pure spirits. To range below them a series of rational creatures would seem to be an easy matter, except that we know nothing about their state. The perplexing point is their relationship to Christ, and this is something I have not seen treated. Although the fact is interpreted differently by the two schools mentioned above, all see the angels as subordinate to Christ. He is given a primacy over all. The entire material creation is understood as involved in his work and destined to be transformed by the glory of his resurrection. This is an anthropocentric view of the universe, based on the primacy of Christ, and Catholic theology has long accepted its application to creatures naturally superior to man, the angels. Must it be extended to embrace other possible rational creatures, so that man would remain, whatever the physicists might say, the centre of the cosmos? He would not be the centre in a physical sense nor according to the natural order, but according to that higher plan or pattern which God has decreed for this universe and which is known to us only by faith. The fact of the incarnation and the exaltation of human nature in Christ would give this man this central position.

Theologically speaking, this view is fairly straightforward; indeed, it would seem to be imposed by the teaching on the primacy of Christ. It is in sharp conflict with the modern mind which, engrossed in the stars, disdains as naïve any anthropocentric account of the universe. But basically the conflict is the same as that aroused by the Christian view of history. Whether we consider the place of Christ in history or in the universe, the presupposition is the same: God has imposed on the development of the universe and on the course of history a pattern and a goal that are not accessible to mere reason but known by faith. Or we may put it another way: all the movements and forces of the universe and history are taken up into a higher integration, which is supernatural and centred on Christ.

But a certain doubt still remains. Is the incarnation unique? If other rational creatures exist, some may well have found themselves in the same need of a redeemer as our own. May not the incarnation have been multiplied? If so, while Christ as God-man would be higher than any mere creature, we should have to qualify our statements about his primacy and we could not speak in the full sense about the universal significance of his work. Our view of the world in the narrow sense would be Christocentric, but not our view of the universe. Christ would no longer be the purpose and goal of the entire creation but an element in a wider plan of which we know nothing. If there are various incarnations, we are quite in the dark concerning their mutual relations.

At this point some readers may give vent to irritation. Perhaps they think we have no right to make these conjectures. We know nothing, they may say, about life elsewhere in the universe, and we certainly know nothing about any other incarnation. To a great extent, let us admit it, their attitude is sound. A mere playing with unverifiable hypotheses is intellectually enervating and useless. But a real issue is at stake here. Our contemporaries are very conscious of the universe. They no longer think in terms of this globe but in terms of the vast universe in which it is but a minute speck. If they venture to offer an account of the scheme of things, a world-view, it embraces the whole of the cosmos such as we now know it to be. When we present our view of things it must be as wide. To say that the universe was created by God is basic but not enough. What is the goal towards which the universe is moving? What is the plan of God for it? Is there a central element which explains and determines the order of all the rest?

The Christian answer to such questions has been to point to Christ. Christ has the primacy over all. He came first in God's plan. Everything is directed to him. The final destiny of all things is to share in his glory at his Second Coming. He is Alpha and Omega. The answer was given when this earth occupied the horizon of men's minds and the rest of the universe was seen as its environment. Do we still maintain it, must we still maintain it, now that the immensity of the universe has been revealed? In other words, is the Christian view of the universe Christo-centric?

What are the alternatives before us? To interpret the biblical and traditional statements about the primacy of Christ as apply-ing to this world understood in the narrow sense. We should then maintain firmly that God created this universe, but admit frankly that we do not know his plan for it. We should thereby admit that we know only in part God's plan for ourselves and for our world, because the universe is clearly a whole and the destinies of its parts must be linked together in the unity of a common destiny. We cannot contract out of the universe and regard our destiny as a thing altogether apart. This would be to deny an in-telligible order in creation. Whatever the total order, it will include us and have its repercussions on our individual development and purpose. And we would be ignorant of that total order. It is true that in any hypothesis our ignorance of God's plan must be profound. But we have generally supposed that the mystery of the divine plan was revealed to us in Christ and that, while it re-mained a mystery, it gave us the main lines of the divine scheme of things. If, however, the divine plan for the universe is not centred on Christ, then we must confess that we are in the dark even in regard to its main lines.

The other alternative is to make the entire universe find its centre in Christ, to put all under him and to grant his work a universal influence. This view, with its anthropocentric conse-quences, cannot be upset by the mere size of the universe. It is not really endangered by the supposition that there are other ra-tional creatures besides man, provided we maintain that the in-carnation is unique. Christ as the God-man would be the highest communication of God to his creation. As such he would be placed above all, and, since the lesser is ordered to the greater in the universe, everything would be ordered to him. He would come first in the purpose of God and would be the end towards which everything would be directed. His relationship to rational beings other than man could be explained along the same lines as his relationship to the angels. It would not be important for us to know anything precise about it. We know little enough about the angels. We could be content with the knowledge that Christ is the centre of the universe. For this would enable us to bring the universe into the Christian scheme of things. It would tell us the divine plan for it and our place within it.

Provided the incarnation is unique. If we suppose other incarnations, the position is altered. Christ would retain his essential dignity as the God-man, but his work would lose its universal significance. We could not speak of his primacy in the same way. We should not know the relationship between the various incarnations nor the divine scheme of things for this universe. The Second Coming of Christ, for example, would not bring about the end of the world and transformation of all by itself but only as a subordinate factor in some higher scheme. We could not speak of the universal kingship of Christ as man. It is well to notice that we do not have to know the fact of other incarnations for these consequences to follow. Simply to suppose them is enough. If we say our Christian faith allows the hypothesis of other incarnations in other rational natures elsewhere in this universe, then we are equivalently saying that the Christian view of the universe is not Christocentric. We are in fact saying that there is no Christian view of the universe, except that it was created by God. Christianity knows only one scheme of things and that is the scheme centred on Christ. If this is not applicable to the universe, then there is no Christian explanation of the universe. Once we begin making suppositions outside the Christian scheme by the hypothesis of other incarnations, we can continue endlessly, because there is nothing to control our hypotheses. It would be better to admit at the outset that we know nothing. But we cannot do this nor can we begin to play with the hypothesis of other incarnations, unless we have first reduced the Christian scheme of things to a merely local significance in this universe.

No absolute impossibility excludes other incarnations. This supreme communication of God by which he subsists in a created nature could be multiplied; it involves no change in God. At the same time, there is no reason to suppose its multiplication. Even had other rational creatures found themselves in a situation similar to our own, that would not be a cogent reason for supposing a similar Saviour. God was not compelled to become incarnate. The incarnation was an utterly gratuitous gift. And he could have saved us without it. That it should be unique would be far from surprising. Can we say that it is in fact unique? We must do so if we are to interpret the statements of Scripture (Col. 1.15–19; Eph. 1; Heb. 1; 1 Cor. 15.27–28) on the primacy of Christ in a universal sense, and I find it difficult to do otherwise. And it would not be exegetically sound nor theologically adequate to refer them simply to Christ as God.

Much of what has been said may have seemed to some a waste of time. Surely we have always taken it for granted that Christ is at the head of the whole creation. I believe we have. I believe that that represents the Christian conviction. But it is not enough to take it for granted. We must consciously reaffirm it in the face of modern knowledge. Our contemporaries have passed from a realization of this world to a realization of the universe. To them, what has happened on this planet is of no importance when compared with the drama of the universe. It is only local history and the history of a tiny locality. Our earth has seen the emergence of intelligent life, but there is no need, they remark, to see in that a unique phenomenon. Now, we cannot afford to ignore this outlook, and we would not be justified in dismissing out of hand the possibility of other rational beings besides man. Must we, then, qualify the usual statements of the primacy of Christ and limit the familiar Christian account of the world to the confines of our solar system? Or is the man Jesus the centre of the universe with a primacy over all? The latter would seem to be the bearing of our faith. I should speak with more confidence if other theologians had tackled the problem. Perhaps the discussions between Thomists and Scotists could be raised to a new level by examining this question. We need to be clear. The primacy of Christ, with the central position it gives to man, is not a doctrine that will be accepted calmly by the modern mind.

What, then, are our findings? We place Christ at the centre. He is the centre of our faith, the centre of history, the centre of the created universe. By Christ we do not mean God the Son considered in his divine nature but the man Jesus, who is God the Son subsisting in a human nature. God was made man to become as man our Lord. To him as Christians we owe our allegiance, and the logic of that allegiance asks from us a surrender to him as a Person. We cannot simply imitate him as a hero of the past; he is living and accessible to us. Our union with him in the intimacy of a personal relationship is our religion. Through him and in him we come to God; for he is the fullness of God's revelation to us. When we look back over the divine revelatory activity we see it culminating in Christ. In Christ alone was its meaning made clear and its purpose accomplished. And this revelation has been in deeds as well as words. God's self-disclosure has been nothing less than his entry into human affairs to direct history to a higher, divinely assigned end and give it a new meaning. This divine involvement in human history reached in Christ its decisive manifestation. Christ is at the centre of that line of divine actions in history which we call redemptive history. He is the definitive intervention of God. He is, therefore, at the centre of human history considered in its entirety, because this is governed by redemptive history and subordinate to it. And redemptive history reaches out to embrace the universe itself and its processes. As the highest communication of God to his creation, Christ is at the head of all and all is subject to him.

In brief, governing history and the universe, everything in it and all its movements, is a divine plan. It is not a plan accessible to unaided reason, because it is an integration of all at a higher, supernatural level. At its centre is Christ. The mystery of the universe and history is simply the mystery of Christ.

CHAPTER XIII

THE TIME OF PREPARATION

Jesus Christ came from above. The Incarnation cannot be explained by what went before; it must be joined by a vertical line directly with God. At a particular moment in time God the Son entered this world in a unique, unprecedented fashion and began to exist as man. But the ground had been prepared. Although Christ is not the end-product of an historical process but a fresh intervention or coming of God, a progressive preparation of long centuries preceded him and gradually established the context for his coming. A horizontal line connects Christ with Abraham and with Adam. The evangelists, Matthew and Luke, were teaching this when they gave their genealogies of Christ. The connexion was a blood-relationship, because Christ became not just a man but a member of this human breed. But the link was also spiritual. Christ came to complete a line of history which found its only meaning in him and his work.

The Old Testament looks forward to Christ. This is a familiar truth and we speak of it very easily. We call it the Messianic expectation. Usually we think of it in this way. The Jews expected the coming of a Messiah. They had many wrong ideas because they misunderstood the prophecies, but the prophets themselves had foretold the coming of Christ with wonderful accuracy. We then ransack the Old Testament to find texts that tell beforehand details about him. We show little concern with the rest, with the sometimes outlandish contexts in which our favourite texts are to be found. Now, this approach is unsatisfactory, and often wrong in its results. And the reasons are these. First, the interpretation of the individual texts is far more difficult than we usually suppose. Even when the Messianic meaning is there, we offend by trying to extract it in too facile a manner. Second, the movement of thought we call the Messianic expectation is very complicated. It includes a bewildering variety of ideas. The expectation of a new era was a more dominant element in it than the expectation of a personal Messiah. And even in personal Messianism there was no single figure awaited by all. Only the actual coming of Christ showed clearly the convergence of what had existed as distinct trends. Third—and this is the key reason— the whole movement of the Old Testament towards Christ is vastly more important than any individual prophecies. The main concern of the prophets was not to predict the future but to shape it by making known to the people the purpose and will of God. Their insight was into the events that were taking place in their time; they saw the true significance of these in relation to the plan of God. They looked to the future because of their realization that there was a divine purpose in history which would be achieved in due time.

This prophetic understanding of God's purpose and of the way it was to be fulfilled was continually deepening. We ourselves now know clearly that the divine purpose was centred on Christ. We cannot, however, forgo a study of the prophets, because to see the Old Testament as leading to Christ, as a prophecy of him, we need their understanding of Israel's role and history, though we can now complete it in the light given by the events of Christ. Once we have made our own the basic insight of the prophets, individual texts will receive a serene and balanced interpretation.

The faith of Israel took its origin from men who enjoyed a special intimacy with God and were made the recipients of divine communications. It was so with Abraham, the father of the Chosen People, who was called from his pagan environment and given an awareness of the true God and a sense of his special destiny. It was so with Moses, the founder of Israel as a nation and the great lawgiver whose work determined ever afterwards the character of its institutions. The memory of his closeness to God was such that this was never considered to have been surpassed. The religious message of these men was preserved in a tradition, and this tradition was frequently revived and enriched by other men raised up by God. Outstanding among these were the prophets, in particular the great line of prophets who dominated the scene from the eighth century until the gradual dying away of prophecy in the period after the Exile. A prophet does not mean a man who foretells the future, but a spokesman of God. The prophets had a vision of the future as we shall see, but only as part of their insight into the purpose and will of God in relation to what was happening to Israel in the present. Their difficult vocation was to be the mouthpiece of God to their contemporaries.

The human antecedents of the prophetic movement are not clear to us, nor do we know very much about the way their message was preserved for us in writing. But the Bible does tell us the kind of men they were. They stood in the tradition of Moses and saw themselves as guardians of the ancestral faith of Israel. But they were not mere echoes of tradition. They were specially called by God; they acted under his influence; they received from him the message they proclaimed. They sharply distinguished themselves from the professional prophets who infested the court and produced flattering predictions to order. What they said came from God; it was his message they uttered, whether or not it pleased the great ones of the world.

Despite their rejection at the time, their influence was ultimately victorious in Israel. Thus, the historical books of the Bible as we have them reflect the teaching of the prophets. They present a prophetic understanding of the history of Israel. The discoveries of the last century and this have made known to scholars the history of the ancient Middle East. With the new data and a rereading of the Bible in their light, it is now possible to write ordinary political histories of Israel. Such histories differ strangely from the biblical accounts. Not that the Bible has been found to be untrue. Far from it, although we are now better able to appreciate the methods and literary forms used by ancient historians. What distinguishes the biblical accounts from our political histories is their religious character. We are offered a religious understanding of Israel's history, and the criteria used in assessing the significance and value of events are drawn from faith. Biblical history is a statement of faith, not a faith that creates events but a faith which sees their divine meaning. And this faith, as we have said, owes its depth to the work of the prophets.

Now, we want to grasp the meaning of the Old Testament in

order to see how it looks towards Christ. We wish to understand the vocation of Israel and how God prepared the way for Christ through the vicissitudes of its history. In fact, we are asking for the message of the prophets; for it was the prophets who pointed out to Israel its vocation and who told the Israelites what God was doing and intended to do. What, then, was the message of such men as Amos and Osee, Isaias and Micheas, Jeremias and Ezechiel?

The groundwork of their thought was the conviction that a divine plan governed history. Underlying the faith of Israel was an original conception of history. Things were not subject to a blind Fate, but to God who was sovereignly independent. For the Israelites, Yahweh was precisely the God who acted in history and directed it to his purpose. He was the Lord of history. Men indeed were free, but events remained none the less under the control of God. He intervened, whether to punish or reward, and ordered everything in accordance with his will. There was a meaning in history, a divine significance in events, because what was taking place was the unfolding of a divine plan. One day this would reach its final achievement.

Coupled with this conviction was the sense of Israel's special relationship with God. Many, unfamiliar with the Old Testament and accustomed to depict its God in harsh colours, are unaware of the depths of intimacy this relationship implied. It is expressed in terms of a covenant between Yahweh and Israel. But let us not be deceived by the legal character of the term. Jonathan made a covenant with David because he loved him as himself (1 Sam. 18.3), and the covenant which God made with Israel on Mount Sinai was an outpouring of his love. God freely chose this people from among the other peoples on the earth and united it to himself by a bond of friendship. He demanded faithfulness, but as a response to his steadfast love. Israel is called the child of Yahweh, but the most poignant descriptions of the relationship are in terms of the marriage union. In vivid sentences, Osee contrasts the unfaithfulness of Israel the bride with the enduring love of Yahweh the rejected bridegroom. Such a relationship carried with it many privileges, but also, as became increasingly clear, a special vocation. Israel was called to a special role in God's plan of salvation for all men.

The covenant at Sinai was but a further expression of the promises made already to the patriarchs. When God called Abraham, he promised him a son, a numerous posterity, and a land. The promises were fulfilled on one level, only for a further level to be revealed. The history of Israel is a dialectic of unfaithfulness and divine promises. The unfaithfulness was punished with disaster, but the disaster never meant complete annihilation but purification. And ever again the divine promises were renewed, each time in a deeper and more spiritual sense. The religion of Israel was a religion dominated by hope. God was the Rock on which that hope rested. He would be faithful to his promises. He would bring salvation. He would achieve his purpose.

The prophets worked with these ideas of the divine plan, the divine promises, the covenant, the hope of Israel, and the faithfulness of Yahweh. Enlightened by God, they interpreted the events of their time against this background. They had a message of present urgency for their contemporaries, whether of warning or of consolation. They drew upon the past and reminded the people what God had done for them. They looked to the future, because they shared and enriched an expectation. The scope of this expectation meant that they saw human history as moving towards a final end in which all would be accomplished. It is their teaching on this final end that particularly concerns us here. It constitutes what is called eschatology or doctrine on the last things. Prophetic eschatology forms the setting of the Messianism of the Old Testament.

The first element in this eschatology is the theme of judgement, associated with the idea of the Day of Yahweh. Judgement had not the same legal sense for the Hebrews as it has for us. It was understood in relation to the covenant. When two parties were joined together in a covenant they had mutual rights and duties. To be just meant to act in accordance with the covenant. To judge was to act so as to maintain or re-establish the order of the covenant. God was the Supreme Judge; his covenant was with Israel. Oppressed by enemies, the Israelites looked to the judgement of Yahweh. The Day of Yahweh would come when he would intervene to judge, that is, to fulfil his promises and save his people and punish their enemies. The popular expectation at the time of the prophets was that judgement meant victory and salvation for the Israelites, defeat and punishment for their enemies. What the prophets did was to deepen the moral content of the notion of divine judgement and alter as a consequence its application to Israel. When Yahweh judged, he would punish, not merely the wickedness of Israel's enemies, but also its own unfaithfulness. The Day of Yahweh to which the people all looked forward would be a day of wrath for them. The writings of the prophets are full of denunciations of the sins of Israel and threats of disaster. All this had an immediate relevance; for the theme of the Day of Yahweh and his judgement was closely wedded to historical events. The various calamities that overtook the people, such as the ruin of Samaria, were so many Days of Yahweh, which saw the exercise of his judgement. But the eschatological aspect became increasingly prominent: the expectation of a final end, *the* Day of Yahweh, in which his judgement would be fully and definitively manifested.

While the prophets uttered threats of disaster and warnings of divine vengeance, while in fact seemingly final disaster came in the destruction of Jerusalem, the prophetic message was a message of salvation and the destruction was never complete. The righteousness of Yahweh was a righteousness that saved from wickedness, not merely punished it. A remnant of the people, they said, would surive. This idea of the remnant received a moral resonance. Israel would be reduced to a stump, which, purged and strengthened, would bear new shoots and inherit the promises. The punishments of God were a means of purification. Salvation would follow disaster. The Day of Yahweh would usher in a new order. The prophets described in lyrical terms the happiness that would follow the judgement. Their message did not take away the hope of Israel but enhanced it and gave it a deeper moral meaning. This second element in prophetic eschatology, the element of hope and consolation, is what we know as Messianism. We shall see later the origin of the word; at the moment it is better to take it in its general meaning. As with judgement so also here we find an intermingling of historical and eschatological perspectives. The thought of a final and definitive salvation was tied to the hope of rescue from imminent disaster and promise of immediate restoration. But historical events themselves uncovered, layer by layer, the divine plan and increased the tension towards the future. One day there would be a complete fulfilment of the hopes so long cherished but never fully realized.

The new order awaited would be a time when God would reign over his people and over all the nations of the earth. Essential to the hope of Israel was the expectation of the coming of God's Kingdom. The idea of the Kingdom of God is not something new in the prophets. Since Sinai, it had served to explain the relation between Yahweh and Israel. Yahweh is King. The word "kingdom" may mislead us. What the original expressions evoke is not the idea of a territory but rather the fact that Yahweh is king; they indicate his royal rule or kingship. God is indeed King by right, but men do not recognize his rule. A time will come when his reign will be acknowledged, his law observed, and his worship accomplished. He will exercise a sovereign rule that will brook no denial. This will be the coming of the Kingdom. The realization grows in the prophets that when the Kingdom comes God will reign, not only over Israel, but also over all peoples reunited under his rule. The privileged place of Israel remains, sometimes very strongly marked, but a religious universalism comes in and complements the national hope of the Chosen People.

There are other ideas used to describe the new order to come. Important among these is the idea of the covenant. The basic religious use of the term is as an expression of the relationship forged at Sinai. But the Pentateuch speaks of two covenants that preceded the one made with Moses: the covenant with Abraham and, significant in its universalist implications, the covenant with Noah as representing mankind after the Flood. The use of the theme in the patriarchal accounts is largely, though not entirely, a projection into the past of the Mosaic covenant. We also read of various renewals of the covenant after Sinai. Understandably, then, the prophets are able to carry the idea into the future and speak of a new covenant. This new covenant will be different from the old. It will be more interior in character, written in the hearts of men. It will be an everlasting covenant. See Jer. 31.31–4; Osee 2.14–23; Ez. 37.21–8.

These passages envisage the restoration of Israel. When we turn to the work of the Second Isaias, we find a wider outlook that embraces the whole human race. This work consists of chapters 40–55 of Isaias; it is often called the *Book of Consolation*. The

Book of Isaias as we now have it is a collection of writings by different authors, though with some affinity to one another. The chapters mentioned are not by Isaias himself, who belongs to the eighth century, but by an unknown prophet of the sixth century. He lived with his countrymen in exile in Babylon and, seeing in the victorious rise to power of Cyrus of Persia a sign that the deliverance of Israel was at hand, addressed this wonderful message of hope to the exiles. The punishment of Israel was at an end and its sins forgiven. Yahweh the Creator, who held all nations in his power, was about to deliver his people by the hand of Cyrus. He is their redeemer and he is going to ransom them from their slavery. It is his steadfast love that has moved him to have compassion on them. The prospect of a new age and an eternal covenant, of a deliverance and salvation, is offered to the exiles to revive their faith in Yahweh and to console them in their dejection. What is immediately envisaged is the imminent return of the exiles from Babylon, but the message has a deeper import as a revelation of the more remote intentions of God. The disappointments of the actual return would make this clear and keep the attention of Israel directed to the future. Particularly notable, however, is the universalism of the message. The vision of the prophet extends beyond Israel and embraces all peoples.

This universalism is most clearly marked in the four Servant Songs found embedded in the *Book of Consolation*. These are usually given as Isa. 42.1–7: 49.1–6: 50.4–9: 52.13–53.12. The beginning of each poem stands out clearly, but the ending of the first three is not so easy to distinguish because these merge into their context without any sharp transition. The relation of these four poems to the book as a whole is disputed. Some make them independent, others stress their close connexion with the rest of the book. Some hold that they are by the author of the *Book of Consolation,* the Second Isaias; others think that they are by one of his disciples. But what matters here is their teaching. We shall return later to the figure of the Servant. We may simply note for the moment the universal character of his mission. He is to be a light to the nations; his task is to re-create the unity of the human race. The salvation here promised is extended to all peoples without exception.

Since many are inclined to underestimate the nobility of Old

Testament teaching, it is well to insist here on the moral and spiritual character of the salvation awaited by the prophets. We need not deny that material and political restoration or prosperity occupied a large place in their thoughts and formed part of what they meant by deliverance and salvation. But the prophets were men of a high moral sensitiveness. They had a deep sense of the holiness of God and of sin as an affront to it. Their sense of sin was no cloistered reverie. They denounced with courage and pointed clarity the sins of their time: oppression of the helpless, cruelty, corruption, avarice and luxury, the impurity of the idolatrous rites, unfaithfulness to Yahweh and lack of trust in him, the formalism of Temple worship. Their hope for the future was inevitably shot through with moral implications. The new order would bring the knowledge of Yahweh and observance of his law. And we must remember that knowledge for the Hebrews was not a merely intellectual affair. Knowledge of Yahweh was a religious attitude that involved faithfulness to him and a response to his love. The new covenant would have its source in the tender mercy of Yahweh and establish with his people a relationship of faithfulness and love. It would be written in the hearts of men and so bring a change of heart, the gift of a new heart. There would be a purification of men and a pouring out upon them of the Spirit of God. Sins would be taken away, and salvation would include the gifts of moral enlightenment and integrity. And the source of this new order would not be man but the holiness, righteousness, and love of Yahweh himself. All these were elements that could be and were taken up into the New Testament teaching on the grace of redemption.

At the same time we must admit that the prophets conceive the happiness of the coming age largely in terms of a happiness here on this earth. This should not surprise us. It is due in part to the slowness with which belief in rewards and punishments after death developed in Israel. Survival in Sheol was a bleak existence, hardly worth the name of existence. Only at the end of the Old Testament period does the idea of a retribution in the next life emerge clearly, and then it is principally associated with belief in a bodily resurrection. We should also beware of neglecting on our part the bodily aspect of redemption. The Christian message of salvation concerns our bodies as well as our souls, and the resurrection of the body and the restoration of this material universe are truths that remain as part of our Christian faith. But apart from the difficulty felt by the prophets of envisaging anything other than an earthly happiness, there was also the impossibility of depicting the last days except in symbolic terms. Hence their use of imagery. These considerations may help us read aright the prophetic descriptions of the new order to come.

They see the promised happiness as a return to the happiness of Paradise. Sin has deprived man of the happiness in which God created him. But in overcoming sin God will restore for man this primeval happiness. A rich imagery accompanies this idea, and the theme of Paradise is developed with the use of the theme of the Promised Land. There will be a pact of peace between man and nature; wild animals will lose their fierceness; the Holy Land will enjoy a wonderful fertility; the new Jerusalem, far exceeding the old in splendour, will become the religious centre of the world. Paradise, the Promised Land, the Holy City: these, especially the second two, are ideas deeply rooted in the soul of Israel, nerve-centres vibrant with memories and religious sentiment. They became the vehicles of its hope.

Every nation has its golden periods that remain indelibly marked in the national consciousness: heights of achievement or turning-points in development. Two such periods continued to live on in the memory of Israel: the time of the Exodus and the apogee of the royal power in David and Solomon. The Exodus saw the origin of Israel as a nation. And more important than this: for the religion of Israel it remained the fundamental experience of salvation. The deliverance from Egypt, the intimate protection given by God in the desert, the revelation and covenant at Sinai: these were for Israel the great manifestation of Yahweh's power, righteousness, and love, and the time of her espousals with him. The Exodus gave the basic pattern of salvation. Hence the prophets saw the salvation to come as a new Exodus. This pattern of thought passed into the Christian message. The work of Christ was seen as a new Exodus and a new covenant. And the liturgy of Easter is still dominated by the theme of the Exodus as the principal type prefiguring Christian salvation. The other golden period in Israel's past caused the prophets to represent the coming age as a new royal period in which the glories of David and

Solomon would be renewed. Connected with this was the expectation of an ideal King, which we have still to examine.

Up till now we have been considering the new order announced by the prophets and awaited by Israel. This expectation of the Messianic times is more prominent in the Bible than the expectation of a personal Messiah. But now we must ask about the one who would accomplish all this. Our first answer must be that God himself would be the author of salvation. Deeply implanted in Israel was the conviction that it was Yahweh alone who saved. But God had been represented in the past by men whom he had raised up to be his spokesmen and intermediaries. Outstanding among others had been Moses and David. Would there be a mediator of the new covenant? an intermediary of God in the establishment of the new order?

Before separating the different strands of personal Messianism we must mention what has been called "Messianism without a Messiah." The prophet Osee so insisted on the action of God that he gave no thought to any intermediary, and many prophetic passages are Messianic in their expectation of the Kingdom of God without being concerned with a Messiah. But more than this, during and after the Exile, a tendency grew in some circles to hope that God would establish his Kingdom himself without the help of any human king. This was a reaction against the royal ideology, which had gathered to itself the national hopes of Israel. The disappointment caused by the kings of the past aroused the desire of a direct theocracy. This current of thought is a development of the very ancient idea of Yahweh as King, but it now takes the form of a transcendent Messianism with the expectation of a direct intervention of God to restore his people. We find this expressed in the "Psalms of he Kingdom," namely, Pss. 92, 95 and 98. This expectation of the coming of God was fulfilled remarkably in the Incarnation, but in a way that was not anticipated.

More widespread was the expectation of an ideal king, a new David. This royal Messianism, as it is called, was a strong current in the Messianic expectation. From it, in fact, came the term "Messiah." Messiah means Anointed; it is a rough transcription of the Hebrew, whereas "Christ," which corresponds to it, is taken from the Greek word used to translate it. In the Old Testament the term designates, in particular, the king of Israel. He was called "the anointed one of Yahweh" with reference to the rite of anointing that marked his investiture and with the implication of a special mission from Yahweh as his representative. The term is also used of priests, because they too were anointed, and occasionally in a wider sense of one to whom God has given a special mission, such as a prophet or even the heathen king, Cyrus. Curiously enough, it is not used in the Old Testament of an eschatological figure. It was in the extra-canonical writings of Judaism before Christ that it acquired its eschatological meaning as a designation of the ideal king of the future. And already in Judaism there was a tendency to connect the various views and titles referring to the last days with this one title, the Messiah. The unification, however, of the various strands in the eschatological hope came only with Christ. In the apostolic Church the term "Christ" became all embracing and the other titles were subordinated to it; it was permanently joined as a name to the name "Jesus." And so, although it owes its origin to what was but one strand in the Jewish expectation, that of royal Messianism, we use Messiah, together with Messianic and Messianism, as a general term to indicate the eschatological figure who was to bring about the fulfilment of Israel's hopes.

It is easy to see the reasons for the origin and development of a Messianic hope centred on the monarchy. The prestige of David drew to him and his dynasty the hopes of the people for the future. The royal house became the centre of the national life. Receiving a religious significance, it was inevitably a focal point for all the ambitions and aspirations of Israel as a nation. The basic text which connects the divine promises made to Israel with the Davidic dynasty, and which, consequently, underlies the whole movement of royal Messianism, is the prophecy given to David by Nathan, 2 Sam. 7.11–16. It promised the perpetuity of the line of David.

At first the hope of an ideal king was historical, not eschatological, in character. In other words, at this stage, the "Messiah" was not thought of as a personage coming in the last days to rule for ever a definitive kingdom. What was in question was an ideal, the model of a perfect king, the portrait of a king according to the image of David, which people continually hoped to see realized in the historical order. Whenever the king was unworthy—a frequent occurrence—people nourished the hope that God would raise up a king after his own heart. Perhaps there was even the hope that one day all the kings without exception would be monarchs according to the mind of God and the example of David. And so an ideal was fostered, applied to historical events, and then, because of repeated disappointments, projected more and more into the future. Thus, we have prophetic passages in which the writers envisaged both the contemporary kings or kings awaited immediately in the historical order and, at the same time, the Messiah or ideal king. To put it in another way, the prophets talk about kings in a way that will be completely true only of an eschatological figure in the future. There is an intermingling of promise or recognition of a good king, description of an ideal king, and hope of a final king. Hence the difficulty we come up against in interpreting the pre-exilic texts or determining the immediate perspective of the prophet. Had he directly in mind the last days? Or was he speaking of contemporary events and personages in terms of a religious ideal which would be actually fulfilled only in the last days? Controversy surrounds certain texts, but usually the second alternative is the more probable. The important texts of royal Messianism are: Isa. 7.14–17: 9.2–7: 11.1–9, Jer. 23.5–6; Ez. 34; Psalms 2: 109.

After the Exile there were some attempts to revive hope in the historical monarchy. The house of David had been destroyed, seemingly completely, but some hope remained that a successor of his line would arise. Thus we see the hopes placed in Zorobabel by the prophets, Aggaeus and Zacharias. Zorobabel was a descendant of David. He became the commissioner of Juda at the time of the restoration and took in hand the reconstruction of the Temple. Ezechiel had described this as a Messianic work, and it led to a sudden revival of the royal Messianic hope, with the two prophets hailing him with Messianic titles. But all this was short-lived. What is more important is that, after the Exile, an eschatological royal Messianism now emerged clearly. There arose an unambiguous expectation of a final king, ideal in every respect, the king of a definitive kingdom, the mediator of the eschatological era. The old royal psalms, such as Pss. 2:71: 100: 109: 144, and others, written during the monarchy with reference to the king, were reread in a new way and given a Messianic meaning.

This royal Messianism came right down to the time of Christ. An outstanding witness to it is the apocryphal work, the *Psalms of Solomon,* written about 60 B.C. Here we have the use of the term "Messiah" in a technical eschatological sense, and the coming of this Messiah, Son of David, is expected and celebrated. This current of thought was increasingly distorted by the hardening of Jewish nationalism. We are familiar with the false political and temporal hopes created by it in the Jews contemporary with Christ.

A very different outlook is found in the four Servant Songs already mentioned. The Songs are dominated by the figure of the Servant, the mediator of the covenant. But who is the Servant? There are a bewildering number of interpretations. Needless to say, all Catholics see these texts as in some way fulfilled in Christ, and this is the teaching of the New Testament itself. All the same, it is still important to determine the immediate meaning these passages had for the prophet himself, for only in this way shall we grasp their full import. Nowadays, the eschatological bearing of the passages is widely recognized but the interpretations of the Servant fall into two groups. The first group takes the Servant as an individual. Starting from some historical personage, such as the exiled king or a prophet or Moses, the author, it is thought, has drawn the features and mission of the future mediator. Those in the second group maintain a collective interpretation. Sometimes they think of Israel as a whole, but more often of Israel in the qualitative sense of the Remnant, the true Israel, realizing in the sufferings of the Exile the mediatorial function described by the prophet and seen as destined to bring about a new order.

The difficulty in choosing from among the various interpretations is that the texts seem to lend their support now to a collective, now to an individual, meaning. There are places where the Servant is apparently identified with Israel as a whole, other places where a part of the people, the Remnant, seems to be meant, and finally places where it is hard not to take the Servant as a single individual person. To be valid, any interpretation must do justice to all these passages. Hence the attractive suggestion of some writers that the three interpretations do not exclude one another. An appeal is made to the Semitic mode of thought. This saw so close a connexion between the individual and the collectivity that a group and its individual representatives were often identified in thought and expression. The Hebrews had what has been called the idea of "corporate personality." A community was seen as being made actual and active in an individual who represented its unity and exercised its functions. The relation between the individual and the group was fluid, and the mind would pass from one to the other without any transition, the attributes of each being freely intermingled. An illustration of this kind of thinking is the place of the king and his relationship to the community as we find it in Semitic thought and expression. If we apply this to the Servant, we can maintain that he is an individual person, but one who represents Israel and, in particular, its purified Remnant, and is so identified with these groups that the author freely passes from him to them without any noticeable transition. Such an interpretation harmonizes well with the fact that the central theological thought of the Servant Songs turns on the principle of representation. The faithful Servant accepts a solidarity with the sinful people whose sins he bears. Representing them, he offers his sufferings in expiation and wins by them the divine pardon. Nor is it surprising that the prophet should have been led to envisage an individual person. The prophets had already considered Israel as reduced to a Remnant which alone could assume and fulfil Israel's role in the divine plan of salvation. What has happened is that the Remnant has now been further reduced, this time to one man, who represents Israel and carries out the implications of its destiny.

The key feature in the mission of the Servant is his redemptive sufferings. But other features should not be missed. His prophetic function as the light of the nations; his role as the mediator of the covenant; his innocence and humble obedience; the universality of his mission; his final exaltation. It is a very different picture of the future intermediary from the one found in royal Messianism. Only the coming of Jesus would show how the two aspects were to be brought together, when by his sufferings he entered into his glory (Luke 24.26).

The theme of the Suffering Servant had but a limited influence in Judaism. It found, however, some echo. The suggestion has been made that it had some influence on the description of the Messiah-King given in the deutero-Zacharias (chapters 9–14) of

the fourth century. There the trait of humility is added to the portrait of the victorious king (Zach. 9.9–10). Psalm 21 received a
new meaning by the addition of verses 28–32. Originally the
psalm had been a cry of distress addressed to God by one of the
poor and oppressed in Israel. The final verses now added—there
had been a previous addition—widen the perspective and give a
vision of the Kingdom of God. The sufferer who speaks in the
psalm is thereby raised to the status of an eschatological personage
like the Servant of Second Isaias. He passes through sufferings
to a deliverance that coincides with the coming of the eschatological kingdom. From such indications, we can suppose that the message of the Servant Songs was cherished by a spiritual few in
Israel.

Certain contacts between the expectation of a Messiah and the
Servant theme have been discerned in some extra-canonical writings, but the Servant's essential task of atoning suffering was not
transferred to the Messiah. At least, any idea of a suffering Messiah remained very exceptional and was confined to the periphery
of Judaism. How difficult it was for the official representatives of
Jewry to accept a suffering Messiah is shown by a rabbinical
Targum on Isa. 53, which identifies the Servant with the Messiah
but then by a most arbitrary twisting of the text avoids attributing
the suffering to him. And we know from the New Testament how
hard it was even for the apostles to assimilate the doctrine that the
Messiah must suffer.

A further and important line of eschatological thought is found
in the apocalyptic writings. The word "apocalypse" is simply the
anglicized form of the Greek word for revelation. What is called
apocalyptic literature is a body of writings, belonging roughly to
the period from 200 B.C. to A.D. 100, which teach the end of the
present world and the coming of a new order and do so under
the form of a series of revelations. The apocalyptists saw history as
a mighty drama in which God did battle with the forces of evil,
particularly in so far as these were embodied in the great pagan
empires. At the height of the struggle God would intervene,
destroy his enemies, and establish his kingdom. The purpose of the
writings was to give comfort in the midst of calamities and persecution. They aroused hope by showing the unfolding of a divine
plan in history and by looking forward to a decisive intervention

by God. They shared this expectation with the prophets, but there was a shift in perspective. The prophetic hope is tied to this historical order. The judgement the prophets awaited was to take place in history, and though there was a tension, increasingly marked, towards a final order, no sharp break is introduced between this world and the new order to come. In the apocalypses the judgement comes at the end of the world; an intervention from on high causes the upheaval of this present order and puts an end to it; there is then set up a transcendent kingdom. A rupture separates this present world and the world to come. This outlook was helped and accentuated by the growth of belief in the resurrection from the dead. It should be noted, however, that for our present purpose the variety of opinion found in the apocalypses has been of necessity greatly simplified.

This supramundane eschatology is taught with the extravagant use of imagery, hyperbole, and allegory, which renders this literature very strange to us. In this respect, it owes much to Babylonian and Iranian sources. The origins of this form of writing go back some way; some passages in the prophets are in the apocalyptic style. The Bible itself contains two apocalypses, one from the beginning and one from the end of the period during which it flourished, namely, the Book of Daniel and the Apocalypse of John. But most of the apocalyptic literature is extra-canonical, though it had an important formative influence as an element in the background of Christianity.

Now, there arose in the apocalyptic school of thought the expectation of a mysterious heavenly figure through whom God would intervene and bring about his kingdom. The first indications are found in the Book of Daniel, written between 167 and 164. In Dan. 7.13–14, we read of a vision in which one like a son of man came with the clouds of heaven and received from God, the Ancient of Days, an everlasting and universal kingdom. The symbol is immediately explained by an angelic interpreter. As verses 18 and 27 make clear, it is the eschatological Israel, the Israel of the last days, the people of the saints, which will overcome the four beasts, representing the four great pagan empires, and will receive the kingdom. "Son of Man" has, therefore, a collective meaning. But does that exhaust its meaning? We are told expressly that the four beasts are also four kings (verse 17—the

Douay wrongly reads "kingdoms"), and the idea is that the kings are the personal embodiment of their empires. The thought of the passage would be more consistent if the Son of Man also was not only the personification of a community but an individual through whom it functions as its organ and representative. What we have said about the idea of corporate personality can be applied here, so that the meaning of the mysterious figure would be twofold; it would bear a collective and a personal interpretation.

Whatever the meaning of Daniel, it is beyond question that later apocalyptic writings understood the Son of Man as an individual and expected him as an eschatological personage. The most striking texts are in the Parables of Enoch (cf. 48, 2–7), which describe a being who is without equal in the world, pre-existing with God as Wisdom, receiving all gifts, with the prerogative of saving men and the task of judging all peoples before reigning eternally with the just. He is called the Messiah, the Just, the Chosen One, and, above all, the Son of Man. This is the most ideal and transcendent type of Messiah conceived by pre-Christian Jewish thought, and it may also be noted that this heavenly figure assumes various characteristics taken from the Servant of Yahweh and the Davidic Messiah. Many scholars have maintained the existence of Christian interpolations in the Parables of Enoch, but their reasons do not seem to be conclusive.

Traces of the same current of thought are found elsewhere, and the expectation of the Son of Man may have been common in esoteric Jewish circles, though it remained alien to official Judaism. Why was this title used? Son of Man is simply an Aramaic idiom for Man. But we can still ask why this heavenly figure was called the Man. The Jewish texts provide no clear answer. It is not unlikely, then, that there was some influence from outside Judaism, and a link has been suggested with the theme of the Primal or Heavenly Man found in Oriental mythology. Any such influence would have been on Judaism and not directly on Christianity. The question is surrounded with uncertainty, and it is important to remember the distinctively Jewish character of the Messianic expectation to which any borrowings were subordinated.

The Davidic Messiah, the Suffering Servant, the Son of Man: these are the principal strands of thought in personal Messianism, and an examination of the claim of Christ is largely a discussion of his attitude to these three titles. Naturally, a fuller account would have to add further details, for the complexity of the Messianic expectation should never be forgotten. A danger to be avoided is an excessive preoccupation with personal Messianism and a neglect of the significance of the general movement of the Old Testament towards Christ. What the Old Testament gives us is not an anticipated revelation of Christ—the foreshadowings were far surpassed by the reality—but a preparation for Christ. It records a progressive revelation which culminated in Christ. The self-disclosure of God made through the events of Israel's history and the teaching of God's spokesmen was completed in Christ, who gathered up all the past into himself and gave it meaning.

It would be relevant here to recount the whole of Old Testament history and see it, in the light of what we have said, as a preparation for Christ. To do that is impossible, but certain features in the movement of the Old Testament towards Christ deserve to be noticed. The first is the sovereignty of God and the freedom of the divine choice. God freely chose Israel from among the nations. His free choice was frequently exercised in the course of its history. Not all the descendants of Abraham were members of the Chosen People. He chose Isaac not Ismael, Jacob not Esau; only Juda was left to inherit the promises, and of Juda only a remnant survived. And this brings us to the second feature. The movement of the Old Testament is a movement from the Many to the One. A principle of reduction is operative. If we take the movement in its full sweep, it passes from mankind to Israel, from Israel to the Remnant, and from the Remnant to the One, Christ. In contrast to this, there is an inverse movement in the New Testament: from Christ to the first disciples, from the first disciples to Christians generally, and from Christians to the whole of mankind.

Finally, the Old Testament drives home the lesson that salvation can come only from above. The very unfaithfulness that mars Israel's history serves the purpose of making it abundantly clear that the religion of Yahweh was not a creation of men, a projection of their own desires, but a call from above drawing them beyond themselves. The repeated disappointments of Israel's hopes hammered home the truth that they were not to expect salvation from military power or political change or any other human resource. God used these to bring from time to time a partial deliverance, but it always fell short of their hopes. The true salvation for which they longed seemed always beyond their grasp. An anxious, urgent question rises up from the Old Testament: when will God speak the word of life? He did so when that saving Word himself became flesh and dwelt amongst us.

CHAPTER XIV

OUR KNOWLEDGE OF CHRIST

We cannot love Jesus unless we know him. Since we are invited to love him as a living Person and not simply admire him as a great hero of the past, we must know him as a living Person. Somehow we must meet him and establish that kind of relationship in which we gradually enter into his mind, share his thoughts and acquire his outlook. We can do this in the Church. It is a mistake to see the Ascension as the complete withdrawal of Christ as man from this world. If we do so, we misunderstand the Resurrection and the sending of the Spirit which resulted from it. Christ is still present. But to grasp this we need to see something of his relation to the Spirit.

From the beginning in the womb of Mary the human nature of Christ was filled with the Holy Spirit. It was in the power of the Spirit that Jesus carried out the work given him to do by his heavenly Father. This possession of the Spirit meant the communication to Christ's manhood of that plenitude of saving gifts which was to bring about the perfect accomplishment of his task, his own glorification and the salvation of the human race. But until the work of Christ was finished the Spirit in him was tied. It was not given in unrestricted abundance. The reason is that in God's plan the Spirit is given only as the outcome of Christ's work. Christ is the Saviour. He must first reconcile men to God and then the Spirit, the gift of salvation *par excellence,* will be given to them. Before this there were but imperfect anticipations of the gift to come. The barrier between man and God was broken through at the crucifixion and the Spirit of God was released upon us. The first effect of his power was the glorification of Christ.

And by his resurrection Christ became a life-giving Spirit, that is, he was so penetrated with the Spirit as to become the unfailing source of the Spirit for all men. When his glorification was completed by his ascension and his exaltation to the right hand of God, he was able to send the Spirit upon his apostles at Pentecost. Since then, the Spirit has streamed forth from him into his Church and into all men who accept his offer of salvation.

Every grace we receive comes to us from the Spirit, and from the Spirit through Christ. The graces we receive are so many outpourings of that fullness which is already found in Christ. We are as it were fitted into Christ, made part of his structure, so that the Spirit that is in Christ is in us too. The Spirit brings us to Christ, joins us to his body and animates us there with his life. We may use an example to illustrate this. When the body of a man grows, the soul continues to give life to the whole of it. There is one and the same life, but now it is shared by more cells than before. Similarly with Christ. We become parts of Christ's body, animated with his life. Christ continues to grow, incorporating men into himself, and the process will go on until he has reached the full stature decreed for him by God. It is not a perfect analogy. We are not joined to Christ like the unconscious cells of a body but in the freedom of a personal relationship. But it serves to bring home to us that the life we receive by grace is the very life of Christ. The Spirit establishes between us and Christ a bond which involves the communication of life. In that way Christ is present to us and we are made present to Christ. Or, in Pauline terms, we are in Christ and Christ is in us. We are speaking of Christ as man. We are referring to the glorified humanity of Christ, through which alone the Spirit comes to us and with which we are made one by the Spirit. The apostles watched Christ go away from them into heaven, but he had comforted them with the promise of his Spirit. The coming of the Spirit has ensured the invisible nearness of Christ to all his followers until he comes again.

Already this much enables us to see how we can know and love Christ. We can analyse it in this way. Sanctifying grace establishes a basic union of life with him. Faith, hope and charity bring that union onto the conscious plane. As our faith develops, we begin to think like Christ; his mind pervades our own and gradually we share his understanding of reality. Hope gives us the same set of values as his. We look forward to the same things, and our lives begin to beat with the rhythm of his plan for ourselves and the world. Charity implies possession. It seals our union with love. Our wills are at one with his and move in unison towards God. And so, we know and love Christ because he reproduces in us what he is.

Yet were this identification with Christ to be brought about simply within our inner experience, we should have to admit a strange inconsistency in the plan of God. By the incarnation God became visible to men. He could be seen and touched. Human words conveyed divine truth and human actions became the vehicles of divine power. It was the climax of a history during which God had made himself known to men through visible signs. Are we to suppose that this process of coming to men across perceptible signs ceased after it had been brought to perfection in the incarnation? It would mean that the departure of Christ into heaven marked the suspension of what we call the law of the incarnation, namely, that the divine reality is accessible to men in the outward forms of visible reality. Since the incarnation itself is permanent and carries with it the necessity of our union with Christ's humanity, we should expect that the manner of our union with Christ would correspond to it. We are led to think that in some way or other our union with Christ is achieved by visible as well as invisible means.

When Christ was on earth, people learned to know and love him by listening to his words and coming into contact with his actions. As he taught them, their minds were opened to a new understanding of God and his redemptive plan. And his teaching was not merely about his mission but also about himself, his own Person, because the two coincided with each other. It is true that at the time they largely failed to grasp his meaning. But the memory of his words remained, and the faith of the Church after Pentecost, its knowledge of Christ, consisted in an insight given by the Spirit into what Christ himself had said. But Christ made himself known by deeds as well as words. His love for men, the redemptive purpose of his coming and the divine power he possessed were shown in his compassionate healing of the sick. How a man came to know and love Christ is described by John in the ninth chapter of his Gospel in the account of the man born blind. Jesus made his first impact upon this man by the action which restored his sight. He then led him by his words to a recognition of his Person. Words and actions: these were the signs through which his first disciples came to know and love Jesus.

And it is the same with ourselves. If we are to know and love Jesus, we have to listen to his words and receive the impact of his visible actions. But where are these now? They are in the Church. Through the power of the Spirit Christ uses as his own the voices of other men. He speaks to us in the preaching and witness of the Church. The words of the Church are the words of Christ. When we listen to the Church, we are listening to Christ, and when we enter into the mind of the Church, we are entering into the mind of Christ. Some will object and say that we should first have pointed to the words of Christ in the Gospels. But we are looking for the living voice of a living man, not a record of the past. This might seem to undervalue the Gospels. It does not do so in fact. At the centre of the preaching and witness of the Church is the inspired record of what Christ did and said while on earth. Christ arranged for this record because of the unique, unrepeatable character of what then occurred. His life was the privileged intervention of God in history and must therefore be preserved for us in its historical reality. But the Gospels come to us not as mere records but as the living voice of the risen Christ because they are read again and again to us by the Church in the name of Christ and in the power of his Spirit. And read in that way they have the qualities of a living voice. They can be explained and interpreted and our questions about them answered. The same is true of all the words of Scripture. They are uttered for us by the Church, and in the voice of the Church we recognize the accent of Christ.

The actions of Christ also are continued in the Church. Above all, this is true of the sacraments. They are actions of the risen Christ. In a sacrament we come into contact with Christ as truly as the men he healed with a touch. But what is true of the sacraments is true in a lesser degree of all the activity of the Church. Christ acts through the Church. Through his Spirit he controls its activity and makes it his own. Here it becomes apparent that in this matter we need the distinctions of theology. There is a human element in the Church. Since in the Church

Christ makes use of the voice and actions of other men without entirely preventing the effects of their sins and weaknesses, we cannot say without qualification that all the words of the Church are the words of Christ and all the actions of the Church his actions. We have to see how far he has made them his own, how far he has guaranteed their Christian authenticity. But the concern here is with the basic principle, not with the distinctions that make it precise. And the principle is: we meet Christ in the words and actions of the Church.

Perhaps we can understand now the manner in which we know and love Christ. We encounter him in an inner experience. The Spirit establishes between us and the risen Christ a community of life. We are bound to him in a vital and at the same time personal relationship. But this inner experience is mediated to us in an outward contact with Christ achieved by words and actions. These words and actions belong to Christ, they express his mind and carry his influence, although they are not spoken by his own voice nor performed by his own body. The Spirit given by the risen Christ to the Church ensures that we do really encounter Christ in her preaching and witness and in her actions. Using the word in a wide sense, we could call the whole process by which we come to Christ sacramental. Whatever aspect of the Church's life we consider, it is always a question of reaching the invisible reality of Christ through outward signs in which he makes himself accessible. The sacraments in the strict sense are simply privileged instances of this process.

How, then, do we increase our knowledge of Christ? Every earnest Christian wants to know more about Christ and know him better at the same time. People seek practical advice on how to set about it. The need is particularly felt by students and other educated laymen, who feel that their knowledge of Christ does not correspond to their general level of knowledge. But all of us have to foster our knowledge of Christ and promote its growth. It helps us in this matter if we realize that the growth is a two-sided process. On the one hand, we must become more and more familiar with what the Church tells us about Christ. Since the Scriptures are in the centre of the Church's message, what is required in the first place is an ever increasing familiarity with them. But we can speak in more general terms and say that we must learn all that we can about Christ; we must meditate upon his words in the Gospels, we must see from the Old Testament how the way was prepared for him, we must find out what Paul and John have written about him, we must make our own the insights which the Church has reached concerning him in her long years of reflexion. It is an endless task, which each must fulfil according to the opportunities given him by God. In a basic way it is fulfilled by taking part in the ordinary life of the Church, and especially in her liturgy. On the other hand, we must give this knowledge life by our openness to Christ and his action. We are not seeking to learn all about a dead person but to meet a living one. It is Christ who is speaking to us in this many-sided witness of the Church. We must go forward to meet him. The action of his Spirit is always there when we study Christ. If we open our hearts to grace, if we go wherever Christ leads, our study of him will become a personal encounter. We shall not simply learn about him but learn to know and love him.

The two sides of the process should run parallel to each other. They do not always do so. The intensity with which Christ is welcomed from within sometimes overcomes the inadequacy with which he is presented from without. And the reluctance with which he is accepted from within can reduce to dead matter the rich information assimilated from without. But we must base our lives on what is normal, and this implies both a resolve to learn about Christ to the measure of our capabilities and a prayer that we may correspond to his grace and thus meet him when we study.

If we now examine more closely the way we learn about Christ, we find that our first task is to know the Gospels. In a sense that is easy enough. They are quite short, and to read and reread them so that the sayings and incidents they contain become familiar, become part of ourselves, is extremly fruitful and necessary. But with many of us, questions soon arise that press for an answer. It is not the details of exegesis that bother us—we must simply work at a commentary for those—but more fundamental questions. What is the nature of these documents? How far are they historical? What about the discrepancies between them?

The Gospels are not histories of Christ in the ordinary sense; they are presentations of the mystery of Christ. Gospel means Good News, and the evangelists did not conceive their task in the same way as a modern biographer but as a setting forth of the good news of salvation. Their starting-point was the faith of the Church, and what they intended to do was to give an account of the life of Christ in the light of that faith. Their purpose was doctrinal. Each had in mind some particular aspect of the mystery of Christ and wrote his Gospel so as to bring that aspect into relief. We can say that each Gospel gives us a Christology, an individual way of viewing the mystery of Christ and his work. The unity of the Bible, guaranteed by inspiration, ensures that the various Christologies are complementary, not contradictory.

This doctrinal bias does not mean for one moment that the evangelists were unconcerned with history. On the contrary, it meant that they were vitally concerned with it. The Christian message is a message about history. A study of that message in the testimony of all the early sources shows beyond doubt that at its very heart was the affirmation of a series of facts. The primitive faith in Christ was not based on a myth or speculation about a divine Saviour but on events witnessed by the apostles and involving the man Jesus whom they had known and with whom they had lived. It arose from what Christ had said and, above all, from what had happened to him. Every presentation of that faith, and the Gospels are no exception, is essentially a history. Its nucleus always consists of testimony to fact. But the history in question is history of a unique kind. It is redemptive history, which means that it is made up of events in which God has intervened with saving power. The events actually occurred in the course of human affairs, but they have a transcendent content and significance. This inner content is grasped by faith. When the evangelists recounted this history, their aim was to present the total event, the inner content as well as the outer crust. We must not see them as chroniclers busy with the bare facts, which equivalently means the facts as judged by merely human criteria and seen in relation to the network of human motives and activities, but as evangelists, which means people anxious to tell the good news of God's saving acts as these can be seen by faith in the events of Jesus Christ.

It is almost impossible to make assertions like these at the present day without causing alarm among believers. The reason is the understandable reaction against the excesses of those biblical critics who emptied the Christian faith of its historical truth. Such excesses still exist, for example in Bultmann, but where they are found the influence of philosophical presuppositions is plain. Nowadays, the main body of biblical critics has adopted a saner attitude and accepts, though in varying degrees, the factual basis of the Christian faith. It is disturbing, however, how many young people, for example undergraduates, refuse without consideration the right of the Gospels to be taken seriously as historical records. We have no alternative but to dub such a refusal obscurantist; it is a refusal to face the evidence. The familiar arguments are still valid: the simplicity and sincerity of the writers; the sources they used; the connexion with the primitive community in which eye-witnesses held the principal place; the verifiable accuracy with which they depict the complicated Palestinian world of the time of Christ, which was so completely destroyed in the year 70 as to make an imaginative reconstruction unthinkable; the confirmed soundness of their geographical information; the perspective in which they place the teaching of Christ, its anti-pharisaic charac-ter for example, which did not correspond to the interests of the Church at the time of writing; and, in regard to the Synoptics, the archaic nature of their portrait of Christ, which contrasts with the theology of Christ that had already developed in the Church before the Gospels were written—see the Pauline writings—and is sometimes in apparent conflict with it. A critical analysis of the Gospels shows that they and the community on which they de-pended were not out of touch with history but faithful to it, fre-quently down to details. At the same time, we must not exaggerate. To treat the Gospels as if they were stenographers' reports of the sayings and deeds of Christ, to use them in the same way as we would a modern critical biography, is critically indefensible and a misunderstanding of their nature. If it is important to affirm the fact of their historical character, it is also important to under-stand the manner in which they are historical.

The first thing that distinguishes the Gospels from a modern life is the fragmentary nature of the material from a biographical point of view. There is so much that we do not know. We are not sure of the length of Christ's ministry. It is impossible to arrange the incidents in a chronological sequence. The attempts to do this are ingenious but, I am afraid, a waste of time. The arrangement in the Gospels is largely editorial. The discourses in Matthew, such as the Sermon on the Mount, are compilations of scattered sayings. Luke, for his own purposes, arranges much of his material in the setting of a journey to Jerusalem. John changes the position of the cleansing in the Temple. And so on. We can, it is true, by critical analysis reconstruct the course of Christ's ministry in its main lines: the baptism by John, the first preaching to the crowds, the misunderstanding of his mission, the turning-point marked by the confession of Peter and the transfiguration, the concentration on a smaller group of disciples, the predictions of the passion, the growing hostility of the Jewish leaders and the conflict with them, and the passion, death and resurrection. The main outline is enlarged or reduced in the ebb and flow of scholarly debate. But if we take what we know at its maximum, we must admit that from the point of view of a modern biographer we have materials for a memoir of Christ, not for a full life.

Next, we must take account of the nature of the material used by the evangelists. The Gospel tradition, the tradition of the sayings and deeds of Christ, gradually took shape in the Church. It had already reached an advanced stage of development when the four Gospels were written. The evangelists had at their disposal pre-existing units in which sayings, parables, miracle stories, and so on, were being handed down in the tradition according to a given literary shape or form. This conglomeration of material in preformed units was diverse in character and the diversity remains within the written Gospels, so that it is necessary to treat different parts of the Gospels in different ways. The vivid directness of some accounts marks them as eye-witness accounts. Some sayings have the rhythm of the oral style, which allows us to see in them the very words of Christ. But other parts have a different character. Some parables are given in a developed form in which their message has been adapted to the situation in the Church; an instance is the parable of the talents. It is also interesting to discuss the reasons that led to the divergent form of the Beatitudes in Matthew and Luke. Sometimes the tradition contained two different accounts of the same incident. The feeding of the five thousand and the feeding of the four thousand are probably different versions of the same miracle. The infancy narratives have not the same historical character as the passion narratives. In other words, we cannot avoid the need for critical analysis if we want to determine the exact character of the different elements in the Gospels. And while we have reasons, both theological and historical, for the soundness and homogeneity of the development in the tradition of the primitive community, we cannot be blind to the existence of such a development.

The evangelists started from the faith of the Church and the tradition as they found it at the time. A good illustration of this is the accounts they give of the institution of the Eucharist. These accounts are reduced to the essentials concerning the Eucharist and do not give us a detailed description of the Last Supper as it actually occurred. If we decide that it was a paschal meal, we have to reconstruct the ceremonial from other sources. Again, the words of Christ are given in different forms. The accounts have in fact a liturgical origin and give the narrative of the Eucharist as it had been simplified and arranged for use in the liturgy. If we examine the differences carefully, we can go some way in determining which of the variations are more primitive and more likely to represent the actual words of Christ.

Enough has now been said to enable us to tackle the question of the discrepancies between the Gospels. Some of these are due to the way each evangelist adapted his material to his individual purpose. These are easier to explain and should cause little difficulty once we have grasped the literary technique of the time, which was different from our own. Here it is far more important to understand what the evangelists were doing than pointlessly to lament that they did not follow the literary procedures of a later age. The more troublesome inconsistencies arise from the fact that the evangelists draw on different sections of the Gospel tradition as it had variously developed. These inconsistencies are often mere differences in presentation and emphasis. Occasionally they involve contradictions, as in the accounts of the blind beggar or beggars outside Jericho (Mt. 20.29–34; Mark 10.46–52; Luke 18.35–43). The evangelists were not always able nor was it always their intention to affirm the accuracy of details. We must read them as we would a modern critical historian.

Some would like to quote the Gospels as if every saying gave us the *ipsissima verba* of Christ and every narrative was a simple account of what had actually occurred. Apart from the untenable character of this position, which a mere comparison of the different Gospels should suffice to exclude, it has unfortunately been the case that insistence on a too narrowly conceived historicity has been accompanied by a neglect of the doctrinal riches to be found in the Gospels when properly understood. They are, it may be recalled, not ordinary histories but presentations of redemptive history, and the purpose of the evangelists is to show us the significance of the events recorded. We can only do them justice if we recognize the distinctive doctrinal purpose of each and follow out its implications.

But how far do the Gospels put us into contact with Christ himself? This can be answered from the standpoint either of theology or of history. Theologically speaking, we can say that we meet in the Gospels the living voice of Christ. He speaks to us in the words of these summaries of the faith of the early Church, which were written down under the inspiration of his Spirit and are read to us by the Church of today. Further, the faith of the early Church, which is ours too, was indissolubly bound up with the historical facts of Christ, his message and his mission. We are assured, therefore, by our faith that the Gospels rest on historical fact and that any development in the tradition they record has remained true to the historical reality which was its starting-point. From the point of view of the historian, it is already of vital moment that the Gospels give us a record of the faith of the first Christians, particularly since this faith lays such stress on historical events. But the reasons already enumerated allow the historian to go further and affirm the substantial historical veracity of the Gospel accounts of Christ. He will not, however, expect the same rigour of historical presentation as in a modern critical history, and he will clearly discern the diversity in the materials used by the evangelists. Critical analysis will enable him to trace the stages in the development of the tradition and determine, though only within limits, its primitive stratum, thus coming close to what Christ actually said and did.

In speaking of the Gospels, I have had in mind principally the Synoptic Gospels. The Gospel of John deserves special consideration. At the same time, much of what has been said applies equally to it. John shares the common Christian concern with the historical reality of Christ. The vivid detail of the narratives reveals the voice of an eye-witness again and again. His topographical information is remarkably good. If we compare his account of the teaching of Christ with that of the Synoptics, we find numerous indications of the essential continuity between them despite the manifest differences. The recent discoveries at Qumran have brought to light Jewish documents containing ideas that remind us of the themes characteristic of John. This has confirmed the opinion of those who stressed the Semitic character of the Johannine thought and has checked the contention that it was a later Hellenization of the Christian faith. It may well be that John depends on a different though authentic side of Christ's teaching from that given by the Synoptics. All the same, we have in the Fourth Gospel a different kind of writing from the other three Gospels. It is a more personal, original and unified work than they. It is dominated throughout by a mature Christology that is even more developed than St. Paul's. The author has not lost touch with historical reality or tradition, but he presents the life of Christ in the light of a personal reflexion of a high order. The inner significance of Christ's actions is made to stand out with clarity, and the meaning of his teaching has been drawn out. In the discourses found in the Gospel we are further from the actual words of Christ than in the Synoptics. When confronted with the declarations of Christ in John, with their developed content and clarity, we are often tempted to ask: what did Christ actually say? The answer must be that we do not know. But need that bother us? We know that the author was close to Jesus and intended simply to understand his teaching and see its implications. Examined historically, his portrait of Christ is in harmony, not conflict, with that of the Synoptics. For us as believers its truth is guaranteed by inspiration and we know further that Christ who is still living speaks to us in the words of the Gospel.

Do not let us always approach the Gospels with the preoccupations of the apologist, regretting all the time what the Gospels do not give us and anxious for whatever will make our apologetic task easier. If we take the Gospels as they are, and as God intended them to be, and try to assimilate them as Christians, we shall begin to see how far more truly and effectively they bring us into contact with Christ than an ordinary history would have done. And I mean into contact with the Jesus of history. It is the Jesus of history who is the Christ of our faith. Precisely because the historical Jesus was in his history a mystery, it is inadequate to deal with him as with an ordinary historical fact. The evangelists, especially John, realized this. The deep insights of John's Gospel bring us closer to Jesus as he actually was and still is than any critical biography would have done. And a less superficial apologetic will frankly recognize this.

If our first and obvious task in trying to learn more about Christ is to study the Gospels, these do not exhaust what the Scriptures have to tell us of Christ. The study of John will, of course, reach out and embrace the Johannine writings other than the Gopel. And the New Testament offers us two further, important fields of study. First, there are the beliefs of the primitive community as these are revealed to us in the first part of the Acts of the Apostles and in certain formularies embedded in the epistles, especially Paul's, and taken over from the inheritance of the community. The earlier discourses given in the Acts (2.14–40: 3.12–26: 4.8–12: 5.29–32: 7.2–53: 10.34–43: 13.16–41) put us in touch with the primitive Christian preaching and show us how the resurrection of Christ and the accomplishment of salvation were first proclaimed to men. In other words, we find in them the apostolic *kerygma* or message as it was first announced. These discourses are not verbatim reports of what was said on the occasions to which they are assigned. We must allow Luke a reasonable freedom in adapting his materials and remember that ancient historians were accustomed to put speeches into the mouths of notable personages. But Luke did not create them out of nothing. Their historical value consists in the fidelity with which they record the themes of the primitive preaching. And critical analysis allows us to go further and say that they preserve the characteristics proper to the individual preaching of the persons to whom they are assigned. Luke probably had access to sources which kept alive the memory of the preaching proper to the various persons and groups of the first community. If we add to them the other information given in the Acts and the traces of earlier formularies of faith and worship found in the epistles, such as 1 Cor. 11.23–5: 15.3–5; Rom. 1.3–4; Phil. 2.6–11; 1 Peter 2.1–10, we can give some account of the faith in Christ as it existed in the nascent Christian community. It is of great interest to do this.

It shows us the central place occupied in the apostolic message by the resurrection of Christ. The *kerygma* was in fact the proclamation of the resurrection as marking the accomplishment of salvation. We can also see how the Church came to a realization of the divinity of Christ through the fact of the resurrection, and we can grasp better the development of Christology by contact with its earlier themes as these existed prior to the reflexion of Paul and John and before the writing of the Gospels. Needless to say, this is a very technical field of biblical study where much is still debated by scholars, but some knowledge of it can enrich and refresh our vision of Christ by the contact it gives with the earliest faith of the Church. A good book on the subject by a Catholic is Joseph Schmitt's *Jésus ressuscité dans la prédication apostolique*.[1]

The second and remaining sector in the New Testament teaching on Christ is filled by Paul's theology. Christ dominates the writings of Paul from end to end; he is the centre on which all the themes of Paul's thought converge. His theology of Christ had its roots in the faith of the primitive community, and we find the same prominence given to the resurrection. There is an added reason for this stress in Paul's own experience of the risen Christ on the road to Damascus. But if his thought is in line with the traditional faith of the Church he joined, he reached new insights which mark a considerable development. Like the first Christians generally, he always viewed Christ in relation to his work, and his great contribution to Christian thought lies in his deep understanding of Christ's redemptive work and of the continuing influence of the risen Saviour. But this went hand in hand with a deeper understanding of the Person of Christ. Fortunately, fine studies of Paul's theology are available, but it is regrettable that for so many educated Catholics the riches of this thought still remain an untouched treasure. We should add, before leaving the New Testament, that the Epistle to the Hebrews contains a Christology that is too powerful and original to be ignored without loss. Since Paul is no longer held to be its author, its thought is not examined in writings on his theology, and existing on the fringe of the Pauline corpus it is somewhat neglected. But a study of the Christology of the New Testament is not complete without it.

[1] Paris, Gabalda, 1949.

With the task of assimilating the New Testament teaching on Christ, already so formidable and with the seemingly endless wealth its pages promise, some may think themselves reasonably excused if they leave aside the Old Testament. Some, indeed, thumbing through these strange writings, may feel that the coming of Christ brought such transformation, such newness, that the Old Testament is no longer relevant to us as Christians, but remains simply as a record of what went before, what is now over and done with. It is a very common mistake, but a mistake none the less. Even though it may cause surprise, we must maintain that we cannot advance in our knowledge of Christ unless we take the Old Testament seriously and become familiar with it. We mean with the whole of it, not simply with a series of proof-texts brandished as prophecies of Christ.

The first reason is that the New Testament is fully intelligible only when placed alongside the Old Testament. Its themes and ideas are the themes and ideas of the Old Testament in a later stage of development. If there is newness, there is also continuity, and the newness is the newness of fulfilment of the old. No one can hope, for example, to understand the theme of the Kingdom of God, which is so prominent in the Synoptic account of the teaching of Christ, unless he has studied it in the Old Testament. And we could continue to multiply examples through the whole range of New Testament teaching. We cannot grasp the meaning of the titles given to Christ, the Son of Man, the Servant, the Son of God, the Word and so on, if we ignore their Old Testament roots. And it is not merely the case that the Old Testament is a kind of glossary in which we can look up the meaning of the terms used in the New Testament. It contains rich doctrinal teaching on these subjects, which is presupposed in the often briefer New Testament statements. We impoverish the New Testament doctrinally unless we can see in its teaching the implications that are due to its connexion with the teaching of the Old Testament. That teaching is still relevant and valid, though it has to be understood in the light of its final development in Christ.

The second reason why we must study the Old Testament is a continuation of the first but carries the matter deeper. What is the perspective in which the New Testament in all its parts presents Christ? It is the perspective of the history of salvation. Yahweh was a God who acted in history. He was the God of mighty deeds who intervened in history and directed it to his saving purpose. Israel awaited the last days in which Yahweh would bring about the final salvation, the new Exodus, the new Covenant, the King-dom of God. Christ came as the fulfilment of God's promises; he brought the Kingdom of God; he was the definitive intervention of God; in him salvation was accomplished. That is the way the New Testament sees Christ and that is the way we must see him if we are to understand him and his work. In short, we must see him in relation to the unfolding in history of God's redemptive plan for the human race. Now, we can never grasp any history in its meaning by studying exclusively the event which forms its climax. If we do that, we shall not see it as a history at all. That in fact is what has happened. Our neglect of the Old Testament has led to a loss of the sense of the history of salvation and the reduction of the Christian message to a timeless relationship be-tween God and men. Hence, we must know the Old Testament as a whole, so as to see the development of God's plan, the pattern of his action in history and the significance of Christ as the cul-minating point. Only thus can we see the basic way in which the Old Testament prophesies Christ: namely, as a line of develop-ment that points to Christ and finds in him its fulfilment. The in-dividual prophecies must be seen in that setting if they are to be rightly understood, otherwise they become, in a rather silly way, riddles which God set the Israelites and solved in Christ. When the first Christians were faced with the mystery of Christ and sought to penetrate its meaning, they turned, as the evidence shows, to the Old Testament and found in it what they needed in order to understand. We must do the same if we are to advance in our knowledge of Christ.

We read the Scriptures in the Church and under her guidance. It is in this way that they become for us the living voice of Christ. In a sense, they contain all that we need to know, for they embrace the mystery of Christ in its entirety. They are an inspired state-ment of the faith of the apostolic Church, and the close of the apostolic age saw the completion of the sum of revealed truth. Since then, God has revealed no further data about Christ. But during her history the Church has never ceased to reflect upon the mystery of Christ. The Scriptures always remain at the centre of that reflexion. They form an endless source from which the Church continually draws new points for attentive meditation and a permanent focus to which she relates the results of her reflexions. But during the process of reflexion questions come to mind that are not expressly answered in the Bible and errors arise that cannot be excluded by the words of Scripture alone, and so the Church struggles forward to new insights and new formulations. And then, revealed truth was given in Scripture in relation to a particular audience, time and place. The permanent value of the words of Scripture as inspired does not exclude the effort or the need to formulate the same truth in different terms, nor should it stifle the endeavour of the speculative thinker to understand and express truths, even revealed truths attained by faith, from a standpoint that is universal.

Consequently, there has taken place in the Church a doctrinal progress, which is enshrined in the decrees of councils and the writings of speculative theologians. A certain biblical exclusivism is sometimes found, mostly among Protestants but occasionally influencing Catholics, which dislikes this fact and wishes to stick simply to the biblical formulation of revealed truth. This is to forget that the Scriptures are not the records of a dead past but the means of a living dialogue with Christ. It is to make the biblical statements items for the filing-cabinet of memory and not, as they should be, food for thinking minds. If we recognize the presence of Christ and the action of his Spirit in the Church, we shall see the validity of that progress in the understanding of revealed truth, which gives rise to new dogmatic formulations and provides room for the speculations of theologians. Such progress is the fruit of the Christian effort, supported by grace, to know Christ better.

Part of our task, then, in learning about Christ is to make our own the insights which the Church has gathered during her history. We do this by studying her official decrees and the works of theologians. We must trace the history of the great controversies that shook the early Church until we reach the formula of Chalcedon (451), which, with its two natures in one Person, has been the basis of all subsequent Christology. Further precisions were added to this, and then there came the profound thought of the medieval theologians and their successors, which has enriched our understanding of the mystery of Christ. We must also take account of developments in the life of the Church which have a bearing on our knowledge of Christ; the devotion to the Sacred Heart deserves a particular mention in this respect.

Some, in studying the theology of Christ, make the mistake of supposing that all they need to do is to learn and accept passively the results of all this thinking about Christ. They learn to manipulate the concepts of nature and person, so as to speak accurately about Christ and avoid any verbal contradiction. It is already much, but it is inadequate. We can assimilate thought only by doing the thinking ourselves. The results of reflexion can be made our own only if the process of reflexion is repeated in our own minds, helped, of course, by what has been achieved by others. The theological statements about Christ will be so much dead matter in our minds, often a hindrance rather than a help, unless we see the problems, ask ourselves the questions and seek to gain for ourselves the insights which are their origin and basis. We shall only profit from theology when we see that a mature faith allows a ceaseless though guided questioning and is not simply a passive acceptance.

To learn about Christ is a work that requires more than a lifetime. Each one of us must be content to do as much as he is able and as God gives him the opportunity to do. It is useful to see the full dimensions of the task and to outline its various parts. But it is important to recall again what it should mean for a Christian. We are not studying a dead person but making contact with a living Person. If we approach the Scriptures and our study of theology with our hearts open to Christ and sensitive to grace, with an awareness of his living presence and our union with him, we shall not merely learn about him but we shall meet him and advance in knowing and loving him. And that, after all, is our aim.

CHAPTER XV

THE RESURRECTION AND
THE ATONEMENT

Most students are disappointed with the treatise on the redemption. They do not find the rich matter and profound thought they expected. Appended to the long developments on the hypostatic union, the pages on the redemptive work of Christ seem thin and shallow. There is an indefinable absence of grandeur. Where is the magnificence of God's love? The epic of a victory is reduced to the payment of a debt. Wonder and joy should fill us when we study how God saved us. But there is no impact.

Jesus Christ is a living person for all devout Christians. They recognize his love. They appreciate that he suffered for them, and they contemplate his death with sympathy and love. No one denies this deep devotion. But in theology the student seeks to understand the passion. He searches for its intelligibility. Why is suffering redemptive? How does all that Christ did fit together? What is the over-all plan of salvation? He is told that Christ's death was a sacrifice and given the concepts of merit and satisfaction to explain its value. He assents, but deep within remains unsatisfied. He is not gripped in any compelling way by the redemptive plan of God. The depths of love he can appreciate in Christ are not matched by any corresponding sublimity he can see in the divine purpose. No clear synthesis brings together all that he knows about Christ. He returns to his contemplation without any real understanding of the mystery.

The plain truth is that the average theology of the redemption is truncated and its intelligibility maimed. The basic reason is the omission of the resurrection. The resurrection of Christ is essential in the mystery of salvation. To attempt an account of the redemption without including the resurrection is to end in an impasse. Some partial insights are achieved, true as far as they go, but a theology of redemption that pays exclusive attention to Christ's death is necessarily unbalanced and impoverished. It is not that there is any opposition between a redemption by the death of Christ and a redemption by his resurrection. Nothing is taken away from the redemptive significance of Christ's death by insisting on the resurrection. On the contrary, it is the resurrection that gives meaning to his death, while his death gives meaning to his resurrection. But both are essential and indissociable.

A stunted theology of redemption gained currency in the West for several reasons. The origins are not entirely clear, but we can trace its main development. After Anselm, certainly, the stress on satisfaction made the resurrection seem incidental to the work of redemption. If redemption equals satisfaction, the resurrection, which is not a work of satisfaction, is not redemptive. St. Thomas, as so often, was an exception. He gave a masterly treatment of satisfaction and related ideas, but he went further. By attributing to the passion, resurrection and, indeed, the whole work of Christ an efficient causality in our salvation, he incorporated into his teaching, in Scholastic terms, themes associated more with the Greek than with the Latin tradition. However, this part of his teaching was not understood by his contemporaries or successors, and only recently has it begun to exert its full influence. The concept of satisfaction, together with the closely related idea of merit, continued to dominate the doctrine in the West. Christ's death was understood as a sacrifice, but sacrifice was seen simply in terms of these notions.

The theology of satisfaction reached its apogee in the writings of Rivière. During the first half of this century he produced a long series of studies on the doctrine of redemption. For him, the concept of vicarious satisfaction expressed most exactly the redemptive meaning of Christ's work. All that Christ did which was properly redemptive could be brought under it. The value of Rivière's work lies in his insistence on the moral character of satisfaction. He distinguished it clearly from penal expiation, with which it had been sometimes confused after the Reformation. The primary or formal element in Christ's satisfaction was his loving obedience. It was a moral reparation. His suffering entered into his redemptive work, but in a secondary way. The notion of satisfaction was thereby purified and restored once more to its true nobility. The offence to our moral sense caused by unhappy rhetoric on the innocent Christ punished in our stead was excluded. But this theology, widely influential, remains onesided. Rivière was blind to other aspects of redemption and regarded a consideration of the glorious mysteries as irrelevant to the problem of redemption itself.

Christ "was delivered up for our sins, and rose again for our justification" (Rom. 4.25). Paul states here clearly enough the redemptive significance of the resurrection and the indissoluble bond joining the death and resurrection in the one mystery of salvation. Yet, theologians were unable to accept this affirmation at its face value. Cajetan gave a roundabout interpretation. Although Christ paid the price for our sins by his death, we should not have been justified unless he had risen, because we should not have believed. He rose in order that we might believe and so come to justification. The resurrection is redemptive as a motive of credibility. This is in keeping with the way theologians have handled the resurrection. It has been considered almost exclusively from the apologetic angle, especially since fundamental theology emerged fully as a separate branch of theology at the end of the eighteenth century. The theologian coming to the treatise on the redemption assumed that the resurrection had been dealt with in apologetics. True, the *Mysterium Fidei* of de la Taille brought out the role of the resurrection as the divine acceptance of Christ's sacrifice. And the development of the doctrine of the Mystical Body has emphasized the present activity of the risen Christ as Head. Again, a limited awareness of recent trends has caused a little more to be added to the mention of the resurrection as the complement of Christ's redemptive work. But the treatise on the redemption remains substantially unchanged. A glance at several well-known and generally praiseworthy manuals will show that only a *scholion,* sometimes of less than a page, is devoted to the resurrection in the section on redemption.

The protest came from biblical scholars. They ascertained that this defective theology does not do justice to the teaching of the New Testament. The discovery was made by Prat. The first edition of his great work on Paul came out a little before the First World War. But it is since 1930 that studies on this point, mostly articles, have multiplied, and the general advance in biblical theology has clarified and consolidated the earlier results. *The Resurrection: A Biblical Study* by Père F. X. Durrwell[1] is an outstanding contribution to this literature. Few books have received such lavish praise on all sides. While it gives a careful exegesis of numerous texts, its particular value consists in presenting a synthesis of all that the Bible says on the resurrection as a mystery of salvation. It is a work of biblical theology, and so the author remains within the world of biblical ideas and expressions. But he was not content to amass the data; he has moulded these data into a doctrinal whole. His book has become the standard work on the subject because of its comprehensiveness and the knowledge and penetration with which it is written.

The dogmatic treatise that takes adequate account of these findings has yet to be written. Speculative theology will take some time to assimilate them. However, a tentative outline may be ventured.

Man by his sin separated himself from God. He fell back into a condition of existence marked by sin, and his sin marred the rest of creation. Sinful man was cut off from God and enslaved in a world of suffering, corruption and death. His slavery was the grip of sin and its effects on the whole of his existence. His world was a world in which the powers of darkness held sway. Theology needs to pay more attention to the biblical notion of the cosmic powers. The present teaching on the angels does not fully cover what is said about the principalities, powers and world rulers of this darkness.

God in his love decided to save mankind. The origin of redemption is the utterly free love of God for his creatures. This love is a self-giving love, for the gift by which God saves is the gift of himself. God's plan is to raise men to the divine level and communicate to them a share in his life and glory. This was the purpose of God from the beginning, but the gift now comes to sinful man as a gift of salvation.

God carried out his plan by sending his Son into this world as man. The incarnation was the supreme self-gift of God. We can

[1] Trans. by Rosemary Sheed (New York, Sheed and Ward, 1961).

conceive no higher communication of God than that by which a human nature exists with the existence of God so that a man is God. The incarnate Son was established as the foundation for the whole structure of the new order God planned. He was to be the source through which every further self-giving of God was to come. The incarnation radically changed the situation of mankind. It inserted into the human race the principle capable of transforming its existence, of overcoming sin, death and the powers of darkness and of leading men into the spheres of the divine glory. As the entry into this world of the divine life and light, Christ possessed the Spirit from the beginning of his existence.

But salvation was achieved by the incarnation in a particular way. As brought about in this historical order, the incarnation was more than the assumption of a human nature; it was the assumption of a redemptive history. By becoming man, the Son entered the world of sin and death. He could not be touched by the moral guilt of sin, but he took upon himself the condition of our sinful existence. He came in the likeness of sinful flesh; he became subject to suffering and death; he was made lower than the angels. The Spirit he possessed did not penetrate fully his created nature. Incarnation into our history meant a self-emptying on the part of the Son incarnate. Christ, as man, renounced the glory that was his due and accepted a solidarity with the sinful human race. This abasement must be taken seriously if we are to grasp the plan of redemption. Usually, theologians are more concerned with the consequences of Christ's dignity as a divine person than with the implications of a redemptive incarnation.

The act of divine love by which we were redeemed is the act which transformed the manhood of Christ, brought him out of this world of sin and death, penetrated him completely with the Spirit and exalted him as Lord of the whole creation. This act has its source in the Trinity. We were saved by the Father, through the Son in the Holy Spirit. The redemptive drama enacted by the saving intervention of God took place first in Christ, but it took place in Christ in such a way that the act which brought Christ from death to life, from this existence marked by sin to the order of the resurrection, is the very act which effects the same transition in us. The Father glorified Christ by the Spirit and in doing so he glorified us with the rest of creation. How can this be so?

Christ is the visible, sacramental expression in this world of the saving act of divine love. With Christ, the divine love and power to save entered this world in a visible, human form. Every action of Christ is an expression of the divine saving purpose and an expression which is an efficacious sign, embodying and conveying the divine power. But this human expression of the divine saving act was not a single, static sign but a history. The whole history of Christ from beginning to end forms a dramatic, effectual sign in which God's saving purpose is set forth and through which his saving act comes to men. This sign found its completion and eternal permanence in the risen Christ, reigning in glory at the right hand of the Father. And so, every mystery of Christ's life is redemptive; in each event some facet of the divine saving love is manifested and every event shares the efficacy that belongs to all together as the effectual sign or sacrament of the divine redemptive act. That is what St. Thomas meant when he said that all the mysteries of Christ were efficient causes of our redemption. A consideration of the various mysteries of Christ's life should be restored to the theology of Christ and not relegated to devotional literature.

But the essential core of this redemptive history was Christ's death and resurrection. That was when the essential transition took place and Christ passed from this world to the new order of creation. The conjunction of this spiritual transition with physical death might be illuminated if we had a more adequate theology of death than is available at present. The transition was a new exodus of which the former was but the shadowy type. In Christ, the conditions of this existence were destroyed, sin and death overcome, the powers of darkness subjugated, the full influence of the Spirit released and the new order of the resurrection established with Christ as the first-fruits. It was a transformation by which the manhood of Christ was brought fully within the sphere of the divine, though in no way losing its proper nature. Notice that Père Durrwell shows that a divinizing transformation of the victim is included in the notion of sacrifice. What was effected in Christ is the efficacious sign through which the same transition is achieved in us. The act which glorified Christ glorifies us, though the actual effect in us is given at different times and places and in different measures according to the divine will. But, before the sign was completed by the exaltation of Christ, only anticipations of future salvation were bestowed. The Spirit was not given until Christ had been glorified.

But we have not yet seen the full mystery of the redemption. Christ was not an inanimate tool in the hands of God or a piece of clay moulded into a sign by the divine action. We must not think of redemption as akin to a biological process. Christ as man was free, and the redemptive purpose was accomplished only through the loving obedience with which he freely responded as man to the divine will. The human act of love in Christ is essential to the mystery of redemption. Christ was the sacrament of the divine love, and the radiant centre of the living symbol was his heart with its depths of charity. The underlying force governing the life of Christ and giving it unity was his love. His life, death and resurrection are the history of the loving obedience with which he accepted the abasement of the redemptive incarnation and made his way back to the Father along the path appointed by the divine will. His death was the lowest point in his obedient self-abasement and the culminating expression of his love. In an act of sacrificial oblation he gave himself into the hands of his Father. So he merited the saving act that would glorify not only himself but also all this brethren. And his loving surrender was of such surpassing moral worth that it more than counterbalanced the weight of moral depravity in the sins of men. The destruction of sin and death by the saving power of God came as its just recompense. Here we may rightly apply by analogy the concepts of merit and satisfaction.

Redemption comes to each of us personally when the divine act, which reaches us through its embodiment in Christ and his work, effects the transition in us from death to life. We die with Christ and rise again with him. But our passage from the world of sin and death to the order of resurrection and glory is not achieved at once. Our Christian life is an advance towards its full accomplishment. Insertion into Christ and his mysteries, and consequently contact with the saving act of God, is made possible by the Church and her sacraments. But we are not saved by being seized by God and subjected to his transforming power without our freedom being engaged. There arises in us a free response of charity. But this charity is itself an effect of the grace of Christ and so a share in his charity. It has the same traits and, in particular, is similarly sacrificial. Our response is joined to the response of Christ through the sacraments. So, the Church, the sacraments, charity and the rest of the Christian life must be seen in the light of the paschal mystery. They are the paschal mystery as it spreads outwards from the risen manhood of Christ into other men.

To pursue these reflexions into ecclesiology and the liturgy would take us too far. Much could be said on the discovery of the central place of the resurrection in the liturgy. More than any other factor the liturgical revival is making ordinary Catholics aware of the resurrection as a mystery of salvation. The consequences of this are so many that we can say that the present renewal in the Church is essentially a rediscovery of the resurrection. An urgent pastoral concern at present is to give Catholics a fresh consciousness of the faith by presenting them with the message of salvation in its full native splendour. They have been too long without it.

CHAPTER XVI

THE STARTING-POINT
OF MARIOLOGY

The harassed seminary professor who has to grapple with the whole of theology, whose course begins with the question "What is theology?" and finishes with the Second Coming, might well have sleepless nights when he comes to Mariology. He is faced with the problem of how to assimilate an overwhelming amount of recent work. Nor can he console himself with the reflexion that the recent flood of writing consists mainly of devotional works that can be left aside by the theologian. That is simply not true. Since about the 'twenties of this century, writing on our Lady has become increasingly doctrinal in content and scientific in method, so that, although books of edification are still numerous, there are only too many works that call out for attention from those who want to keep in touch with significant present-day trends in Mariology. Several sectors of theology are very active today, but that is particularly so with this branch; and the activity has led not merely to a greater quantity of books but also to a marked increase in the quality of the writing. The doctrine on Mary is being presented less and less as an isolated account of her privileges, and what is being said affects the other parts of theology. Questions such as the nature of the Church, the economy of salvation and the development of doctrine are involved. That is why the discussions now taking place are so interesting.

This does not mean that the theology of Mary has lost its contact with Christian piety. On the contrary, the new depth and balance of the treatment should exert a wholesome influence on the devotion of Catholics—the theologian still feels very close to the piety of the ordinary faithful when he deals with our Blessed Lady. Now, it is not the ambition of this chapter to display adequately the riches of this writing—an impossible undertaking within the limits of an essay. The purpose here is more modest: it is to discuss three books that confront us with the problem of the marked development of Marian doctrine in the Church. These books provide the opportunity of studying the starting-point and the laws of this development.

The truths concerning Mary taught by the Church are part of the Christian revelation. At once it is clear that the Church has advanced considerably in her understanding and proclamation of that revelation; for truths such as the Immaculate Conception and the Assumption have been recognized only at the end of a long process of development. To explain that development is one of the biggest tasks facing theologians today. There are two parts in the problem: how in fact, in what order, by what stages and through what factors have the Marian doctrines become explicit, and in the light of what principles is this development to be theoretically justified and explained? Our knowledge on the first point is rapidly increasing as the works of history and positive theology on this subject are multiplied; it is pleasing to note that these show a greater use of those critical methods adopted more rapidly in other parts of theology.

The second question is trickier and it involves the whole problem of the evolution of dogma. The definition of the Assumption has brought this matter very much to the fore, and theologians have realized that some of the previous theories about it, elaborated *a priori,* are too rigid. Non-Catholics are suspicious of the Catholic attitude here, but there is nothing strange about it on the basis of ordinary Catholic presuppositions. The present belief of the Church is infallible. The theologian, therefore, knows by faith that the Assumption is a revealed truth. It follows that it belongs to the revelation of Christ, which has closed with the apostolic age. No new revelation has come to add anything to the primitive deposit of faith handed down from the apostles, nor even indeed to clarify that original revelation. The suggestion made in some quarters that theologians might reconsider the binding force of the teaching that revelation was closed with the apostolic age has met with no support and has been rejected as inadmissible. The truth of the Assumption, like other truths, has been made explicit by a process of development that leaves untouched the essential immutability of the original Christian revelation.

Now, the problem caused by the gradual unfolding of revealed truth is not a new one; but in the period after Trent the discussion of it was largely confined to the function of theological reasoning and the definability of theological conclusions. This is too narrow an approach to account for the advance in our understanding of Mary, and the attention of theologians has been directed to other factors, in particular the *sensus fidei,* which have helped to draw out the implicit in the object of faith. Hence, the further widening and renewal of a problem which other influences also, such as the advance in our historical knowledge, have made one of the preoccupations of our time.

It is not surprising, then, that theologians have warmly welcomed two outstanding studies recently devoted to this matter. The first is *Le sens de la foi et le progrès dogmatique du mystère marial* by the Redemptorist, Fr. Clement Dillenschneider.[1] By far the more important of the two, it can be acclaimed without fear of contradiction one of the most significant books on Mariology that recent years have given us. The second, *Esquisse du développement du dogme marial* by Mgr. Charles Journet,[2] is slighter, but it is instructive to place this parallel but very different treatment alongside the first. A reading of both will confront the student with every aspect of this basic and absorbing problem.

Underlying Fr. Dillenschneider's treatise is the conviction that the method of logical analysis and deduction is insufficient to establish the various truths concerning Mary that have become explicit in the Church. In particular, he states with a courageous clarity that the Immaculate Conception and the Assumption cannot be proved by a rigorous deduction from any prior data about Mary. The arguments for these privileges put forward by theologians are persuasive only; they have not of themselves a compelling force. It is the frank recognition of the inadequacy of formal theological reasoning in this domain that has led him to

[1] Romae, Academia Mariana Internationalis, 1954.
[2] Paris, 1957.

investigate in detail the more hidden paths by which these truths made their way into the clear consciousness of the Church. After all, even the most syllogistically-minded theologian would acknowledge the part played in the development of these dogmas by the piety of the faithful. What kind of activity is in question? The Holy Spirit enlightens the believer and brings about an ever deeper insight into the truths of faith. He causes an advance in the understanding of revealed truth in a way that goes beyond what can be set down in the formulas of human reasoning. The subject of the treatise is this Christian insight, this sense given by faith, and at the end of his analysis he defines it in this way: "The intuitive supernatural sense of the believer, the fruit of the vigor of his faith and of the gifts of the Holy Spirit, through which he is endowed with a facility in discerning, within the communion of the Church, what is implicit in the revealed truth objectively proposed to him by the magisterium."[3]

The standpoint of Mgr. Journet is at first glance very different. His book is abstract in character; there is great play with notions and distinctions; and the author remains at a greater distance from the concrete data of Mariological development than does Fr. Dillenschneider. In keeping with this he makes much of theological reasoning. He maintains that all the truths concerning Mary can be drawn in an absolutely rigorous way from the notion of the divine motherhood, provided that this notion is grasped according to its revealed content. Seemingly, the two authors are directly opposed. Yet, they are not so far apart as might be supposed. Several strands are entangled here that need to be separated. There is a decided difference between them on the question of a first principle in Mariology. It is a point that has been much discussed lately, and a return will be made to it.

Is there or is there not a primordial truth concerning Mary from which all her other privileges and functions can be strictly deduced? Mgr. Journet says Yes and Fr. Dillenschneider, with greater justice, says No. But granted this admittedly basic dif-

---

[3] "Le sens intuitif surnaturel du croyant, fruit de la vigueur de sa foi et des dons de l'Esprit Saint, par quoi il est habilité à discerner, dans la communion de l'Eglise, les virtualités du donné révélé qui lui est objectivement proposé par le Magistère" (p. 327).

ference, they are nearer than at first seems on the present issue, namely, the process by which revealed truth is made explicit. Both speak of a divine logic which goes beyond the mere resources of human reason and is bound up with the insight given by faith, but they look at this in different ways. What Mgr. Journet stresses is the initial grasp of the revealed data from which the theologian starts; this calls for the assistance of the Hoy Spirit and the magisterium if it is to be maintained correctly. The theologian who has that and keeps it can then proceed to construct his speculative synthesis with reasoning absolute in its rigour. Fr. Dillenschneider is more impressed by the transcendent character of the mental process concerned. He emphasizes the fact that the divine light renders perceptible implications and connexions in a way that cannot be adequately formulated in the terms of human reasoning. As formulated, our arguments remain persuasive only; they are arguments of fitness, of suitability. It is the magisterium with the special guidance given to it that must finally judge that the convictions thus formed in the Christian mind represent truly the content of revelation.

To choose between these two points of view is not easy; does not each stand for a different but perennial temper of mind in the appreciation of the value of formal reasoning? Nevertheless, the very fact that so distinguished and learned a Mariologist as Fr. Dillenschneider—and there are others of like mind—cannot see in the arguments adduced for the Immaculate Conception and the Assumption more than a persuasive force shows sufficiently that these formal proofs are but the sign and incomplete representation of a far more complex mental process which lies behind them and which must be allowed for in judging their value. And no disciple of Newman would disagree or find any difficulty with that.

Fr. Dillenschneider's book has three parts. The first of these is called methodological; in it we enter into the problem and become acquainted with the author's intentions. He himself describes the purpose of this part as the determination of the place that belongs to the sense of faith in the explicitation of the mystery of Mary. He does this in three steps. He begins by giving us a historical account of the problem of dogmatic development and its treatment. This well-documented survey will be a boon to students, who often get lost in this complicated subject. He then establishes the objective starting-point, the initial deposit, that lies at the origin of all the subsequent dogmatic progress concerning Mary. Finally, he determines the factors that have brought about progress. He gives the views of theologians about this, and then goes on to make clear his own position. This grants a part to the logical process in doctrinal development but denies its adequacy. The living tradition of the Church shows a progress in the understanding of God's truth which outstrips the reasoning powers of theologians. That living tradition is nothing other than the consciousness of the faith in the Church—the whole Church, the Church taught as well as the Church teaching, but in each in a different way. Hence the need to examine more closely the nature of the Christian sense of faith.

Of particular interest is the author's view on the initial deposit from which all the dogmatic development concerning Mary takes its origin. He gives it in these terms: "At the base of the dogmatic development in Mariology, we shall place the scriptural Marian datum in its integrity and its organic unity."[4] He assigns this biblical basis without dwelling on the relation between Scripture and tradition. His preoccupation in this chapter is with other problems; in particular, with the connexion between revelation considered as reality and revelation considered as teaching. But he returns to the question of Scripture and tradition in his more recent book, *Le principe premier d'une théologie Mariale organique* (pp. 89–93),[5] and Mgr. Journet in his book discusses the matter in some detail. He expressly assigns a biblical foundation for all the subsequent Marian development, without any appeal to a parallel oral tradition as providing supplementary data:

. . . The first revealed foundations of the Marian doctrines of the Immaculate Conception or the Assumption we shall seek, along with the best and the greatest majority of theologians, not in an oral tradition

---

[4] "A la base de l'évolution dogmatique en Mariologie nous placerons donc le donné marial scripturaire dans son integrité et son unité organique" (p. 55).

[5] Paris, 1957.

parallel to Scripture, but in Scripture itself, in which is condensed the tradition or *paradosis* of the apostles, read by the primitive Church in the light of the Holy Spirit which assists her.[6]

The attitude of these authors reflects, as they themselves explain, the return to the older view on the relation between Scripture and tradition that is taking place in contemporary theology. Scripture and tradition are the two channels of revelation, each transmitting to us in its own way the revelation of Christ: Scripture is the inspired Word of God and tradition has its own peculiar and indispensable authority. But does that mean that they are parallel and separate sources in the sense that the body of revealed truth is contained partly in Scripture and partly in tradition? In particular, does the existence of tradition necessarily imply that the Scriptures contain only incompletely the deposit of faith and that there are some revealed truths that are in no way found in them? No; Scripture and tradition each gives us fully, though in a way proper to itself, the revealed deposit of faith, as we have tried to show in Chapter VII.

The New Testament must be seen as the inspired crystallization of the apostolic preaching, and it represents adequately the belief of the primitive Church. God intended the Scriptures to remain in the doctrinal heritage of the Church as a record enshrining in a permanent form the body of revealed truth such as it existed during the period of revelation which closed with the apostolic age. To fulfil this purpose he gave them a plenitude in this sense: they state expressly all the fundamental truths, the principles of faith, from which everything else in Christian teaching can be drawn, so that the entire body of revealed truth is contained either explicitly or implicitly within the sacred pages. The Bible remains the permanent starting-point to which the Church must always refer, the perennial centre around which her teaching must always revolve, since it possesses the never-ending riches and the inex-

[6] ". . . les premiers fondements révélés des doctrines mariales de l'immaculée Conception ou de l'Assomption, nous les chercherons, avec la meilleure et la majeure partie des théologiens, non pas dans une tradition orale parallèle à l'Ecriture, mais dans l'Ecriture elle-même, condensant en elle la tradition ou *paradosis* des apôtres, et lue par l'Eglise primitive avec la lumière de l'Esprit saint qui l'assiste" (p. 40).

haustible fecundity proper to the inspired account of Christian teaching in the unique and privileged period of its origin. (Attention is being paid here directly to the New Testament, but the Old Testament is not left aside; for it was taken over by the revelation of Christ and became part of it.)

But it was the oral tradition that created the Scriptures and formed their living context, and this oral tradition has continued its life unbroken. It is this oral tradition which gives the Bible its full intelligibility, which draws out and displays its full riches, and which provides its divinely authorized interpretation. Of itself the letter is dead. The soul that animates the Scripture and makes it here and now the living Word of God to men is the tradition of the Church. Through tradition the truth of Christ lives on in the Church, the body of Christ; and in the life of the Church that truth continually unfolds its virtualities. Nevertheless, in its doctrinal life the Church incessantly looks back to the Scriptures, the starting-point of all development, the inspired record making permanent for Christians the primitive preaching as it fell from the lips of Christ and the apostles. Scripture and tradition are not two separate sources. They interpenetrate one another, each dependent on the other and forming one organic whole.

The point to be stressed here—and surely it is of key importance that it should be known to Catholics in this century—is that leading Mariologists today unambiguously affirm that the initial deposit from which all the revealed truth on our Lady is derived is given in the Bible. Let us understand clearly where we differ from non-Catholics. This is how Mgr. Journet sees it:

If the Protestants on one side and Erasmus on the other understood by "scriptural principle" the principle according to which Scripture is normative as the "theological source *containing* revelation" in this sense: that it comprises in itself the fundamental truths of the revealed deposit from which the whole content of the deposit of faith can, with the assistance of the Holy Spirit, become eventually explicit— then there would not, on this point, be any controversy between them and us. The two questions which would remain debatable would be, as we have said, to know (1) what is the initial meaning of the revealed deposit as it is epitomized in Scripture and (2) whether there is an infallibly assisted authority for safeguarding and explicitating this meaning in the course of the centuries.[7]

An appeal to oral tradition as providing additional revealed data not found in Scripture is as out-of-place in Mariology as elsewhere.

The second part of *Le sens de la foi et le progrés dogmatique du mystère marial* is historical. It puts us into close contact with the factual data of Mariological development. The author confines his attention to the truths that have been already defined as dogmas by the Church: the Virginal Motherhood, the Immaculate Conception and the Assumption. He examines the manifestations of the sense of faith concerning these truths, taking in turn the liturgy, the catechetical teaching of the Church and the consciousness of the faithful. In that way he sets forth in abundant detail the role actually played by this factor in the unfolding of the mystery of the Mother of God. Apart from its immediate purpose in this treatise, this historical section forms in its own right quite a good account of the development of belief in these privileges, and at the end of it the reader feels that he has been made conversant with the way that these doctrines evolved. The third part of Mgr. Journet's study covers briefly a little of the same ground, though in a more abstractly analytic manner. One interesting observation he makes is that the growth in the testimony to Mary's sanctity that took place in the East was accompanied by a forgetfulness of her redemption (p. 114).

It is the last part of Fr. Dillenschneider's book which is the key one; having thoroughly prepared the ground, he is now able to set out the nature and value of the *sensus fidei* as a factor in doctrinal development. After a glance at the remarks of Scripture and tradition on the understanding imparted by faith, he brings

---

[7] "Si les protestants d'une part, et Erasme d'autre part, entendaient par 'principe scripturaire' le principe suivant lequel L'Ecriture est normative comme 'lieu théologique *contenant* la révélation,' en ce sens qu'elle renferme en elle les vérités fondamentales du dépôt révélé, à partir desquelles le dépôt révélé tout entier peut, avec l'assistance de l'Esprit saint, s'expliciter ultérieurement,—il n'y aurait pas, sur ce point, de controverse entre eux et nous. Les deux questions qui resteraient à débattre seraient, nous l'avons dit, de savoir: 1° quel est le sens initial du dépôt révélé tel qu'il est résumé dans l'Ecriture? 2° s'il y a une authorité infailliblement assistée pour protéger ce sens et l'expliciter au cours des siècles?" (pp. 39–40).

into prominence the decisive role that must be assigned to the
Holy Spirit in all dogmatic progress. It is not a question of anything equivalent to a fresh revelation or of any touching-up of
the primitive deposit; the original revelation remains what it was,
unchanged. But the Holy Spirit manifests to our understanding
the depth of meaning in that revelation and unfolds for us its
implications. The author goes on to discuss the exact role and
value that the liturgy has in this matter. This section is necessarily
less original because the doctrinal value and function of the
liturgy have been much studied in recent years. Attention is,
however, given to some special problems connected with the feasts
of our Lady. More important is the chapter devoted to the Christian sense as manifested in the consciousness of the ordinary faithful. The nature of this insight is first analysed—an analysis summed
up in the definition already quoted. A further point to be noted
is the insistence of the author that the sense of faith possessed by
Christians is not a mere passive receptivity to the teaching of the
magisterium; it enjoys an active role in the transmission and unfolding of the Christian message, though always in dependence on
the authoritative judgements of the magisterium. Then comes an
enumeration of the conditions necessary to ensure the dogmatic
efficacy of the insight of the faithful: it must have an objective
basis in revealed truth; it must concern a point within the grasp
of the faithful generally; and it must be universal in character.
Each of these conditions is appreciated nicely. The second is of
some interest. It means that one can invoke the attitude of the
faithful only in favour of a point that is within the interest and
understanding of the mass of them. Many will wonder as a consequence how far this factor—at least as yet—is relevant to the
discussions about Mary's part in our redemption.

The next section of this chapter deals with the value of the
sense of faith as a criterion of revealed truth. When it is truly
universal it enjoys infallibility, not the infallibility proper to an
authoritative judgement but the infallibility of a living and active
testimony to the Christian faith given by believers. Hence:

When the sense of the faith, operating on the revealed deposit proposed by the magisterium, has in dependance upon this same magisterium become established in the whole believing Church, pastors and

faithful alike, then it enjoys the infallibility of an active testimony and constitutes, without any authoritative determining by the teaching Church, an indisputable factor of homogeneous dogmatic development.[8]

This conclusion leads the author by a natural sequence to examine in a separate chapter the magisterium and its relation to the sense of faith found in the Church. There belongs to it in the first place the task of watching over and guiding it, vigilant in doing so for the purity of doctrine and guarding against all mistaken excesses. "An experience of many centuries indeed bears witness to the almost irresistible attraction for the mass of the faithful of all that magnifies, or seems to magnify, the Blessed Virgin. If ever the vigilance of the magisterium is called for, it is here."[9] Then it should make enquiries concerning it in preparing its doctrinal decisions. But notice: "The Christian sense is not a norm for the magisterium to observe but an objective datum for it to understand"[10]; and the authority of its decisions is not derived from the investigations that precede them. Nevertheless, the decrees of the magisterium are not arbitrary and cannot therefore be dissociated from the belief of Christians. Finally, through the special gift with which it is endowed, the magisterium is alone able to judge with finality this sense of faith and discern infallibly in a given case its dogmatic and universal character. The author grants to the magisterium a positive power of discernment whereby it can perceive and judge that a tenet current among the faithful represents in fact the living tradition of the Church and is an expression of revealed truth, even when there are not decisive theological arguments to verify this. Fr. Dillenschneider would not support those who stress the negative character of the charism of infallibility.

8 "Le sens de la foi, qui porte sur le dépôt révélé proposé par le Magistère, lorsqu'il est devenu, sous la dépendance de ce même Magistère, le fait de toute l'Eglise croyante, pasteurs et fidèles, jouit d'une infaillibilité de témoignage actif et constitue ainsi, avant toute fixation autoritative de l'Ecclesia docens, un facteur indiscutable d'évolution dogmatique homogène" (p. 341).

9 "Une expérience de plusieurs siècles atteste en effet le penchant quasi irrésistible de la masse de croyants pour tout ce qui grandit ou semble grandir la Vierge. Si jamais la vigilance du Magistère est de rigueur, c'est ici" (p. 348).

10 "Le sens chrétien n'est pas pour le Magistère une norme à suivre, mais une donnée objective à connaître" (p 349).

How does all this affect the position of the theologian? This question is answered in the final chapter of the treatise. The answer comes to this, that the theologian must not abstract from but must keep in touch with the present living tradition of the Church. It is within that tradition that he must pursue his thinking as a theologian. He is indissolubly both theologian and believer, and he must find the normative rule of his theological thought in the living tradition of the Church, which is constituted precisely by the universal Christian sense as guided and formed by the magisterium.

The volume of Fr. Dillenschneider just analysed plunges the reader into all the intricacies of the problem caused by the marked development in the Church's teaching about Mary; his more recent study, *Le principe premier d'une théologie mariale organique,* will put the student in touch with another basic problem, one less likely to attract the attention of the non-specialist but arousing much discussion among theologians at the moment. What is at stake is the organization of the treatise on Mary. The speculative theologian must order his matter, observe the connexion between the different truths and construct a synthesis that respects their intrinsic relationship. To do this requires the choice of a first principle, some fundamental datum on which all else can be made to rest, some central idea around which everything can be grouped. In what sense is there such a principle in Mariology? What is, or should be, this principle?

In answer to the first question some theologians claim a first principle in the narrow sense of a basic truth from which every privilege, grace and function of our Blessed Lady can be logically derived by a series of rigorous deductions. Fr. Dillenschneider sets his face against such an attitude. What reason is there to suppose that God in his plan for Mary limited himself to the bestowal of graces bound to each other by a strict necessity? The gratuity of God's plan, the freedom of Mary's co-operation and the ineffectualness of the inferences brought forward to prove some of her privileges show that the search for such a principle is a mistake. Does it follow that there is no first principle in any sense and that all efforts to construct a truly systematic treatise on the Virgin Mary are misguided? The conclusion is unjustified. There is ample cause to seek a principle of unification around which we

can group all we know about Mary. God may be free in the grant-
ing of his graces, but he is also wise. The theologian is right to
seek the intrinsic finality of the mystery of Mary. It is this that
will provide him with a principle of intelligibility which will
clarify all the assertions concerning her and enable him to perceive
their fundamental unity. This first principle will be, not an axiom
excogitated by human speculation, but a datum drawn from revelation. What is sought is the basic intention of God in regard to
Mary—something only known to us by his Word.

Having stated the problem and chosen his standpoint, the author
passes in review the solutions already proposed. This part of his
book may be recommended to those who wish to enter into the
present *problématique* of Mariology; for the attitude of writers to
this point is closely bound up with the attitude they adopt to the
various questions concerning our Lady's position under discussion
today. The solutions given fall into two groups according to the
perspective in which they choose to view the mystery of Mary.
Alongside the older and still vigorous tendency that sees Mary
primarily in her association with Christ and takes as the fundamental principle of Mariology her motherhood, analysed in different ways, or her role as Second Eve, there have arisen those
who put first her relation to the Church or to redeemed mankind
and seek the first principle for their theological synthesis on this
side of her mystery. For example, Semmelroth gives as principle:
Mary is the prototype of the Church. Fr. Dillenschneider's com-
ments on the various views are generous and balanced. He tries
to see the contribution each can make to our understanding of
Mary, but he criticizes the deficiencies and exaggerations with
which this insight is often accompanied. He is led by his examination of the current opinions to conclude that one should not give
up the divine motherhood as the basic principle and substitute
for it any other, but that this motherhood must not be taken in the
abstract but in its integral reality as found in the actual economy
of our salvation known to us by revelation.

The theologian's choice of a first principle should not be a
mere matter of personal preference; it should be governed by an
examination of the biblical data which reveal to us the vocation
of Mary in this present order of our salvation. In order to establish
positively his conclusion, the author proceeds to an investigation

of the biblical revelation on Mary. This section of the book corresponds to the second part of the study of Mgr. Journet mentioned
above, in which he analysed the content of the deposit of faith.
Put both together and a fair insight will be gained into the way
leading Mariologists today handle the biblical texts.

What is important is not the detailed conclusions but the general
approach. "Today one finds quite stunning," writes Fr. Dillenschneider, "the placid assurance with which, in the domain of
Mariology, certain theologians of the past brought forward such
or such a truth concerning the Blessed Virgin as formally taught
by the inspired writings."[11] Exegetes need not fear that the insistence on the plenitude of Scripture noted above involves necessarily
exaggerated claims to *prove* everything from Scripture alone.
Recent studies have indeed shown that the statements in the Bible
concerning Mary are more meaningful than many have previously
suspected. The advance in biblical theology, with the consequent
stress on the unity of the Bible and the continuity of its themes,
has done more than the individual exegesis of isolated texts to
uncover the germinal richness of those statements. We understand
better than before the meaning of Luke and John.

All the same, it remains true that Scripture is a starting-point,
not an ending. As has been said, it is a perpetual starting-point
with which the Church must ever keep in contact, but it is a point
from which there has been, as God intended, a continual doctrinal
progress and effort at formulation. Revelation was closed with the
apostles, but revelation was not given to men as a dead letter but
as living truth capable of development or unfolding in the Spirit-
guided consciousness of the Church and under the infallible authority of her teachers. This fact must inevitably affect the exegete
and the theologian. The exegete cannot ignore the living tradition
of the Church; he must take cognizance of it and work within it.
But at the same time the theologian must recognize the limitations
of the proof from Scripture and not seek in the text alone precisions
that only came—often centuries—later. Very often all that the
exegete as such can say is that the biblical texts indicate a direc-

---

[11] "On est stupéfait aujourd'hui de la tranquille assurance avec laquelle,
dans le domaine de la Mariologie, certains théologiens d'autrefois déga-
geaient telle ou telle vérité concernant la Vierge comme enseignée formelle-
ment par l'écrivain inspiré" (p. 93).

tion with which recent doctrinal developments are fully in accord. The theologian then shows how the Church followed that direction and was led gradually to perceive the full implications of the original statements and find the more precise formulation. (It is for hermeneutics to analyse this handling of the biblical data in terms of biblical senses.)

Mgr. Journet finds in Scripture express statements capable of giving rise by development to the entire body of doctrine on Mary, but he acknowledges frankly that nothing is said explicitly about the Immaculate Conception, the mediation of Mary or her Assumption; and Fr. Dillenschneider, who does not find the scriptural arguments for these privileges decisive in themselves, is in agreement with this. Paradoxical though it may seem to some, the more flexible approach to the biblical texts in which scientific exegesis goes hand in hand with a profound meditation on the germinal biblical data is far more satisfying in its results than the attempt to prove apodictically every Marian doctrine from a few isolated texts.

After analysing the scriptural data concerning Mary's vocation in God's plan of salvation, the author elaborates in detail what he considers is the first principle of Mariology. The affirmation he found to be primary in all the texts was that of the Messianic Motherhood of our Lady. That, then, is the fundamental principle: the Messianic Motherhood taken in its full concrete reality with the threefold dimension that belongs to it, namely, personal, soteriological and social.

Thus, these three books taken together provide us with a basic standpoint from which the whole richness of Marian doctrine can be studied in a way that harmonizes with the understanding of the Bible and tradition which has been regained in modern theology.

CHAPTER XVII

THE MASS AS THE ASSEMBLY OF CHRISTIANS

The task that faces us in the liturgical apostolate today is to persuade the faithful to take again a fully active share in the celebration of Mass. If our efforts are to bear good fruit and not do harm, the faithful must answer the priest, join in the singing and perform their ritual actions, not because we have told them to do so but because they have become aware of the value of all this for their Christian life and have learned to want it and seek it as fulfilling a spiritual need. Only in that way shall we canalize into the new forms of celebration the devotion, often intense, which they already have to the Holy Mass. The vital factor is always, not the practical details of ritual technique, but the spiritual consciousness of our people.

Now, the enrichment we are seeking to give them is a reawakened sense of the assembly of Christians as a sacred reality: the inadequacy we are trying to overcome is a loss of an understanding of the assembly as a basic reality of the Christian life. When we try to explain active participation, we have to come back again and again to the truth that at Mass we are gathered together as a community, as the assembly of God's People, and that in the communal celebration each one has a part to play, a part that corresponds to his place in the Church. We are not there as isolated individuals but as forming an assembly convoked by God and we share in the Mass through our membership of the Christian Church, present there in the concrete in the congregation with its presiding priest. We are not disturbing the habits of our people in order to make sure they are praying or because we want them to follow everything that is going on—such motives are secondary and insufficient of themselves, even where they have some importance; our basic purpose is to make the assembly come alive again as a meeting of Christians in Christ and to give a new force to the function which the Eucharistic assembly was designed by Christ to fulfil: namely, the function of expressing visibly and realizing effectually the community of Christians in the one Body of Christ.

If we turn to the New Testament, the first Church Orders and the writings of the Fathers, we find clear evidence that the regular assembly of Christians is a basic institution of the Christian religion. This pattern for the life of the Church was set by the appearances of the risen Christ to the apostles gathered together in one place and by the gift of Pentecost which was given to the first Christians as an assembled community. The Acts of the Apostles tells us of the concern of the first believers to share a common life, how they listened to the apostles' teaching and met together for the breaking of bread (2.42); and later on the same book describes a Sunday assembly at Troas (20.7–12)—the bearing of the text indicates that this was a regular practice. We know how St. Paul refers to the assemblies of the Corinthians in order to correct abuses (1 Cor. 11.17–34: 14.23–40); but his rebukes presuppose that the assembly itself is an essential feature of the Christian life. St. James also had to remind the faithful that their common life in Christ made distinctions of wealth or class of no account, and in doing so he bears witness to the regular assembly as a feature of the life of the Church. His remarks are still relevant today: "Brethren, you believe that all glory belongs to Our Lord Jesus Christ; do not combine this faith of yours with flattery of human greatness. Suppose that a man comes into your place of meeting in fine clothes, wearing a gold ring; suppose that a poor man comes in at the same time, ill clad. Will you pay attention to the well-dressed man and bid him take some place of honour; will you tell the poor man, Stand where thou art, or Sit on the ground at my footstool? If so, are you not introducing divisions into your company? Have you not shewn partiality in your judgement?" (2.1–4, KV). And the Letter to the Hebrews warns Christians against neglecting the assembly: "Let us keep one another in mind, always ready with incitements to charity and to acts of piety, not abandoning, as some do, our common assembly, but encouraging one another; all the more, as you see the great day drawing nearer" (10.24–5, KV). Notice the significance of the assembly as the way in which we wait for the coming of Christ.

The patristic writings give the same impression of the importance of the assembly.[1] The stress St. Ignatius of Antioch in the early second century lays on gathering around the bishop and doing all in common is well known. But also in the fourth century St. John Chrysostom returns again and again to the subject of the assembly in his preaching, seeing in its exterior unanimity the manifestation of the unity of Christ's body and declaring that Christ is present in the midst of the gathered community. The *Didascalia Apostolorum* of the third century, a key document because of its widespread and prolonged influence in matters of Church discipline, counsels the bishops about the need to urge the people not to fail to come to the assembly, lest the assembly be diminished by an absentee and the body of Christ lack one of its members. Undoubtedly, a prominent characteristic of the liturgy in these early centuries, a characteristic of which the Christians were aware and which they prized, was that it involved the coming together of the Christian people for a communal celebration in an assembly. That is why the word *synaxis,* meaning "assembly," became from the fourth century the current term for the Eucharist in the East; it remained so for a long time until it was displaced by the word *liturgy.*

The part that belongs to the assembled people in Christian worship is also shown by the basic idea of a church (in the sense of the building) in the Christian scheme of things. The ancient pagan cults did not generally allot to the people any part in the sacrifices and prayers of the priests, and no space was provided for them in the interior of the temples. The temple was simply a room for the idol, and its architectural splendours were on the outside with its colonnades and sculptures. This is true to some extent of the Old Testament order itself. But a Christian church

---

[1] For the details and texts, see four articles of A. G. Martimort, to which this chapter owes much, although I have adopted a different approach to the theology of the assembly: "L'Assemblée liturgique," *La Maison-Dieu,* 20 (1950), 153–75; "L'Assemblée liturgique, mystère du Christ," *ibid.,* 40 (1954), 5–29; "Dimanche, assemblée et paroisse," *ibid.,* 57 (1959), 55–84; "Précisions sur l'assemblée," *ibid.,* 60 (1959), 7–34.

is essentially an interior space for the accommodation of the Christian people. It was called the *domus ecclesiae,* the house of the assembly, and then took the name of the assembly itself, *ecclesia.* The material structure is but the shelter for the spiritual temple formed by Christians themselves. They are one with the risen body of Christ, which is the temple of the new covenant, and all share the priesthood of Christ.

When we examine the meaning of Sunday as understood and observed through the centuries, we are again faced with the central importance of the assembly. Sunday, the Day of the Lord, the memorial of the resurrection, the Eighth Day inaugurating the new creation, is unquestionably an unalterable institution in Christianity, one going back to the beginnings of the Church. But if Sunday essentially demands the celebration of the Eucharist, it also demands by its nature the assembly of the community. The two requirements, Eucharist and assembly, are two elements forming the total reality of the Sunday celebration. To observe the Sunday was not originally merely a question of attending Mass wherever that might suit the individual; it was understood that everyone should come together for one communal celebration, since Sunday was the day for the plenary assembly of the local community. At first this had to take place in the early morning before the dawn, because Sunday was an ordinary working-day. When later the Church was able to affect public life, the hour of the assembly was transferred to nine o'clock in the morning, the hour at which it was customary to transact important business.

Right until the latter part of the Middle Ages, the accepted principle was that a Christian should be present at the one assembly of his local community, not just attend Mass anywhere. The perfection with which the underlying principle—that Christians dispersed during the week should flock together for a communal celebration on Sunday—was realized down the centuries varied from the ideal of a gathering around the bishop, which lasted longer than is often thought, to a rather rigidly conceived system of parochial rights, but the sense that the Sunday Mass was the assembly of the community endured. It receded into the background when from the fourteenth century onwards the rule about attending Sunday Mass in the parish church was gradually modified under the influence of the Mendicant Orders and then finally abolished. Only a relic of the previous legislation remains in the restrictions governing private oratories. The Sunday obligation has ceased to involve presence at a common assembly: the meaning of the Sunday and the need for Christians to come together regularly remain valid none the less for that.

We are faced, then, with the fact that when we look at the reality of the liturgy in tradition, a prominent feature of it, stressed in practice and in teaching, is the assembly. How did it come about that Christians lost that sense of assembly and its importance in the Christian life? We can hardly deny that is has been lost, or at least pushed very far into the background. Suppose a Christian today were able to attend Mass on his own every Sunday, would he feel any genuine sense of loss? Is he not perplexed when he finds he cannot fulfil his obligation by attending Mass in a private oratory? Again, it would be difficult to explain to many that one of the reasons why a televised Mass is not enough is that the Mass calls for the coming together and active participation of a community. At church the attention of our people is so absorbed by the mystery of what takes place at the altar that they remain unaware of the mystery of the assembly itself, a mystery which has its own importance and which does not diminish but enhances what occurs in the sanctuary. Letters to the Catholic papers, protesting against the introduction of a full active participation, show a lamentable ignorance of the communal nature of the Eucharistic celebration. Many see nothing anomalous in the fact that our assemblies are a formless mass of individuals ignoring each other and regarding communal responses and actions as unwarranted intrusions on their private participation in the Mass. Our communicants are as indifferent to each other as solitary eaters in a restaurant, without finding it odd to carry out in that way a common sacred meal meant to express our union with one another and to anticipate the wedding-feast of heaven.

There is no need to be wrongly fanatical about particular forms of external participation to see in that attitude—and it is the spiritual attitude that really matters—a sad inadequacy in our present Christian outlook and to deplore its various manifestations as a distortion of the sacred reality of the assembly. And are priests themselves properly conscious of the fact that they are not only offering a sacrifice for the community but also presiding over the assembly? The recognition of this latter function involves an attitude of mind in celebrating Mass, the lack of which can easily wreck any attempt to establish a fully communal celebration. We joke about priests who complain that a dialogue Mass distracts them and interrupts their devotion, but that such complaints are even conceivable shows how far we have lost that sense of the assembly and its mystery which Christian tradition demands that we regard as an essential ingredient in any properly formed Christian consciousness.

The remote origins of this situation have been traced back to various causes—apart from the general decline in liturgical life and understanding. The principal cause, however, was a development that in itself was sound and that gave us valuable doctrinal insights, but which, as is often the case with such developments, produced a onesidedness, against which the Church is now reacting in order to restore a true balance. Originally, liturgy and assembly were co-extensive: wherever there was liturgy there was an assembly of the people and, likewise, whenever a local community came together for worship, the common worship was liturgy. The liturgy, the public worship of the Church, was understood in the concrete in a simple and obvious way. This has changed and our notion of liturgy is more developed and more complex. The change was brought about by the growth of a liturgical worship carried out in the name of the Church by lawfully appointed persons but without any assembly of the people and then, owing to the strict determination of the liturgy by the Church, the development of collective forms of prayer that are not liturgy. Liturgy and assembly are no longer co-extensive; hence the danger of concluding that the assembly is unimportant in the liturgy.

Let us consider first the development of a liturgy without an assembly. First, the prayer of monks and the clergy gradually became an official prayer, recognized by the Church as her own. From being a merely private prayer, it assumed a liturgical character until the hours observed became liturgical or canonical hours in the full sense. Of itself this prayer does not involve an assembly of the people; indeed, on occasion these are excluded. Despite this, it is a properly liturgical prayer, since it is carried out in the name of the Church in virtue of an express appointment by the

Church. When a priest recites his breviary alone, it is an act of public worship offered to God by the Church; it is part of her liturgy, though accomplished in a vicarious way by a member lawfully appointed to do this.

The second and more significant development was the growth of what were formerly called private Masses. (Since the Instruction *De Musica Sacra* abolished the term "private Mass," no suitable term has been suggested to replace it. Perhaps "simple Mass" would serve well enough.) Such Masses cannot be traced back further than the sixth century, although there were instances of Mass being celebrated for very small communities on the occasion of a funeral or other event, and it is possible that even before the sixth century personal devotion may have led a bishop or priest to celebrate Mass alone. The real increase in these Masses, however, came with the early Middle Ages, and since then they have been a regular part of the life of the Church. Now, the Mass celebrated with or without an assembly is always of its very nature a liturgical act in the strict sense. The priest offers sacrifice in the name of the Church in virtue of a divine appointment given by the character of Holy Orders. When the priest offers Mass, the whole Church is necessarily involved in the offering, since it is offered in the name of the Church by a divinely deputed minister and, likewise, the whole Church benefits from the offering. It is and cannot be otherwise than an act of public worship.

We all know how Pope Pius XII reacted strongly in *Mediator Dei* against the mistaken depreciation of "private" Masses into which some had been led. There is no need to enlarge upon the point here. Such Masses are not only fully justified doctrinally but also have a definite and honoured place in the life of the Church. The increase in their frequency has enriched our understanding of the liturgy, making us better aware that the Mass, the sacrifice of Christ, is a gift to the Church and that in the liturgy the action of Christ, mediated through his minister, comes first and precedes our response. Nevertheless, the prominence given to this form of Mass led to a neglect of awareness of the assembly. Priests forgot their role as president of the assembly when the faithful were present and the faithful thought of themselves as assisting at Mass rather than as taking part in it, as being outside rather than inside the Eucharistic celebration. Thus the assembly was broken up into individuals; and the communal character of the celebration was further damaged when Low Mass, a form adapted for celebration without a congregation, was taken over for use as a public celebration. Hence the need to right the balance and stress again the part of the assembly.

The fact that the Mass is a valid and integral sacrifice when offered without an assembly and that such a celebration has a legitimate place in the life of the Church does not mean that the assembly is outside the Eucharist. To say this would be like arguing that, because the Communion of the faithful is not necessary for the integrity of the Mass, when they do go to Communion, their Communion is not part of the Mass. Not only must we refuse to strip down the sacraments to what is necessary for validity, but also we must recognize that there is a certain flexibility in the way a sacrament may be celebrated. Communion under both kinds or under one kind, one anointing of the sick person if time presses or several anointings in a more leisurely celebration, baptism by immersion or by pouring, and so on: these are instances of the way the celebration of a sacrament may vary. Various forms of celebration may exist contemporaneously, each having a place in the life of the Church. This is so with the Eucharist. The part of the deacon at High Mass enters into the Eucharist and is done by him in virtue of the character received at ordination, although it is not found at a Sung Mass. The part of the faithful in a communal celebration enters into the Eucharist and is done by them in virtue of their baptismal character, though it is not found (except, according to the law of the Church, in the server) when a priest celebrates Mass alone.

What is more fully sacramentalized, or given fuller expression in the sacramental sign, when the assembly is present, is the part of the Church in the Eucharist. The Church, modern theologians are telling us, is the basic sacrament—not as a substitute for Christ, who is the Great Sacrament, but as his Body, the continuation of his incarnate existence, representing him and bringing us into contact with him. As the basic sacrament, the Church is the ground in which the seven sacraments are rooted. The seven sacraments are seven actions which the Church does as the basic sacrament. They bring into action in a given situation, for a particular community or person, what the Church is permanently and essentially. If all the sacraments must be seen as actions of the Church, a bringing into actuality of the Church as the basic sacrament, this is particularly true of the Eucharist. The Eucharist is the sacrifice of the Church, intended as the expression and cause of her unity as flowing from the mystery of Christ. All the members have a part in it. The priest alone has the power to consecrate, and therefore he alone performs the sacrificial action, not as a delegate of the community but as the ordained minister of Christ. But the faithful offer through and with the priest, who represents them, and the Mass is the offering of the whole Church, of the entire assembly. The part of the Church in the Eucharist receives a minimum sacramental expression in the minister when he celebrates without a congregation, but it is given a greater sacramental expression when the faithful are assembled. The same applies with some modifications to the other sacraments.

The need to avoid any depreciation of Masses without a congregation must not make us overlook that such Masses have a meaning only against the background of regular Eucharistic assemblies in the Church. The fact that the Mass is the sacrifice of the Church, the public worship of the Church, demands that it be regularly celebrated with an assembly of the Church, so that all the members of the Church can take part in it personally. It can *also* be celebrated without a congregation by a minister representing the Church; but it would be an odd kind of Church in which public worship was carried out only in a vicarious fashion. And we must say that the assembly belongs to the Eucharist by the very institution of Christ. When he gave the Eucharist, he intended that there should be regular Eucharistic assemblies as the centre of the communal life of the Church. This intention does not exclude Masses without an assembly, but it does exclude any hypothetical order in which there would be only such Masses. We can say that the assembly is essential to the Eucharist as given by Christ, provided we understand the statement correctly so that it allows "private" Masses as an added enrichment of the liturgical life of the Church.

Besides a liturgy without an assembly, there have developed in the Church forms of collective prayers that are not liturgy. Only from the later Middle Ages have there been popular devotions designed for use by a congregation gathered in church and led by a priest. In principle, approval by the bishop, the head of the local church, would be sufficient to make a given form of prayer part of the liturgy or public worship of the Church, but the Council of Trent removed the liturgy from the legislative power of bishops and reserved it to the Holy See. That is why episcopal approbation cannot now constitute a prayer or devotion as liturgical and the liturgy is confined to what is contained in the official liturgical books approved by Rome. Everything else, according to the clear division of the Instruction *De Musica Sacra,* comes under the heading of *pia exercitia,* or pious practices; and however striking may be its communal character, it is not liturgy or the public worship of the Church. These pious practices prolong the liturgy and prepare the faithful for it; and they are particularly necessary at the present time, because the difficulty of language hinders the immediacy with which the liturgy can nourish the piety and faith of the people. However, it is better to reserve the term "assembly" for a celebration that is properly liturgical. This will avoid any debasement of a venerable word and any confusion in explaining the theology of the assembly. But if every *liturgical* gathering is an assembly, we are right in seeing the Eucharistic assembly as the assembly *par excellence.* It is the summit towards which all the liturgy leads and which brings all the rest to full realization. In it, then, we find verified most perfectly what we mean by an assembly, and it is with reference to it that we may go on now to consider more fully the nature of the assembly.

The assembly is the visible expression and the effectual realization of the Church. It is significant that the same word *ekklēsia* was used in the early centuries, in Greek and Latin, both for the Church as a permanent community and for the regular assembly of the faithful. The permanent Church and the transitory assembly are the same sacred reality but existing on two different levels of actuality. The assembly may be called the epiphany of the Church in so far as the word implies the deeper and more active presence of the reality as well as its external manifestation. To understand the assembly, we must first look more closely at the mystery of the Church.[2]

[2] For the rest of this chapter I have drawn freely on passages from chapter four of my *Liturgy and Doctrine* (Sheed and Ward, London and New York, 1960), though with many additions.

Through its use in the Septuagint, the Greek word *ekklēsia* when applied to what Christ came to establish connects his work with certain decisive moments in the history of the Chosen People, moments marked by what the Bible called the "Assembly of Yahweh." The first and basic assembly was that of Sinai. God convoked that assembly. It was the Assembly of Yahweh because he had the initiative. By it the rabble of Hebrews was transformed into a people and a nation. God spoke to them and made a covenant with them, which was sealed in a sacrifice. The other great assemblies of Israel reproduced the essential characteristics of that of Sinai and served to renew the existence and consciousness of Israel as a people. Of particular importance were the assembly under King Josias (4 Kings 23) and that under Esdras (2 Esdras 8–9). Through the sending of Christ, God again convokes an assembly. This time the call is addressed to all men. Called together by God, men are welded into a People of God. A new covenant is established, and the new relationship between God and man is achieved and ratified by a sacrifice, the sacrifice of Christ. The new people called together and given existence as a people by God is the Church.

The Church is from God. It is not the creation of man; it is not a society due to human initiative, brought into existence by the coming together and self-organization of those who wish to follow Christ and are interested in his teaching. The Church comes from above and is due to a divine intervention in human history. But the Christian revelation demands that we understand this in terms of the Trinity. The first origin of the Church is from God the Father. He it is who sends the Son to be head of the Church, and when we call the Church the People of God we are referring it back to God the Father, who sent the Son. The sending of the Son was a call to men to share in the life of the Son and to enter into relationship between the Son and the Father. Christ prayed "that they may all be one; that they too may be one in us, as thou Father, art in me, and I in thee" (John 17.21, KV). We are invited to share the life of the Trinity, to participate in the current of life that flows from the Father to the Son. The mission of the Son is the origin of the Church; as the Son has his origin from the Father by whom he is sent, so the Church has its origin from

God the Father by receiving a participation in the mission of the Son.

Christ is Lord of the Church, and men belong to the Church only in so far as they are one with Christ. But Christ became Lord of the Church by his death and resurrection. In the present economy of a redemptive incarnation, Christ was able to draw all men to himself and impart to them a share in his own life only by overcoming sin and death by his death and resurrection. The Church, then, owes its existence to the mystery of Christ's saving work. Risen from the dead, the first fruits of a new creation, Christ was now the source of the Spirit, through whom he incorporated men into himself and gave them a share in his life. So the work of establishing the Church was completed and enduring existence given to it by the Spirit released from the risen Christ. Father and Son send the Spirit, and through this sending the Church is given the indwelling presence of the Holy Spirit. The Spirit is the dynamic principle uniting the Church to Christ, conveying the life of Christ to the Church and drawing the Church back through Christ to the Father from whom it came.

Thus, in seeking to penetrate the mystery of the Church, we are led to the mystery of the Trinity and the mystery of Christ. The Church comes from the Father through the Son and exists in the Son, sharing his relation to the Father. The Spirit, the soul of the Church, animates the Church and gives it its union with the Son, and by the Spirit the Church returns in a movement of love to the Father through the Son. Hence the Church has a Trinitarian structure and exists in the inner life of the Trinity. But this has been made possible only by the mystery of Christ. The Son, whose life the Church shares, is the incarnate Son, Christ. But Christ became the source of life for men by his death and resurrection, and the risen Christ remains as our permanent mediator with the Father. So the death and resurrection of Christ is the radiant centre from which the Church draws its life and on which it never ceases to depend. The relation of the Church to the Spirit ensures that it possesses permanently the inner Trinitarian life of grace; but its relation to Christ, from whom it receives the Spirit, means that the Church exists visibly as a sacrament, with a visible structure and organization, prolonging as his Body the incarnate life of Christ, who is the Great Sacrament of salvation.

Such, very briefly, is the wonderful mystery of the Church. Now, the sacred and mysterious reality of the Church as inserted into the historical order and present here in this world is given existence on two levels. It exists as a permanent reality and then, with regular frequency, in the greater presence of an event. We are very conscious of the Church as a permanent reality in the world, and we know how recent theology has drawn attention to the full depth of its mystery; but we are less conscious of the Church as realized anew in our assemblies, and that makes our preaching of the Mystical Body very remote and unreal—and needless to say very ineffectual.

Yet it was the will of God that the mystery of the Church should achieve again and again an even greater presence in history, a fuller actuality, in the manner of an event in which its permanent reality would be more clearly manifested and, at the same time, strengthened and created afresh. This event is the liturgical assembly and, in particular, the Eucharistic assembly. Since the assembly exists in the sacramental order as the realization of the Church, the basic sacrament, we may consider first the sign and then the reality made present in the sign.

The assembly is the sign of the Church and should be a worthy expression of the Church. This statement is heavy with practical consequences. Only a few remarks are possible here. The assembly must reflect the universality of a Church that embraces all races and classes. Although the distribution of Christians into parishes and other groupings ought to take into account geographical and social factors, there is no place in the Christian scheme of things for any division of the faithful into separate assemblies according to race or social class. Further, any distinction of class or wealth introduced into our assemblies impairs their meaning, as St. James already reminded the first Christians. Again, the Church is hierarchically ordered; so also must be the assembly. A true appreciation of the assembly will never lead to a false confusion between the priest and the people. This hierarchical order is reflected in the structure of the church building, which is, first and foremost, a place for the assembly of the Christian community. There must be two distinct parts: the sanctuary or place of the celebrant and his ministers and the nave or place of the faithful. But if the distinction between the clergy and the laity is basic, the laity, on their part, do not form an amorphous mass of individuals. They are a community; and if the assembly is to be a worthy expression of the Church, all those gathered together must be welded into an acting community and drawn up into a communal celebration.

When we are considering the various forms of active participation, we should not ask merely if the faithful already know what is going on or if they are already praying, thinking that there is no need to do anything when the answer is Yes. We must ask ourselves, when we look round our Sunday assemblies, whether we can see reflected in them the life of the Church as a community. The efforts to restore a more active participation are primarily efforts to reanimate the structure of the assembly so that it may fulfil more faithfully the purpose intended by Christ of being a vivid sign of the communal life of the Church and thus able to realize more effectually and convey more readily that communal life. We find in fact that the general life of the Church and the manner in which the assembly is carried out are closely interrelated. The tendency to identify the Church with the clergy and see the laity as passive recipients from the Church rather than active sharers in its life and work has been reflected in the liturgical assembly, which has become largely a clerical affair with the laity as passive onlookers. We are inconsistent and wasting our breath if we preach on the importance of the lay apostolate and ignore the need for active participation in the liturgy. The assembly is the Church in its fullest manifestation and greatest actuality, and the life of the Church flows from the assembly; if a Christian is passive there, he will be passive in other respects also.

If the congregation at Mass is to be shaped into an acting community, there must be a differentiation of functions. The celebrant is not only the priest who accomplishes the sacrificial action but also the one who presides over the assembly. He is assisted by the ministers and servers. Then come the commentator, who helps and leads the participation of the people, the readers and the choir. Finally, the congregation as a whole has its part. The people are drawn into the communal celebration by seeing and hearing. They should see the altar, the celebrant and the actions: they should hear the Scripture readings, the words of the preacher, the

prayers and the chants. They join in by ritual actions such as standing, kneeling and sitting, by acclamations or responses, by singing
and by silence. Their participation reaches its climax in Holy Communion. Thus is achieved a community of expression which presupposes but at the same time helps and strengthens that internal
participation which gives it value. And the communal celebration
becomes a vivid sign of the communal life of the Church.

In this sign the sacred reality of the Church comes to a fuller
actuality as an event. The Church, a basic and permanent sacrament, moves into act in a given time and place and realizes by
actions what it is permanently by essence. What happens in the
assembly is similar to what happened in the Assemblies of Yahweh,
which were so important in the history of Israel: a proclamation
of the Word and a joyous response of the people, an act of sacrifice
and a participation of all in that sacrifice.

The assembly is the privileged place for the proclamation of
the Word. The Word comes to us in other circumstances also,
but the assembly remains the principal occasion for its proclamation. The Word comes to us from the Father. He sent us Christ,
and Christ is the very Word of God. It is Christ himself with his
message that is now proclaimed. And it is the living Christ himself who speaks to us when the Scriptures are read and the homily
preached, even though he now uses the voice of his ministers.
The ministers of the Church are his representatives; they speak in
his name and with his power. Consequently, there is a sending of
the Spirit. When the Word is proclaimed, the Spirit is present,
opening our hearts, provoking our response and re-creating us as
a community of believers. The Church as the Body of Christ, able
to act in the name of Christ and with his power, and the Church
as the Spouse of Christ, able to respond to his grace and enter
into union with him, is actualized in the event of the proclamation of the Word.

/ But our union with Christ is not established simply by faith
in his message but by effectual contact with his redemptive acts.
The saving activity by which the Church continues the work of
Christ does not consist solely in the Word as preached but in
the Word as sacramentally efficacious. So, in our assembly, the
reading and preaching of the Word is followed by the Eucharistic
celebration, in which the mystery of Christ's redemptive work is

sacramentally renewed, so that we can take part in it and be drawn deeper as a community into the death and resurrection of Christ. And again, the Church as the Body of Christ, acting in his name and with his power, and the Church as the Spouse of Christ, answering his love and entering into union with him, is actualized in the sacramental action of the Eucharist. ⁄

The Eucharistic assembly, however, does not simply realize in act what the Church already is. It is the cause of the continued existence of the Church. The life of the Church is created ever anew and the sacred reality of the Church inserted ever more deeply into a particular time and place. Just as the Church owes its origin to a call of God the Father, coming to us through the Son whom he sent and who died and rose again and to the action of the Spirit poured out upon us from the risen Christ, so the Church owes its continued existence to the sacramental renewal of that total mystery in the Eucharistic celebration. We come together at Mass in response to a call of God the Father. Our assembly is created from above by his summons. He has promised to send Christ, his Son, when we gather together to hear the Word and to celebrate the *anamnesis,* or memorial of the passion, death and resurrection. And when we do so, we are joined to the mystery of Christ—which is the source of the life of the Church—by the action of the Spirit sent into the midst of our gathered community. Thus the enduring existence of the Church in Christ and, through Christ, in the Trinity is secured. The Church would cease to exist, were our Eucharistic assemblies no longer held.

We are aware of the mystery of what takes place at the altar. Let us not impoverish that mystery by ignoring the assembly that is part of it. A deep appreciation of the sacred character of the assembly will make us see to it that it is carried out more worthily. Instead of bearing a resemblance to a theatre crowd, our Sunday assembly will become a joyous and resounding expression of our common life in Christ and of our share through Christ in the very unity of the Trinity.

CHAPTER XVIII

SACRAMENT OF THE SICK
OR OF THE DYING

Many priests wish they could give their people a deeper appreciation of extreme unction. Surely, they think, more could be made of this sacrament. What might be a wonderful pastoral opportunity often becomes a drearily dissatisfying occasion, because there is no real awareness of what is being done and why. Yet, if an enthusiastic priest resolves to do something about this, it is an easy prophecy that he will soon be pulled up short. The obstacle that will face him is that the theology of this sacrament is not clear. Make no mistake: the problem here does not only affect the student at his desk. The preacher cannot get this sacrament across to the people and give them a living and lasting appreciation of its value, unless he can state in plain and forceful language its purpose. He must tell them without involved and obscure qualifications what it is intended to do, or, to put it in another way, what are its effects. Now, if he goes beyond the colourless and ineffectual summary of the average handbook, where the difficulties are eluded at the expense of clarity and force, and tries to get to grips with the theology of extreme unction, he will find out before very long that the effects of the sacrament are wrapped in the obscurity of a highly complicated and very tricky discussion. As a result, the powerful sermon he intended on the subject remains undelivered, and priest and people continue in their vagueness concerning a sacrament that is in fact a moving example of Christ's love and solicitude for his own. Can we obtain some help by going on a tour of the theological world and discovering what is at present afoot? That, at any rate, is the purpose of this chapter.

A key question must be confronted. The priest must have an answer to it if what he says is to make sense to an ordinary congregation and not form a cloud of misty verbiage. Is this anointing a sacrament of the dying or a sacrament of the sick? No question is being raised here for the moment about the recipient of the sacrament. Let it be granted without comment that it is only for those who are in danger of death from sickness. Our problem is: what is the anointing intended to do for the recipient? Does the priest come first and foremost to prepare him for death? The anointing, in that case, is given as a final cleansing. By it, the person is purified from all that would hinder his entry into heaven. The thought that dominates is death, and all is seen in that perspective. The anointing is a consecration of the Christian's death, an anointing for glory. Or, does the priest come in the first place to offer relief in bodily sickness to a person who is weighed down by it? The anointing, in that case, is directed to the needs, both bodily and spiritual, of a sick person as sick. The thoughts that dominate are those of reinvigoration, restoration and recovery.

Which is right? Should the priest keep in the forefront the thought of death and the help given by this sacrament in meeting it? The bodily effects are then kept in the background as occasional occurrences that should not be made too much of. Or, should he stress the relief of sickness and point boldly to the hope of bodily recovery? Some readers will protest—perhaps indignantly—that a false dilemma is being created. This is not so. No unreal problem is being needlessly erected. Sufficient proof of this is that we meet on our theological tour two quite different attempts in recent times to renew the appreciation of this sacrament. Undeniably, the priest on the mission is faced with a choice between two approaches to this sacrament, approaches that are very unlike each other, and it is pointless to pretend that the choice he makes will not affect considerably the way he presents this sacrament to his people.

A book that an enthusiastic priest, anxious to strengthen the sacramental life of the parish, is likely to pick up is *Of Sacraments and Sacrifice,* by Fr. Clifford Howell, S.J.[1] It is a book of many excellences. What does it make of extreme unction? A nod is given to the possible bodily effect, but what is emphasized and enlarged

[1] Collegeville, Minn., Liturgical Press, 1954.

upon, what the author is concerned to hammer home, is the efficacy of this sacrament in preparing the Christian for death. This is how he sums up the meaning of anointing: "The sacrament of the last anointing is the rounding off or consummation of the Christian life. It is the consecration of the Christian's death in Christ. Our Lord said in his own last moments: '*Consummatum est*—it is finished.' The anointed Christian, as he dies in union with Christ, can make those words his own." No doubt whatever; according to this account, the sacrament is primarily concerned with death.

The few pages of Fr. Howell are noteworthy because they openly attempt more than a repetition of familiar truths. They have the excitement and vigour of a new statement. The author writes with the knowledge that what he is saying will be found surprising by many. This sacrament has been undervalued, we must change this, is his cry. But how? By returning to the older view of its effectiveness as a final cleansing. This sacrament is no less than an anointing for glory itself; it prepares the soul for immediate entry into the glory of heaven. Received with good dispositions, it ensures escape from purgatory. The assumption made by the average Catholic that he will have to put in a fair time in purgatory is unwarranted pessimism. Extreme unction, the anointing for glory, is a sacramental means of avoiding purgatory. The anointed "leap, so to speak, out of their death-beds straight into their thrones in heaven!" This, we are told, was the common opinion of theologians from the patristic age to the Council of Trent. After Trent, the need to defend the existence of purgatory caused a fear of stressing the power of anointing, and this obscured the truth. What we have to do is to get back to the older optimism. That is the way to overcome any neglect or lack of love of this sacrament and to make it vivid in the consciousness of our Catholic people.

No priest will deny that such a presentation of the sacrament is likely to have a popular appeal. Purgatory occupies a prominent place in the minds of the faithful, and they would welcome such an easy and assured escape from it. What makes priests reluctant to preach this view with unambiguous clarity is that they suspect its truth. Is their suspicion justified? The view goes back in modern times to Kern's treatise, *De sacramento extremae unctionis* (Ratisbonae, 1907), although the Jesuit theologian seems to have been more cautious than his popularizers in insisting on the need for a full co-operation with the grace of the sacrament if the full effect were to be received. Since Kern, the opinion has received a fair amount of serious theological support. It has, besides, been written up for a popular public in an excited and unqualified manner by a number of writers, particularly in America. Fr. Howell's own exposition rests, as he tells us, on a paper read by Fr. Reinhold at the National Liturgical Week held in 1941 at St. Paul, Minnesota.[2] The paper cannot be passed over without comment.

A student of the liturgy reading through this plea for a better understanding of extreme unction will find it very odd. The approach is ostensibly through the liturgy, the aim to find out if the liturgical movement has a new angle on this sacrament. We are told we ought to study the liturgical texts themselves and urged to recognize the "self-explanatory character of the liturgy." Then we are given an account of the sacrament that is certainly not derived from the liturgical texts and is to all appearances out of keeping with them. No attention at all is paid to the bodily effects; apparently, Fr. Reinhold regards these as much too uncertain and rare to be a motive of any enthusiasm for the sacrament. What matters is the way this sacrament prepares us for death and glory. This effect is painted in such glowing colours that the reader cannot but feel that were a person placed in a state of such readiness for heaven a recovery from his illness would be a matter for great regret. What a different impression is given by the liturgy! In the texts for this sacrament there is not a single mention of death; on the other hand, the prayers that follow the anointing are full of the thought of deliverance from sickness and restoration to bodily health. The symbolism of oil and the prayers by which it is blessed have the same bearing. Whatever else may be said for this opinion, it does not rest on the liturgical texts. It comes, not from a study of the liturgy, but from theological speculation; and it has indeed as a point against it that its almost exclusive concern with death is out of keeping with the liturgical rite.

What about its claim to be traditional? The sweeping statement of Fr. Howell that it was the common opinion from the patristic

---

[2] "The Sacrament of Extreme Unction in Parish Life," *National Liturgical Week, 1941* (Newark, 1942), pp. 135–41.

era to the Council of Trent is without basis. It is not until the
Middle Ages that anointing is regarded as a preparation for death,
and Master Simon in the twelfth century is, as far as our knowledge goes, the first to teach that the purpose of anointing is to
prepare the dying for the beatific vision. Admittedly, after that,
the idea was taken up by the great Scholastics. These, despite their
disputes concerning the exact nature of the principal effect of
anointing, agree in teaching that the general purpose of the sacrament is to prepare the soul for glory, to remove what might impede his immediate entrance into heaven. This is a context into
which the thesis of Kern can fit without difficulty. To that extent
at least it can rightly claim support from the Scholastic writers.
Nevertheless, it is debatable whether even they would have given
the conclusions of Kern, and *a fortiori* those of his more ardent
disciples, their full approval. Kern looks at this sacrament chiefly
as a means of escaping purgatory, and he stresses in particular its
efficacy in remitting the total debt of temporal punishment; the
Scholastics were not so preoccupied with purgatory and temporal
punishment. The principal effect of extreme unction as an immediate preparation for glory was given either as the remission of
venial sins (the Franciscan school) or as the removal of the
debility called the remnants of sin (the Dominican school), and
it can be and is argued that they considered this final cleansing,
together with any remission of temporal punishment, to be proportionate to the varying dispositions of the recipient and not total
as a matter of course.

That leads us to take our criticism of Kern's opinion deeper.
What is wrong is his basic approach. To suppose that a sacrament
has been instituted primarily as a means of avoiding purgatory is
to misconceive the general purpose of the sacraments. Fr. de
Letter in an article on the meaning of extreme unction[3] puts this
well:

Moreover, a deeper and more fundamental error is at the root of this
idea. For it tacitly supposes that the sacraments primarily aim at the
next life, while in fact they have in view our present life on earth where

[3] "The Meaning of Extreme Unction," *Bijdragen*, 16 (1955), pp. 258–70.
An abstract of the article is given in *Theology Digest*, 4 (1956), pp. 185–8.
The first quotation given is from the abstract, the other two from the article
itself.

we are souls-in-bodies. Their result for the future life is evidently only an effect of the specific fruit they yield in our souls during this lifetime. It is wrong, therefore, to reason to the specific purpose of a sacrament from its ultimate effect in the next world. The reverse procedure is the right one, and extreme unction is no exception to the rule (p. 188).

A sacrament to escape purgatory is the wrong banner under which to promote a new appreciation of this sacrament—or of any sacrament.

What have we so far ascertained in this attempt to guide the busy pastor? That it would be a mistake to arouse enthusiasm for this sacrament by preaching the popular version of Kern's theory. The last anointing does prepare the soul for glory, and with its cleansing is connected a remission of temporal punishment. Granted. There is not, however, sufficient theological backing to preach unhesitatingly that those who receive the anointing with average dispositions go straight to heaven. But this has not yet answered our question: is this sacrament a sacrament of the dying or of the sick?

There are those who reject the thesis of Kern, at least in its popular unqualified form, and yet continue to keep this sacrament firmly and almost exclusively in the perspective of death. The article of Fr. de Letter is very interesting in this respect. As we have seen, he forcibly rejects Kern's point of view; but he likewise rejects the other new trend. This trend we have still to consider; it insists that this sacrament is primarily the sacrament of the sick, not of the dying. Fr. de Letter will not have it that here is any necessary choice between two alternative meanings for this sacrament. He urges:

Extreme Unction must be said to be neither simply the sacrament of the dying nor simply the sacrament of the sick. It is not the sacrament of the dying, because the grace it confers, according to St. James interpreted by Trent, does not only regard the moment of dying but also and perhaps even more, the preparation for that moment during the illness which is eventually to lead to it. It is not the sacrament of the sick, if by sickness we mean the state of bodily debility and of spiritual incapacity without any reference to its eventual outcome, death, but rather with a view to its effective removal: because its sacramental grace of spiritual strength, a help no doubt for the present corporal and spiritual weakness, is particularly meant for the great spiritual struggle which approaching death usually entails.

Accordingly, by combining the positive elements of each of the two positions their one-sidedness will be remedied. Extreme Unction is the sacrament of the sick in danger of death (p. 262).

Does Fr. de Letter really succeed in having it both ways? No; it becomes clear to anyone who considers his article closely that he has not brought together the two alternatives but has taken his choice between them. Whatever his protestations, for him, without a doubt, this sacrament is a sacrament of the dying, not of the sick as sick. "To enable a sick man, in spite of weakness and spiritual danger, safely to go through the ordeal of the last struggle of this earthly life, such is the specific sacramental grace of Extreme Unction" (p. 269). Death envisaged as the outcome of the illness is made essential to the meaning of the sacrament; the sickness comes within its scope only in so far as it is a preamble to death. Plainly, the purpose given to the anointing is not to help and strengthen the sick in their sickness, but to assist the dying in their death. It is concerned with sickness, not as hindrance to normal activity, but as the antechamber of death. The person is reached by the sacrament precisely and formally as dying, not as sick. In a word, it is not seen as the sacrament of the sick in danger of death, but as the sacrament of the departing when they are dying from sickness.

Before we pass to the writings of those who regard this conception as untraditional and unsatisfactory, let us acknowledge its nobility. A very attractive presentation of it can be found in the *Katholische Dogmatik* of Professor Schmaus.[4] His whole treatment of this sacrament is brought under the idea that it is the consecration of death. He speaks in excellent terms of the meaning of death and its significance for the union of the Christian with Christ. The death of the baptized is already as such the death of those united to the crucified and risen Christ, but the sacramental order includes a further gift. The sacrament of extreme unction unites the dying Christian in an even deeper way to the death of Christ. When the author comes to discuss in detail the various effects of anointing, all that is said is governed by the

[4] *Katholische Dogmatik,* IV, 1 (München, 1957), pp. 614–35.

conviction that the purpose of this sacrament is to make the death of the anointed a participation in the death of Christ. The possibility of a bodily healing is dealt with at the end of the section on the effects. Even here, preparation for death is seen as the ruling purpose. When the salvation of the person calls for the postponement of death, the sacrament will bring about a recovery. The anointing is still an anointing for death, but in this instance for a good but postponed death. The reader is left with the marked impression that no effort has been spared to bring this sacrament in its total meaning under the heading of a sacramental consecration of death.

While one cannot but admire the thought of Professor Schmaus on the deep significance of Christian death and the encounter with Christ it brings, there is some cause for wondering whether he has not attached his reflexions to the wrong sacrament. To judge from the liturgy, the sacrament of a Christian death is not anointing but viaticum. All that is said about death for the Christian goes admirably with the Eucharist in this its final role. It does not go so well with anointing, which is refused to Christians faced with even certain death, if the death is not from sickness. On this point, it is somewhat piquant to observe that Professor Schmaus, in dealing with the effects of the sacrament, quotes extensively from the commendation of a departing soul, but does not cite the prayers that immediately follow the anointing. These, it will be remembered, ask for a recovery. This prompts the reflexion how misleading is the place of viaticum in our present ritual. Up to the close of the twelfth century, the order of the last sacraments was anointing and then viaticum. That gave to viaticum its full significance as the Church's parting gift, with the commendation of the dying as its complement. Then the order was changed, and viaticum yielded to anointing its position as the final climax of the Church's sacramental ministrations to the dying Christian. Anointing took on the appearance of the final preparation for death. That is still the order in the Roman Ritual; but not now in all the new vernacular rituals approved by Rome. The American, the French (revised edition) and the German rituals restore the older order and viaticum follows the anointing. The significance of this return to the older tradition is not reflected in Professor Schmaus's account.

Our busy pastor, who is probably rather worried by now, could draw from Professor Schmaus material for a moving and yet deeply doctrinal sermon on Christian death. He could present extreme unction as the sacrament of such a death and put it before the faithful as a wonderful gift which the Church can give her children when they come to die. Would not many priests, however, hesitate to adopt this approach in the same exclusive way as Professor Schmaus? When attempts are made from time to time to persuade people not to delay this sacrament, these frequently use the possible bodily effects as a motive. This fact keeps alive in the minds of priests an awareness that there is another side to the sacrament. They would feel vaguely uncomfortable at making it so exclusively a sacrament of death. Besides, they would fear that the inherent logic of the view would encourage people in delaying the sacrament until death was imminent; and, despite the urging of these authors that the sacrament should be received at an early stage, the past history of this opinion and its influence amply supports such fears. What, then, is our pastor to do? Talk equally of death and recovery, and leave people in the usual mental fog about what this sacrament is really intended to do? As Dom Botte vividly puts it, the average compromise account of the sacrament reminds one of a request to sit between two chairs.

It is time to turn to the other recent attempts to restore this sacrament to its proper place in the sacramental life of the faithful. Another book that a priest might very well turn to in search for enlightenment is Fr. Roguet's *Christ Acts through the Sacraments*.[5] The anointing of the sick is dealt with in a vigorous chapter that strikes a new note.

Extreme Unction, in spite if its name, is not exclusively, or even principally, the sacrament of the dying. Afterwards we shall see what are the helps which the Church reserves for people on their deathbed. For the moment, let us content ourselves with seeing Extreme Unction as the sacrament of the sick. And this is the reason—let us make the point once and for all—why we ought to drop the term "Extreme Unction," which is unsuitable and relatively modern, in favour of the more accurate and more traditional "anointing of the sick."

[5] Collegeville, Minn., Liturgical Press, 1954.

The meaning of the sacrament is explained in an exposition that begins with the attitude of Christ to the sick and infers from James that the primary effect of the sacrament is the physical cure of the sick. We are told that the medieval theologians burked this truth because they wondered how a sacrament could have a physical effect. But this hesitation is due to a misunderstanding. The sacraments are aimed at man as a single whole made up of body and soul, and sickness has spiritual repercussions. Anointing is then compared with viaticum, which is in truth the sacrament for death. However, the author at the end briefly indicates the role of extreme unction when it has to act as a sacrament of the dying.

A remarkable piece of work this chapter, but disappointingly brief for those to whom the approach is new and who are therefore avid for more detailed support and information. Another and brilliant presentation of the sacrament along the same lines (Fr. Roguet is a co-author) is given in the *Album liturgique* which the periodical *Fêtes et Saisons* has prepared on the sacrament of the sick.[6] Many know by now the format and technique of illustration used by this outstanding series. The doctrinal content of this album corresponds to Fr. Roguet's chapter. The sacrament is presented unhesitatingly as a sacrament of healing, with the fact that the sick are not always delivered from their sickness explained in reference to the present economy of salvation. Yet all partisan shrillness is avoided, and everyone, whatever his theological opinions, can profit from the rich and skilful exposition. What is also of interest is to learn from the album that there is in France *La Ligue de saint Jacques Apôtre* with the purpose of making this sacrament in the common estimation the sacrament of the sick, instituted with a view to recovery, not death.

We have undoubtedly encountered here a new trend of some significance. It is not confined to France. Dr. Rudolf Peil, expressly opposing Professor Schmaus, insists with marked emphasis in his liturgical handbook for the catechist and teacher that this is the sacrament of the sick not the sacrament of death.[7] The same view is taken as correct in a short article in the *Liturgisches Jahr-*

---

[6] *Le sacrement des malades* (Paris, 1957).

[7] *Handbuch der Liturgik für Katecheten und Lehrer* (Freiburg, 1955), pp. 151–5. An English translation is now available: *Handbook of the Liturgy* (New York, Herder & Herder, 1960).

buch,[8] where the references to other writers make it clear that the opinion has gained some currency in German catechetical circles. Its influence is not surprising. Few can fail to find this approach to the sacrament attractive, and there is hardly need to mention how rich it is in pastoral possibilities. It has also the right ring about it, whereas the Kern-Howell opinion seemed reminiscent of the wrong kind of piety. But how does it stand in the theological world? Has it solid backing?

A justification of the approach is given by the liturgical scholar, Dom Bernard Botte, in *La Maison-Dieu.*[9] His article is an appeal to tradition. All the liturgical evidence up to the twelfth century shows that this sacrament was regarded as a sacrament of the sick, directed to the healing of the sick person, although not to the exclusion of spiritual effects. Then came the theological speculations of the twelfth and thirteenth centuries which led to the bodily effects being pushed right into the background. The anointing of the sick became a sacrament of the dying, indeed of the agony. How could the principal effect be bodily healing? the Scholastics asked; the effect of a sacrament must be a grace. Their systematization of sacramentary theology caused a distortion in the attitude to this sacrament. But the Holy Spirit was still with the Church, as is clear from what happened at Trent. The Council was presented with a draft text which was a sanction pure and simple of the idea that this sacrament was the sacrament of the agony, and one in which any normal effect of the anointing on the health of the sick person was excluded. This text was rejected and another adopted which, while stressing the important role of the anointing for the dying, left its wider efficacy intact. Hence the possibility of a renewed understanding of its function as the sacrament of the sick. Dom Botte also argues from the attitude of the Holy See to the practice of the Eastern Church that the danger-of-death requirement in the Latin Church is a disciplinary matter. He then draws some practical conclusions, all directed to the purpose of giving back to this sacrament its true character as the sacrament, not of the agony, but of the sick. Among them is a

---

[8] Heinrich Spaemann, "Die rechzeitige Spendung der heiligen Krankensalbung," *Liturgisches Jahrbuch,* herausgegeben vom Liturgischen Institut, 8 (1958), pp. 147–9.

[9] "L'Onction des malades," *La Maison-Dieu,* 15 (1948), pp. 91–107.

forcibly worded request for the dropping of the name *extreme unction* and the use instead of the older title, *anointing of the sick*.

Dom Botte's article is informative and stimulating, but not altogether satisfactory. This is due principally to his intemperate tone. A theologian does not like to rush his fences and he jibs when people try to make him do so. No doubt some such reaction provoked the article of Fr. Leurent, "Le magistère et le mot 'Extrême-Onction' depuis le Concile de Trente."[10] The Jesuit writer leaves the major problem aside and confines his attention to the question of title. He takes up the remarks of Dom Botte and others, who have directed severe criticisms against the more usual name *extreme unction,* and asks how far it is permissible to reject it or ignore it. The most useful part of the article consists in some interesting titbits about Trent, drawn from the recently published Acts of the Bologna interlude. But all that emerges is that the Council chose the title *extreme unction* with deliberation. No decisive doctrinal reason seems to have been involved, and use was made at the same time of other titles, including *anointing of the sick.* What becomes clear in passing is that as yet we are badly informed about the relevant fourteenth session of Trent; for more information we have to wait for the publication of further volumes of the Acts by the *Görresgesellschaft.* From Trent the author turns to the later usage by the magisterium. What strikes the attention here is the great reticence of recent popes over the name *extreme unction* and their preference for other titles. It remains, however, the term used in canon law. A glance is then taken at the practice of the French bishops.

What results from all this investigation? With one conclusion that the author draws there ought to be agreement: the use of *extreme unction* by Trent and other documents compels one to treat it with respect. Some of the critical remarks that have been directed against it have been regrettably excessive. It is always wise in theological matters to be wary of negative attacks; theology usually advances by widening the point of view and introducing complementary aspects, rarely by mere destruction. At the same time, Fr. Leurent goes too far and tries to prove too much. He admits that the term has not the solemn approval given to *tran-*

[10] *Problemi scelti di teologia contemporanea. Analecta Gregoriana,* 68 (Romae, 1954), pp. 219–32.

substantiation; he admits too the reserve of recent popes and the free use made by the Church of other titles for this sacrament; he rightly concludes that in his general pastoral work a priest is quite free to give his preference to *anointing of the sick;* but he makes the reservation that *extreme unction* must retain the first place in catechetics. As regards at least this last point, I find myself at one with the Dominican scholar, Fr. Gy, who for his part dismisses the author's whole vindication as unconvincing.[11] Nothing in the data adduced by Fr. Leurent justifies his contention. It is perfectly possible to treat the term *extreme unction* with respect as expressing one aspect of this sacrament, its significant role in the last sickness, and yet to recognize that this aspect has received too exclusive a stress and to regard the name *anointing of the sick* as entirely preferable, since it expresses in a fuller and more balanced way the meaning of the sacrament. A return to this title has been made in the new German catechism and in the German diocesan prayer-books. To work and hope that this should happen in other countries seems entirely legitimate. A lesser aspiration for this country, which is merely a matter of euphony and linguistics, has yet to be fulfilled: the ousting of the ugly transliteration *extreme unction* by the English *last anointing.*

Fr. Leurent confined his attention to words. Can we find anything to second Dom Botte's historical and doctrinal observations? Yes; *Theological Studies* has published an important article by the Jesuit, Fr. Palmer, which confirms what Dom Botte had maintained.[12] It is pitched, however, in a lower key, and so is less likely to disturb those whose pious ears are highly sensitive. The author starts with a statement of Kern's view and goes on to say that his aim is to question the basic premise on which it rests: namely, that the purpose of extreme unction is to prepare the soul for immediate entry into heaven. He grants that such was the purpose accepted, despite their differences, by the great Scholastic doctors, but does it truly represent the older tradition of the Church? His investigation begins with the text of James and goes through the various documents on this sacrament. What he finds up to the Carolingian period is summed up in this way:

---

[11] *Revue des sciences philosophiques et théologiques,* 39 (1955), p. 688.
[12] "The Purpose of Anointing the Sick: A Reappraisal," *Theological Studies,* 19 (1958), pp. 309–44.

Up until the period of the Carolingian reform, which begins at the close of the eighth century, there is no certain evidence either in the liturgies or the writings of ecclesiastical authors that the sacrament of unction was ever regarded as a preparation for death or that the rite of anointing formed part of the Church's last rites for the dying (p. 321).

During the Carolingian reform, the anointing of the sick became a normal complement to penance and viaticum in the rites for the dying, its administration however preceding viaticum. Yet, the earlier emphasis on anointing as a remedy for restoring health was not thereby lost, and the ritual of anointing that has come down to us from that period, the earliest full ritual we have and an ancestor of our present rite, contains no reference to death and leaves the definite impression that anointing is the sacrament of the sick and is not primarily concerned with the dying.

It was the middle of the twelfth century that saw this sacrament receive the name *extreme unction* and become the last sacrament, the final preparation of the person for glory. By the end of the century the last anointing had ousted viaticum from its final and climactic position in the rites for the dying. Fr. Palmer traces the change of attitude in the early Scholastic period, when the context was established in which the debates of the great Scholastics took place. The writers of the thirteenth century considered this sacrament simply as the sacrament of the dying. That is why they all agreed that its purpose was to prepare the soul for glory, although they divided into two main schools in determining this effect more precisely. What many readers of his article will find quite startling is the logical conclusion which the Scholastics themselves drew from this view of the sacrament: they insist that it is to be received only when death is imminent, when the recipient is in fact departing from this life and passing to another state. Here indeed is a sacrament of the agony.

Against this background the decree of Trent is altogether remarkable. The author briefly discusses what the Council declared and—what perhaps is more significant—what it did not. Also worthy of note is the attitude of the Catechism of the Council of Trent with its unexpected inculcation of confidence in the efficacy of this sacrament for a recovery of health. Fr. Palmer's judgement on the post-Tridentine period is very enlightening. The medieval outlook has been gradually modified. What was regarded as the sacrament of the departing has very slowly come to be understood as the sacrament of the seriously sick. That is the real reason why the anointing-for-glory idea which Kern tried to revive fell into abeyance. The interpretation of the danger of death required for anointing became much wider, and the view prevailed that it need not be proximate but might be remote. Some now even maintain that a probable judgement of danger of death is enough for validity and lawfulness, even if an objective and real danger is not actually present. This is equivalent to saying that the actual degree of sickness does not affect the validity of the sacrament, although a prudent judgement of danger of death on the part of the priest is necessary for lawfulness. And Fr. Palmer argues that this means in effect that the prescription of canon law about the requirement of danger of death is not a doctrinal demand affecting the validity, but a disciplinary measure controlling the lawfulness, of anointing in the Latin Church. This, he remarks, helps us to understand the history of the sacrament and also explains the attitude of Rome to the Eastern Church. He thus makes the same judgement as Dom Botte, though he reaches it in a different way.[13]

Fr. Palmer's conclusion is the rejection of Kern's view. The chief fruit of his article is the conviction, solidly established, that anointing is the sacrament of the sick. For that we must be grateful.

The busy priest who has consented to come on this theological tour can rightly feel that he has now the answer to the key question with which we began. Anointing is the sacrament of the sick. There is indeed the last sickness. No excessive reaction should make us forget that this sacrament has a particularly important role to play at that critical time; but even then it is concerned with the sickness rather than with death. We may, then, safely and comprehensively present it as the sacrament of the sick. But this has not yet solved all the difficulties involved in conveying plainly the meaning of this sacrament. How are we to describe

[13] A canon law thesis presented recently at Washington University maintains quite definitely that danger of death is not a condition affecting the validity of this sacrament. See *The Recipient of Extreme Unction* by Charles George Renati, The Catholic University of America: Canon Law Studies, n. 419 (Washington, D.C., 1961).

its effects? To make its main effect the recovery of the sick person, his physical cure, seems, let us admit it, an exaggeration. No one would wish to be lacking in faith, but all save the most robust of the clergy get chary about raising false hopes. There is in any case something inherently awkward about presenting vigorously an effect that might not take place. After all, the Scholastic search for an infallible sacramental grace connected with the supernatural life was not unjustified. The question remains: what precisely does this sacrament do for the sick?

The book of Fr. Roguet and the album of *Fêtes et Saisons* give useful hints on the presentation of this sacrament, but the treatment of the effects does not entirely satisfy. We have reason, then, to thank Fr. Alszeghy for grasping this theological nettle firmly. His article in the *Gregorianum* is an outstanding contribution to a difficult question.[14] He sets himself the task of determining the bodily effects of this sacrament. The problem is clear: it is grace the sacraments cause, but the sources seem to indicate that the effect of this sacrament is health of body. How are these points to be reconciled? What exactly is the bodily effect of anointing?

He first examines the sources on the subject of the bodily effect. As will no longer surprise us, the conclusion emerges that there is a decided difference between the ancient texts and recent theology. The former expresses an optimistic attitude towards bodily healing as an effect of the anointing, the latter timidly includes a very conditional expectation. The author then turns to the question of the spiritual grace given by this sacrament. Even the early sources make it clear that the sacrament produces also a spiritual effect. Quite apart from the remission of sins that is given if needed, the anointing is intended as a spiritual aid to the soul. Fr. Alszeghy insists on the presence of this aspect in the documentary evidence on this sacrament. He thus corrects the onesided interpretation of the early tradition found in some writers. The anointing of the sick was never directed solely to a bodily healing. Its spiritual effects were recognized from the beginning, and their existence became at Trent a dogma of faith.

What is the relationship between these two sides of the efficacy

[14] "L'Effetto corporale dell'Estrema Unzione," *Gregorianum,* 38 (1957), pp. 385–405.

of anointing? That is the next problem tackled by the author. Are they two parallel effects? In the sources when the effects of this sacrament are being prayed for or described, it is often impossible to distinguish what refers to the soul and what refers to the body. Is this due to a confusion, to an unfortunate lack of clarity? To think in that way is to fall into the error attributed to Descartes and destroy the unity of man. Our concept of a living man is not a confusion due to a failure to distinguish clearly soul and body. In reality what exists is man; and in man as a biological and spiritual unity the anatomical, physiological, psychological and spiritual aspects exist in continuous relation and mutual interaction, so that to speak of one of these alone is to make an abstraction. Such an abstraction will always be partial, since during life we can never completely distinguish spiritual and bodily life. Man is not a body nor a soul nor a confusion of both; man is a corporal and spiritual unity. Such is man, such likewise is therefore the help given to aid man in sickness. What is given by this sacrament is a grace that affects man as a whole. In the "salvation" given to the sick man there is a unity between the bodily and spiritual aspects. Why should this seem strange to us? It is in keeping with sacramental efficacy in general. When the priest administers the sacraments, he is concerned with man as a whole, man as a psycho-somatic unity or totality, and the efficacy of the sacraments affects both body and soul. The anointing of the sick does not, then, exercise an influence on the soul considered apart from the body nor on the body considered apart from the soul, but on the living unity which is the whole person. That is the way we must think of the anointing as helping the sick person.

Nevertheless, this does not prevent us from distinguishing the spiritual and bodily aspects of the sacramental influence and trying to find out all that is involved. The help which this sacrament gives to the sick man can be taken to mean in general that his spiritual and corporal faculties are influenced in order to offset the sickness and give him freedom of action. The problem of the bodily side of this is that, while the sources maintain that such an effect is produced, a clinical or medical cure is exceptional. It is the author's contention that this apparent contradiction is to be avoided by seeking a bodily benefit given to the sick person but distinct in itself from a clinical cure. How does he do this?

The effect of this sacrament is a strengthening of the whole person. What are the needs of a sick person? There results from sickness a weakness, an unfitness, a lack of vigour in regard to the supernatural life. This is a spiritual matter, but it is also bound up with the physiological state of the person. If we place in a wider theological context the harmful repercussions of sickness on the supernatural life, we see them as due to the loss of original integrity. The difficulty caused by sickness is another example of the weighing down of the will by bodily factors and comes under concupiscence, if this is understood in a wider sense than is usual. The sacramental grace of anointing is a remedy against this. It restores to the sick man the force to live the supernatural life and thereby gives him back part of original integrity. Such a restoration affects the person as a whole and has repercussions throughout his faculties, both spiritual and corporal.

What, then, is the grace of the anointing of the sick? It is a help granted to the person to live intensely his supernatural life, despite the special difficulty of sickness. This grace has a spiritual aspect, which is summarized in the declaration of Trent. Its bodily aspect can be described as a comfort or relief given to the body in order that it should no longer impede the soul; a help, namely, which partially restores order between the various faculties in regard to the total finality of the person. In some instances such a restoration of order will result in a clinical cure; in other instances such a healing will be required as the condition of that restoration. If a clinical healing is involved in either way in the grace of this sacrament, it will be given by the anointing. There will, however, be some instances where no advantage for the medical health of the person will be implied in the restoration and strengthening given by the sacrament. Fr. Alszeghy, in stating that such cases are certainly more numerous and in assuming that in these cases the recipient will die, is accepting too readily a very restricted use of this sacrament. However, we may without difficulty endorse his final remarks on the relevance of the sacramental grace, as he has analysed it, for the last sickness and the agony.

We have come to the end of our tour of the theological world, and it is now necessary to state as plainly and simply as possible what we have discovered concerning this sacrament. One point at least is clear. This is the sacrament of sickness, not of death.

There is a last sickness, and the sacramental grace of anointing has an especial significance when given to those who in the midst of sickness and by means of it have to prepare themselves for a Christian death and make their death a personal and Christian act. Nevertheless, the anointing is still given to them because they are sick, and not precisely because they are facing death. The sacrament of Christian death is viaticum, with the other prayers and rites that the Church herself has added for the help of the dying. It is true that anointing can be given only to those who are in danger of death, but this is interpreted generously by moralists and canonists today. The requirement is a way of controlling the administration of the sacrament, limiting its use to those who are seriously ill. The import of it seems to be disciplinary rather than doctrinal. Certainly, the anointing, according to approved present-day casuistry, may and should be given to those whose recovery we hope for with a natural confidence and pray for without asking for the miraculous. There is no obstacle to a frank recognition that this sacrament is the sacrament of the sick, and the recent work on this subject enables us to embrace this conclusion without fear.

It need hardly be said that the danger-of-death condition must be interpreted according to the mind of the Church. We must go to moralists, not to doctors, for its precise meaning. It is particularly important to remember this at the present day. The criterion was easier to apply in the past. Most of the really serious illnesses unquestionably involved danger of death. The danger would have been admitted frankly on all sides. Today, drugs are so powerful and surgeons so skilful that people do not readily admit danger of death except where medical science can do no more. A doctor is reluctant to speak of death until there is little hope left. These facts demand that we insist with emphasis that the danger required by the Church for anointing need not be a proximate danger. It is not necessary for it to be very serious; it is enough if there is some probable danger. And, to remove all anxiety in our use of this sacrament, we can point to reliable moral teaching that the danger need not be objectively real for the validity of the sacrament; all is well, if we prudently think there is such danger and in doubtful cases the anointing can be validly and lawfully given.

At the same time, it would be a mistake to proclaim a physical cure as the principal effect of this sacrament and to try to make it a rite of healing in the medical sense. Apart from the obvious impossibility of offering such healing as an infallible effect, this attitude would not do justice to the full significance of this sacrament. The spiritual side of the efficacy of anointing has been acknowledged, and it may be taken for granted from general principles that any bodily effects must be subordinated to the recipient's supernatural life, with which all sacraments are concerned. Consequently, the sacramental grace of this sacrament can best be seen as strength and relief given to the sick person to live a full supernatural life, despite his sickness. This grace is given to man as a living unity of body and soul and has repercussions, spiritual and bodily, throughout the whole person. On the bodily side, it implies a restoration of order and unity that might—and often does—involve a cure in the medical sense. We know enough nowadays on the one hand about the complicated causality behind sickness and on the other hand about its repercussions on the various levels of man's life not to be surprised at this. But sickness has a multiple role in the present order of salvation, and God's sacramental grace to the sick man may have varying results. It may be given for a short, severe sickness, where the relief given by the sacrament is striking in its effects. Yet, God's will may be a prolonged sickness, where the effect of the sacrament may be an intense supernatural life in a person whom the natural weight of illness would otherwise have wearied and weakened into inertia. Finally, the sickness may be the preamble to death, where the ability, sacramentally given, to rise above the burden of bodily break-up may enable the person to crown a life of virtue with a new intensity of love or rectify a life of vice by a lovingly endured expiation. To postpone the sacrament to the end of the last sickness is to deprive the person of a much-needed sacramental aid, and partially to frustrate the purpose of the sacrament. In brief, the sacrament of anointing is intended to help our Christian life in all the difficulties and problems caused by sickness.

What a wonderful gift of God! Yet, what a cloud of misunderstanding and fear surrounds it! Much can be and is being done, especially in France and Germany, to restore a true appreciation of this sacrament. But, perhaps, as a French writer remarks,[15] only an initiative from the Holy See similar to the initiative taken by St. Pius X in regard to frequent communion will give this sacrament once again its full place in the Christian life.

[15] F. Meurant, "L'Extrême-onction est-elle le sacrement de la dernière maladie?", *La Vie spirituelle* (March 1955), pp. 242–51.

CHAPTER XIX

THE RESURRECTION
OF THE BODY

What is usually expected from a theologian in an essay on the resurrection of the body? Chiefly a discussion of how it comes about. How can God restore to us again these identical bodies? Certain bizarre difficulties arising from cannibalism or from animals eating men and being eaten in their turn by men come at once to mind. Then the exact nature of the risen body intrigues us: when we transfer ourselves from place to place with the gift of agility, will we pass through the intervening space? Does the endowment of subtlety allow us to penetrate other bodies? In brief, our approach to the resurrection of the body is philosophical; our concern is with the how of it, with its mechanics. All this is very fascinating, and within limits useful and necessary; but in our preoccupation with this side of the doctrine we often miss what is more important: the place and meaning of the resurrection in the history of salvation and in the redemption of each one of us.

Exspecto resurrectionem mortuorum. Is the resurrection of the body a real and living object of our hope? We speak continually of saving our souls and of going to heaven; that would seem to be the limit of our desire. It is not the full Christian hope. It is true that our destiny is determined at death, when the soul leaves the body. But Christ came not to save souls but men, and his redemption extends to the body as well as to the soul. Both are saved, as both were involved in the catastrophe of sin. Again, it is indeed a dogma of faith that the just who are completely purified receive the beatific vision without delay[1]; yet before the resurrection even these are not in their definitive state but in a state of expectation. When the soul is reunited to the body and man in his complete being as a person is restored by God, the beatitude already possessed reaches a new perfection. Despite the present popularity of the contrary opinion, it seems preferable to regard this increase of beatitude at the resurrection as an increase in its intrinsic perfection or intensity and not as a mere extension to the body of an already perfect beatitude. That at least was the patristic teaching, as Fr. Lennerz noted[2]; and, if we accept the textual emendation put forward by Mgr. Glorieux, it remained the constant view of St. Thomas.[3] Perfection in activity follows perfection in being. The soul reunited to the glorified body will be more perfect in being and in activity than the separated soul. Our state in heaven is not, then, the fullness of our final destiny; it calls for a complement. In heaven the just are already the blessed. They are with Christ, and faith has given place to vision, but they look beyond their present state to the fulfilment of the history of salvation and their share in that consummation.

There is more in this than meets the eye. It is possible for the clear grasp we now have of the spirituality and natural immortality of the soul to lead us unwittingly to adopt a world-view that is not Christian—that is in fact incompatible with the biblical and Christian world-view. The idea that death is the liberation of the soul from the body, and that immortality or the after-life is the blossoming into full flower of the natural life of the soul, now no longer impeded by matter, is alien to Christianity. In this sense one can say that immortality of the soul and resurrection of the body represent two outlooks on the meaning of life and two accounts of man's destiny that cannot be harmonized.[4] It is not suggested that any Catholic expressly understands the immortality

---

[1] See the definition of this in the Constitution *Benedictus Deus* of 1336, Denzinger, 530.

[2] *De Novissimis,* ed. 4a (Romae, 1940), p. 134.

[3] "Saint Thomas et l'accroissement de la béatitude (Étude sur le Somme, Ia-IIae, q. 4, a. 5, ad 5)," *Recherches de Théologie ancienne et médiévale,* XVII (1950), pp. 121–5.

[4] The book needs qualification and completion, but M. Cullmann's *Immortalité de l'âme ou Résurrection des morts?* (Neuchâtel, 1956) makes some good points.

of the soul in the way just explained, but such an outlook can be present in tendency. There can be an excessive concentration on the soul. It is more a manner of speaking than a teaching, but it can beget a mistaken mentality. It must not be forgotten that the apostolic preaching was a proclaiming "in Jesus the resurrection of the dead" (Acts 4.2). If we see in the resurrection an unimportant adjunct to the salvation of the soul, something no doubt welcome but rather superfluous or perhaps, though we suppress the thought, considered *de trop,* there is a serious danger of misconceiving some fundamental Christian truths.

A difference between Greek thought and biblical thought is that the future life in the Scriptures is connected with the history of salvation. It is not based on a study of man's nature, nor seen primarily as individual fulfilment, but it finds a place as part of God's all-embracing plan of cosmic redemption. "Christianity," writes Mgr. Guardini, "is not a metaphysics; it is the witness to Himself of the true God. It is the proclamation that God has seized upon earthly existence and will carry it on to a new state in which nothing of the old is lost but rather will receive its ultimate meaning. All of this is bound up with the body."[5] The faith of the first Christians in the work of Christ was faith in an intervention of God that concerned the history of salvation as a whole before it concerned individuals. It was the same with their faith in the resurrection of the body: this was less a yearning for perfect individual happiness than an awaiting the final accomplishment of God's plan for the world and the definitive victory by Christ over the powers of evil. Put it in this way. The Greek philosopher serenely awaited the liberation of the soul from the body and his passing in this way from one level of existence in this present universe to a higher level. The Christian sees death as an evil due to sin, but joyously and courageously meets it, confident in the power of Christ, who has overcome this present corruptible universe affected with sin and death and inaugurated a new creation. To this new world the Christian already belongs in part, but it is with the resurrection of the body and the restoration of all things that it will be fully revealed and established. The future life is for the Christian bound up with the whole drama of

[5] *The Last Things* (New York, Pantheon, 1954).

salvation; that is why the resurrection of the body is essential to it.
It is a question of passing not from one plane of existence to
another, but from this world affected with sin and death to that
world to come in which all things are to be made new. Neglect
the resurrection of the body and you neglect both the social character of redemption and the redemptive character of the future
life. The future life must not become a mere individual survival
due to man's nature, though embellished with certain additional
gifts by God; it must be seen within the framework of salvation
as a cosmic history centred on Christ.

Centred on Christ! Our salvation is a share in what Christ
personally did and achieved. Now Christ's redemptive act included
not only the passion and death but also the resurrection and
glorification. The resurrection is an essential part of the mystery
of atonement. Leave it out and there is left a mutilated picture—
something that defies exposition in biblical terms. A realization of
the place of the resurrection of Christ in objective redemption
should make us give a greater place in subjective redemption to
our own resurrection than we usually do. Sin affects both body
and soul, and the salvation of Christ is for body and soul. This
is in part the meaning of Christ's miracles of healing. For St.
Paul the fullness of our sonship waits upon the resurrection of
the body (cf. Rom. 8.18), and here and now our bodies, as well
as our souls, share by anticipation the redemption brought by
Christ.[6] Reflexion on this bodily side of redemption can influence
the whole approach to the Christian life.

One point it certainly helps us to grasp is the true reality of the
sacramental order, and in particular that of the Eucharist. Our
share in Christ's life comes to us through our union with his life-
giving body. The sacramental economy means that it is through
our bodies that the life of Christ is conveyed to us, and in each
sacrament our bodies are brought into vital contact with the power
of Christ's risen body. That body itself in its full reality is present
in the Eucharist to be our food, and through the intimate union
thus established we are given strength and life. The effect is not

---

[6] On this point M. Cullmann's essay "The Proleptic Deliverance of the
Body according to the New Testament," in *The Early Church: Historical and
Theological Studies* (Philadelphia, Westminster, 1956), has been widely re-
marked.

confined to our souls, and Scripture and tradition emphatically tell us that the resurrection of the body is due to the Holy Eucharist.[7]

The body, then, in the Christian scheme is not a nuisance from which we hope to be freed. Man as a whole has been weighed down and affected by sin: man as a whole has been redeemed. Both body and soul share the Christian life, and our salvation remains incomplete until the resurrection of the body. The dogma of the resurrection is not a minor doctrinal matter; it is of key importance in understanding the social character of salvation as world history and its total character as affecting man in his entirety.

The Jewish and Christian doctrine of the resurrection of the body is eschatological and not philosophical. By that is meant that it does not spring from reflexion on man's nature but from Israel's hope in a definitive salvation, coupled with reflexion on the demands of God's justice. Basic in the Old Testament is the idea that God intervenes in history, and hence the ideas of a divine plan and divine promises. Human history is conceived as moving towards a final end. It is teaching on this last end or definitive redemption that is called eschatology. This is the setting in which we must place the doctrine of the resurrection in its origins. It was seen as something due to the divine intervention and called for because otherwise God's justice could not find fulfilment. The basis for the hope was not a developed anthropology; indeed it couldn't have been, since this was something the Hebrews didn't have.

The Hebrews did not make our distinction between body and soul.[8] They thought of man simply as one and did not distinguish, as we do, two essential constitutive principles. Even less did they think of one part of man as immortal by nature and the other doomed to destruction. For them, man was a living unity, and it was man as a whole that suffered death. They referred to various

[7] For a forcible statement of sacramental realism, see "The Holy Eucharist," by P. Benoit, O.P., in *Scripture*, IX (1957), pp. 5–8.

[8] An excellent account of Old Testament ideas on man and on the future life is given in *Théologie de l'Ancien Testament, Tome II, L'Homme*, by P. van Imschoot (Tournai, 1956). Then Fr. Sutcliffe's *The Old Testament and the Future Life* (Heythrop, 1946) is still valuable.

constituents of man: *basar* or flesh; *nephesh* or soul, *neshamah* or breath, and *rûach* or "spirit"; but these are not clearly distinguished and opposed to each other. They are designations of man under a given aspect. It is a mistake to speak of a trichotomy or dichotomy in regard to Hebrew anthropology. Man is conceived simply as a unity. He is "an animated body, and not an incarnated soul,"[9] a psycho-physical organism. What survives in Sheol is not the soul, but man according to a weak and unsubstantial, not immaterial, existence. The dead are not souls but the *rephaim* or weak. Under Greek influence we do find in the Book of Wisdom and in later Judaism the distinction between body and soul, and the doctrine of the immortality of the soul. Even so, the immortality of the soul taught by the Book of Wisdom is a gift of God. The doctrine is not built on a philosophical basis; the perspective remains religious and biblical. The future life is still seen as part of the history of salvation—something due to the intervention in human affairs of Yahweh and his merciful justice. The theologian thus faces the task of welding together the biblical doctrine of the resurrection and our more developed ideas on the nature of man and on the state of the separated soul. These latter ideas are not without their support in the Scriptures, but the place accorded to them even in the New Testament is a modest one. The subsequent development must not cause us to lose the biblical thought-structure, with its dominant idea of salvation as history directed to its final end by God.

In examining more closely the teaching of the Old Testament on the future life, it is necessary to separate different strands of thought. Belief in a survival after death seems always to have existed among Hebrews and the Semitic peoples generally. The idea of retribution in the next life, of rewards and punishments hereafter, was only a gradual development that emerged quite late in the Old Testament. Again, the express formulation of the doctrine of the immortality of the soul is found only in the Book of Wisdom. Finally the belief in the resurrection of the body arose only at the end of the Old Testament period. It is in fact true to say that there is in the Old Testament no properly worked out

---

[9] The phrase is Dr. Wheeler Robinson's. It is quoted in *The Body: A Study in Pauline Theology*, by John A. T. Robinson (Naperville, Ill., Allenson, 1957).

and coherent doctrine on the lot of individual men after death.

To take now the line of thought that concerns the resurrection[10] The idea of a bodily resurrection is first found in the accounts that tell us how the prophets Elias and Eliseus raised certain people from the dead (1 Kings 17.17–24; 2 Kings 4.18–37; 8.21); though it must be noted that these miracles involved only a restoration to the conditions of this present existence. Then the theme of a resurrection was used on the level of imagery and literary expression; it served as an image to describe the future restoration of the Chosen People. The great example of this metaphorical usage is the vision in Ezechiel 37 of the plain of dry bones and their dramatic return to life. The bones in the valley represent God's people and their resurrection is a symbol that it will be restored. Many authors, such as Martin-Achard, think that the earlier pre-exilic text of Osee (6.1–3) uses the idea of the resurrection in a similar way; others, for example van Imschoot, do not find any resurrection-image in the text. The fourth Servant Song (Isa. 52.13–53.12) speaks of a posthumous restoration of the Servant of Yahweh; after the mention of his death and burial, it is said, "he shall see his offspring, he shall prolong his days" (verse 10, RSV). Some maintain that the text supposes a resurrection, although there is no express reference to one. Needless to say, there is further the perennial problem of the identity of the Servant. In Isa. 26.19, however, resurrection for the slain Israelites is clearly given as a hoped-for future reality, as part of the promised restoration: "Thy dead shall live, their bodies shall rise, O dwellers in the dust, awake and sing for joy! For thy dew is a dew of light, and on the land of the shades thou wilt let it fall." (RSV) The text can also be interpreted as expressing merely a wish, and Martin-Achard takes it in that way. The context shows that this resurrection is seen as a privilege reserved to certain members of the Chosen Race and denied to the pagans and the unjust. Something called for by God's justice, it is due to the divine intervention and part of the eschatological hope. The date of the text is uncertain. It occurs in the Apocalypse of Isaias (chs. 24–7), the latest section of that book. Martin-Achard regards it as probably of the fourth century.

[10] The most recent study of this is *De la mort à la résurrection d'après l'Ancien Testament* by Robert Martin-Achard (Neuchâtel, 1956).

That brings us to Daniel 12.2–3, the first clear affirmation of the resurrection, and one which extends it also to the unjust, although the perspective is not yet universal. "And many of those who sleep in the dust of the earth shall awake, some to everlasting life, and some to shame and everlasting contempt. And those who are wise shall shine like the brightness of the firmament; and those who turn many to righteousness, like the stars for ever and ever." (RSV) The just who will rise are those pious Jews, the Hasidim, who remained faithful to the Law and who were the leaders in resisting the Hellenization imposed by the Seleucids, in particular Antiochus Epiphanes. Were these leaders of the resistance the only ones who were to rise? And the renegade Israelites the only unjust who were to do so? The text doesn't tell us.

The Book of Daniel was composed between 167 and 164, during the persecution of Antiochus Epiphanes and the revolt against him but before the successes of the Maccabees. Some decades later, the same teaching on the resurrection appears in the Second Book of Maccabees (ch. 7). The perspective remains the same: martyrs faithful to the Law will rise again. The same privilege is, however, extended to warriors slain on the battlefield—despite their transgression of certain precepts (12.43–6 and 40). Nothing is said expressly about Israelites who died naturally and about pagans —except for the persecuting king (7.14). The express statement of a universal resurrection of the dead is found in certain apocryphal and rabbinical writings and in the New Testament.

Belief in the resurrection was bound up with belief in the restoration of Israel. The idea first occurs as a symbol of this and then as part of it. Its origin lies essentially in Israel's belief in the justice of Yahweh and in the Messianic restoration. It was a homogeneous development of Israel's faith and not a borrowing from without. Nevertheless, there is no need to exclude all influence of surrounding cultures in leading Israel to formulate and to clarify its faith.

The belief was not accepted universally among the Jews; we are all aware of its rejection by the Sadducees. Jewish eschatology immediately before Christ presents a picture of complicated diversity. There was the theme of a resurrection, but also the development of the idea of retribution immediately after death, with an evolution in the traditional notions about Sheol. In some circles the teaching on the immortality of the soul led in Greek fashion to the exclusion of the resurrection. This is not so in the Book of Wisdom; it is not concerned with the resurrection, but this is not excluded. Nor is it true of the manuscripts of Qumran.[11] It is true of the Book of Jubilees, belonging to the second century. Sometimes, as in the Ethiopic Book of Enoch, the idea of some immediate retribution is combined with belief in a later resurrection. The various notions and the meaning attached to the different terms still remained fluid at this time.

Christ made clear his acceptance of the doctrine of the resurrection in his dispute with the Sadducees (Mark 12.18–27; Matt. 22.23–33; Luke 20.27–40). They put to him their problem. In order to obey the law of the levirate, a woman has married in succession seven brothers. To whom will she belong in the resurrection? In reply Christ emphatically affirms the fact of the resurrection, but at the same time he rejects their gross interpretation of the doctrine. The resurrection is not a return to the conditions of this life; it involves a transformation of earthly existence. "Jesus said to them, 'Is not this why you are wrong, that you know neither the scriptures nor the power of God? For when they rise from the dead, they neither marry nor are given in marriage, but are like angels in heaven'" (Mark 12.24–5, RSV). After giving the solution to their problem, he then attacks directly the position of the Sadducees: "And as for the dead being raised, have you not read in the book of Moses, in the passage about the bush, how God said to him, 'I am the God of Abraham, and the God of Isaac, and the God of Jacob'? He is not the God of the dead, but of the living; you are quite wrong" (vv. 26–7, RSV). In these words Christ introduces a new consideration into their discussions over the resurrection. Yahweh, the God of the Exodus, the God of the Patriarchs, could not be called after the dead unless he intended to restore them to life again. He connects the promises made to Israel and the merciful protection shown to the chosen people with the more recent belief in the resurrection; this latter is but a new aspect of Israel's traditional belief in the living God of mighty deeds.

[11] Cf. M. Delcor, "L'immortalité de l'âme dans le livre de la Sagesse et dans les documents de Qumrân," in *Nouvelle Revue Théologique*, 77 (1955), pp. 614–30.

But Christ did not merely announce the resurrection, he brought it. In his own resurrection he inaugurated and made possible the resurrection of mankind. The resurrection of Christ is the great central fact of history and the good news of salvation. Nowadays when we speak of the Gospel of Jesus Christ we are generally thinking of the public life and teaching of Christ, and we regard the resurrection as coming after that Gospel as its seal and proof. That is not the standpoint of the New Testament, and it does not represent the approach of the apostolic preaching. In the primitive Christian message, the resurrection was not seen as a seal or confirmation added to the Gospel but as the central affirmation of the Gospel. The resurrection of Christ is the very content of the preaching of the apostles. The Gospel of Jesus Christ was not merely a teaching but the coming of the Kingdom of God; a Gospel not in words only but in deeds. It was Jesus himself in his life, death and resurrection; these are the mighty deeds God wrought in him for our salvation. The resurrection is the crowning act. It brought the Messianic age; it was the vindication and exaltation of Christ, and through the risen Christ came the outpouring of the life-giving Spirit.

In proclaiming the resurrection of Christ, the apostles announced our resurrection in him. Their theme was that salvation was accomplished in the death and resurrection of Christ. His resurrection and his exaltation were the certain pledge of his second coming in glory to establish his kingdom and raise the dead. The thought and impatient expectation of this return, the Parousia, constituted the eschatological hope of the first Christians. They awaited the resurrection, and the outpouring of the Spirit was the anticipation of the end in the present, enabling Christians to share already in the life of the risen Christ. It is this basic outlook that is taken up and preserved intact in the more developed theologies of Paul and John.

Paul's teaching on our resurrection is amazingly rich. The difficulty is to disengage it from those other points of his teaching with which it is so closely connected. To bring out the full bearing of his thought on this subject would be to expound the whole Pauline theology of redemption. The glorified body of Christ, the body of Christ which is the Church, the Eucharistic body of Christ, and the resurrection bodies of Christians: all these are in

a very true sense one total reality; the teachings on all are
variations on a single theme. Perhaps enough can be said to show
the place of the resurrection of the body in this conception of the
whole.

Paul is thoroughly Hebrew in outlook. His anthropology in
particular is not Greek but Semitic. His view of man follows that
of the Old Testament, and consequently he saw man simply as a
unity. A realization of this should prevent us misinterpreting his
thought. A theme basic in Paul, developed by him with a fullness
not found elsewhere, is the antithesis of flesh (*sarx*) and spirit
(*pneuma*). This antithesis is not, as people so often think, an opposition between matter and spirit or the immaterial—in other
words, an antithesis of body and soul. "Flesh" does not stand
for a part of man; but for man in his entirety, but seen under a
given aspect. It is man in his weakness and mortality, in his
distance from God; man, then, in his solidarity with a sinful and
corrupt creation. "Spirit" is man as open to the divine life and
as belonging to the sphere of the divine; man, then, under the
influence and activity of the Spirit. Flesh and Spirit are conceived
after the manner of two active principles, affecting man and
struggling within him.

Unredeemed man is for Paul enslaved to an existence in sinful
flesh and under condemnation of death. How did Christ redeem
him? He entered into this world of sin and death, took on "the
likeness of sinful flesh" (Rom. 8.3, RSV), accepted a solidarity
with our wretched state, and then transfigured it in himself and
made it possible for us to do the same by incorporation into him.
In his death Christ put off the flesh, died to the Law, and in
dying broke the power of death, because by his resurrection he
passed through death to a new existence. He rose the Son of God
in power and became by his resurrection a life-giving spirit to
justify and give life to those who are made one with him. Now we
have to make the transition from the body of the flesh to a life
in the risen body of Christ.

A key concept used by Paul in expounding his thought is that
of the body or *soma*.[12] The way he uses it is peculiar to himself,
and through it his thought is given unity. "Body" in Hebrew fashion
stands for man as a whole, in his concrete reality as a living person.

12 On this, see John A. T. Robinson, *op. cit.*

But, unlike flesh and spirit, it is a neutral word, and so it can be thought of as the territory on which flesh and spirit struggle; man, then, in the solidarity of creation considered as intended for God.

Body can be then, and is by Paul, identified with flesh in all man's sin and corruption; it has become the body of the flesh, the body of death. It can also be the bearer of the resurrection, and Paul uses the term to expound his gospel of Christ, the Church, and eternal life. Central in that gospel is the resurrection of Christ. Christ by his death and resurrection put off the body of death and became a spiritual body. It is with that body of the resurrection that we must be united.

Incorporation into Christ, becoming one body with Christ, is the basic teaching of Paul on the Christian life. Through baptism, but particularly through the Eucharist, we become one with the body of Christ. The Eucharist means that our bodies are nourished on the body of Christ and become one with it. That accounts for the realism of Paul's Eucharistic teaching and for the close bond he sees between the Eucharist and the Church. The Church is the body of Christ. It is becoming increasingly clear from recent Pauline studies[13] that what is basic in this theme of the Church as Christ's body is not the Hellenistic comparison of a society to a body, not the idea of the Church as a unified and organized group of men under Christ, but Paul's conviction of the union of all Christians with the personal body of Christ. The Church is the body of Christ because it is the glorified individual body of Christ with which Christians are now united, and through this union made one with each other. The current metaphor of a social body is brought in simply in a secondary way to illustrate the unity among Christians that is a result of their common oneness with the body of Christ.

It should be clear from this brief glance at the theology of Paul that for him our resurrection has already begun. We have in a true sense already risen with Christ: "and you were buried with him in baptism, in which you were also raised with him through faith in the working of God, who raised him from the dead" (Col. 2.12, RSV). It has already been remarked that this anticipation

[13] Cf. P. Benoit, O.P., "Corps, tête et plérôme dans les Épîtres de la captivité," in *Revue Biblique*, LXIII (1956), pp. 5–44.

of the resurrection affects not only our souls, but also our bodies. Man is still seen as a unity; there is no antithesis of body and soul. It is man who receives in the Spirit and by union with the body of Christ this foretaste of the resurrection. But our incorporation into Christ awaits its full manifestation. Our present share in the risen life of Christ does not remove the need for the resurrection at the Parousia, and the eschatological tension of early Christianity is present strongly in St. Paul. When Christ comes again, the dead will rise from the tomb and the living will be changed, receiving without death the fullness of the new life of the resurrection. The texts are well known; the longest and most important is the fifteenth chapter of 1 Corinthians.[14]

It is easier to put briefly the thought of John, profound though this is. A major theme of his Gospel is that Jesus is the Life. God, the absolute master of life, has communicated this power to the Son, who gives eternal life to those who believe in him. He does this through the Spirit. Jesus then is the Life. That means he is for us who are under the power of death the Resurrection. He will raise us up on the last day (6.40). Notice the connexion made between the resurrection and the Eucharist (6.55). Now it is a characteristic of John's thought to see as already given in the present, as actual now, the eschatological reality of eternal life. The same applies to the resurrection. The believer possesses already in himself by his union with Christ, the Resurrection and the Life, the principle of his own resurrection. From now he has

---

[14] After this essay was written, I received the following article by A. Feuillet, P.S.S.: "Le mystère pascal et la résurrection des chrétiens d'après les épîtres pauliniennes," in *Nouvelle Revue Théologique*, 79 (1957), pp. 337–54. It makes these points among others: the resurrection of Christ was the inauguration of the general resurrection; our baptism is already a resurrection; the difference between the Greek and the Christian approach to the after-life must be kept clear. To give one quotation on this last point: "On ne soulignera jamais assez en effet combien les idées des chrétiens sur l'au-delà diffèrent de celles des Grecs. Partant d'une analyse des éléments du composé humain, les unes aboutissent à l'affirmation de l'immortalité de l'âme, radicalement distincte du corps. Les autres s'appuient avant tout sur l'histoire du salut telle que la fait connaître l'Ecriture et sur l'événement crucial de cette histoire, le miracle du matin de Pâques. Selon la Bible, la mort n'est pas en soi un bien et une liberation, comme elle l'est dans la philosophie dualiste de Platon. Etrangère au plan salvifique primitif, elle est tout au contraire la grande ennemi dont le Christ a triomphé le premier et dont ses disciples espèrent triompher à leur tour" (p. 348).

eternal life. The account of the raising of Lazarus was not meant
merely to reinforce the existing belief in the resurrection on the
last day; it was intended to show that in Christ there is present
already the resurrection and the life. "Martha said to him, 'I
know that he will rise again in the resurrection at the last day.'
Jesus said to her, 'I am the resurrection and the life; he who believes in me, though he die, yet shall he live, and whoever lives
and believes in me shall never die'" (11.24–6, RSV). Death has
become unimportant for one who adheres to Christ.

It would be interesting to follow this biblical revelation of the
resurrection through the patristic and Scholastic periods and to
see how each Christian generation has assimilated it, reflected
upon it, and set it forth in different ways. In an already lengthy
essay it is not possible to do this, and it is necessary to be content
with an account of how speculative theology at the present day
tackles this doctrine.

The Church's dogma of the resurrection includes three points:
at the last day men will rise from the dead; this resurrection is
universal, and even the unjust will rise; men will receive again
their identical bodies. Theological reflexion on the first two points
will be largely concerned with the place of the resurrection in the
history of salvation. This has already been dealt with; it could
receive more attention from theologians. The third point presents
a difficult speculative problem, and those with a philosophical bent
of mind have a right to have their questions considered.

We shall rise with these selfsame bodies. The strict or numerical
identity of the risen body with the body of this life is a truth of
faith. There can be no doubt or question about it. The problem is
to decide how this identity is realized. What is the basis in reality
that secures such an identity? Even in this life, there is a similar
problem. The human body remains one and the same despite a
continuous flow of change in all its elements. The parts and cells
of our bodies are frequently renewed and are in a state of constant
change. What maintains the body as the same body? There is an
even deeper problem in the identity between a risen body and a
body that has disintegrated in corruption.

A first solution, put forward formerly, may be quickly passed
over; it doesn't seem to be held nowadays. According to it, there are
a number of basic particles essentially belonging to each individual

man. They remain intact in him from conception to death, whereas all the rest of the body is subject to change. Only these are required for the identity of the body, and after the death of each man they remain in the universe as his by right. God in his omnipotence will gather them all together at the last day. As to the rest of the matter required, that can be supplied without detriment to the individuality of the body by whatever matter is available. This theory lacks any philosophical or empirical basis.

The second solution has been, and still is, the more common opinion. Indeed many theologians reach for their list of theological censures when anyone departs from it. In this explanation, what the soul receives again is the same quantified matter which it had in this life. It is the popular idea; the soul takes up the same matter it left to corrupt as a corpse in the tomb. To put it more technically: an appeal is made, in order to ensure identity, to a phenomenal and historical continuity between the risen body and the past mortal body. There is no question now of any unchanging basic particles. It is admitted that the entire matter of each body is in a state of continuous change. But the risen body will be the same as the body of this life because it will be made out of historically the same quantified matter into which the mortal body disintegrated.

Easy to imagine, this theory is philosophically more complicated than at first sight appears. Suppose one rejects any atomist theory—that is, the idea that matter consists of permanent incorruptible particles that remain the same under the processes of change: in what sense then can one speak of the reconstruction of a body from the same matter? If material things are constituted of prime matter, which is pure potency, and form, and if a substantial change causes a new form to arise, in what sense can the same identical matter ever be retrieved, once such a change has taken place? Unless there is a permanence of elements at least on the phenomenal level, the same matter can only be retrieved, after substantial change, in this limited sense: the new things generated by the corruption give back a part of their substance proportionate to the quantity they drew from the corrupted thing.

The point may be illustrated in this way. Throw a drop of water in a lake and suppose it loses completely its individuality in the lake, that same drop cannot be recovered. All that is possible is to take out of the lake a drop equal in quantity to the one put in. Reject all atomism, and that is what happens in substantial change. A new form takes over, and the identity of the previous thing is entirely lost. If some form of atomist theory is admitted—at the very minimum, a permanence at the level of empirical characteristics—then the divine power can gather together the same atoms or particles which made up the body in this life. The holders of this opinion do not demand that all the matter which enters into the constitution of the body in this life should be revivified at the resurrection. In view of the fact that the matter of our bodies is constantly renewed, any such demand would give us at the last day rather more than we could cope with. Enough matter is taken up in the resurrection to constitute a satisfactory body. Preference is usually given to the matter finally left aside at death; according to many authors, this alone is concerned in the resurrection. It is also added that it is sufficient for identity if part of the risen body consists of matter informed during this life. There would otherwise be no answer to the difficulty about the risen bodies of those born prematurely or to the more unreal difficulty of those nourished exclusively in this life on human flesh.

Is this solution satisfactory? Tradition puts it in a very strong position, but it reveals troubling weaknesses when examined speculatively. If what ensures the identity between the risen body and the mortal body is the historical and empirical continuity between the matter in both, then where that continuity is partial, the identity can only be partial. There will not then, for example, be a strict identity but only a partial identity between the risen body and mortal body of a deformed infant that died at birth. Surely identity must be secured at a deeper level. Further, even if the historical continuity is fully verified, it would not ensure the strict numerical identity of the risen body and the mortal body. It can be convincingly argued that the reconstituted body would inevitably be a numerically different body. Suppose a statue made of bronze is melted down and then re-cast from the same bronze. It would not be the same statue, but a new and similar one. The resurrection in strict identity of animals was considered an impossibility by St. Thomas, because no numerical identity of form could be obtained.

The point is this. Matter marked out by quantity is the principle of individuation, but this designation of a part of matter must include the relationship to place and time and also the relation of the piece to the other individuals with which it is connected. There cannot be a strict identity between material things that arise at different times, in different places, and from different antecedent things. Let us suppose that all the original elements of a body have been gathered together by a miracle. Even if there is a permanence of all and each of the atoms and these are arranged in exactly in the same way, the body produced is still a body made at another time, by another cause, from different antecedents, and consequently not the same identical body. It is indeed similar to the former body, but it is not numerically the same body. Unless, that is, one can point to some higher principle securing identity.

What does the third solution offer? This puts the reason for the strict identity of the risen body with our present body solely in the identity of the spiritual soul. This remains uninterruptedly in being, and is as form that which gives to the body its being and its unity. If one holds the Thomist doctrine that there is only one form in man, the problem we are struggling with ceases. Man is made up of prime matter and a unique form, the spiritual soul. The soul is the one determining principle that constitutes man in his entire being. It determines him, not merely as man, but also as animal, as living being, as body, as substance, even as being. The soul is the source of every perfection and determination in man. The real distinction in man is not between body and soul, but between soul and prime matter. Philosophically then for the Thomist, nothing else is required for the identity of the body than the identity of the soul or form. The soul immediately informs prime matter; as soon, then, as the soul takes over and informs a certain quantity of matter, this becomes the self-same identical body previously possessed. The unity and identity of a thing comes from the form; where there is numerically the same form, there must be numerically the same thing. From the metaphysical point of view the notorious statement of Durandus was perfectly sound, in which he said that if in the resurrection the soul of Peter was united to the corpse of Paul, and the soul of Paul to the corpse of Peter, the corpse of Paul would at once become the body of Peter, identical with his mortal body, and the corpse of Peter the body of Paul, identical with his mortal body.

An attractive solution. Nevertheless, theologians fight shy of it; it is untraditional, they urge. The principle behind it is found in St. Thomas, and he uses it as a partial solution, but it was Durandus who first put it forward as a complete solution. Its great exponent in modern times has been Cardinal Billot, and he has had a few followers, but most theologians continue to view it askance. The very fact that it solves the difficulty is considered an argument against it, since this is taken as an indication that its understanding of the resurrection is not in keeping with tradition.[15] Here, however, I am of the minority view. Frankly, if one holds Thomistic philosophy, there can, it seems, be no other basic explanation. Moreover, it would be difficult, I think, to establish that tradition taught as revealed doctrine, not only the strict identity of the body, but also a particular explanation of this. At the same time, Fr. de Broglie[16] is right to insist on adding a qualification to this solution. In the resurrection of the body, the soul will in fact take up again the person's own remains, when these still exist in some recognizable way at the end of the world. This is not metaphysically necessary, nor will such a re-assumption be always possible. It is but incidental to a true resurrection. But God is not moved by metaphysical considerations alone, and there is a fitness in the use of the personal remains, when these are still extant, which should lead us to assert with tradition that God will in fact act in that way.

The resurrection is the restoration to us of our same bodies, but these will be received in a new state; they will be glorified. (I may leave aside here the resurrection of the damned; this is different in its significance.) It is wrong to think of the resurrection after the

---

[15] See, for example, this passage of Fr. Lennerz, who usually weighs his words carefully: "Praeterea concedendum est, difficultates in hac explicatione evanescere; sed hoc ipsum magnum est praeiudicium contra hanc sententiam; nam inde videtur apparere, resurrectionem et identitatem corporis in hac sententia non iam ita concipi, ut Patres et theologi communiter concipiunt. Hinc quoque est, quod haec sententia ad testimonium Patrum provocare non possit. Immo Patres, ut dictum est, alio modo identitatem corporis intellexerunt. Theologi, postquam haec sententia proposita est, quasi omnes erant contrarii, ii quoque, qui unicitatem formae admittunt" (*De Novissimis*, p. 181).

[16] Throughout this part of the paper I am greatly indebted to the treatment of the resurrection in Fr. G. de Broglie's *De Fine Ultimo Humanae Vitae: Pars Prior, Positiva* (Paris, 1948). It is the finest available.

manner of the raising of Lazarus. A sign teaching us that Christ came as the Resurrection and Life, this miracle was none the less in a different order to our resurrection. Lazarus came back to this earthly existence and remained subject to corruption and death; we pass into a new order of existence. The resurrection is the reintegration of ourselves as men; nothing is lost of our identity and nature. Yet as men, body and soul, we are transformed. Our being passes into a new and higher existence, a share in the divine life. In other words, there takes place the full deployment in our being of the life of grace, and this involves a transmutation or sublimation of our bodies and our bodily life.

What does that mean? Revelation gives us very little information about the glorified body. In Paul's great chapter on the resurrection, the fifteenth in 1 Corinthians, he calls the risen body a spiritual body: "It is sown a physical (*psychikon*) body, it is raised a spiritual (*pneumatikon*) body" (v. 44, RSV). The Pauline term must be properly understood. This becoming spiritual is in no way opposed to the idea of a truly corporal resurrection. It means that the risen body is transformed by, is penetrated with, the Spirit. For us, spiritual means immaterial, but that is not what Paul has in mind. For him, Spirit is the divine power, light and holiness. The stress is on what we nowadays call the supernatural. His teaching is that the risen bodies are brought within the divine sphere and share the divine qualities of power, glory, splendour and holiness.[17] "What is sown," he writes, "is perishable, what is raised is imperishable. It is sown in dishonour, it is raised in glory. It is sown in weakness, it is raised in power. It is sown a physical body, it is raised a spiritual body" (vv. 42–4, RSV). And then a few verses later: "Just as we have borne the image of the man of dust, we shall also bear the image of the man of heaven" (v. 49, RSV).

This last text reminds us that in the resurrection of Christ we have the exemplar and cause of our own. It must be stressed again and again that the resurrection of Christ is not simply a miracle proving his claims. It is a turning-point in world history; it is the beginning of a new existence for Christ, and the risen

[17] Cf. L. Cerfaux, *Le Christ dans la théologie de Saint Paul* (Paris, 1951), p. 64, n. 3. Eng. trans., *Christ in the Theology of St. Paul* (New York, Herder & Herder, 1959).

Christ is the image and the type, the first-fruits of a new world; in him was inaugurated a new state of creation. Our resurrection bodies will be similar to the glorified body of Christ; for by our resurrection we share fully in the risen life of Christ.

What was the risen body of Christ like? Well, it was clearly a body in the sense of a tangible and extended reality. Further, it still possessed the characteristically human shape and form. Attempts to over-spiritualize the risen body, to volatilize away its materiality, always come up against the experience of the Apostles that the risen Christ had a true human body. However mysterious and far-reaching the transmutation of our bodies in the resurrection, the Christian tradition affirms quite clearly that they retain a true corporeity in human shape and structure.

The Fathers and theologians go on to speak of the integrity and natural perfection enjoyed by our risen bodies. The principle is unassailable; patently, a risen body cannot be mutilated or incomplete. At the same time, the attempts of curiosity to apply the principle in detail should be restrained. The common teaching tells us that difference of sex is preserved, though a number of the Fathers would not have agreed. Beyond that, the further inferences concerning a so-called perfect age and stature are valueless.

Our bodies then, profoundly changed, will remain truly bodies, perfected in their corporal reality. Yet the risen body of Christ, although in some way present to the apostles in space and time and inserted into the texture of our world, was of a different order of existence and no longer bound down by the laws of this universe. The appearances of Christ to his apostles were not the same as mystical visions; they were encounters with the objective reality of Christ's body. But if for the apostles they were perceptions, the narratives show that they were perceptions of a unique kind. So far this has not provoked much reflexion on the part of theologians. The valuable pages on this subject by M. Guitton[18] may stimulate some further efforts. The accounts give the impression of an irruption into this world of something from a different order, and the perception of the risen Christ seems to have been a privilege that required in the recipient an openness to the higher order thus manifested. M. Guitton goes so far as to say: "But it would seem to me that if Tiberias or Tacitus, if Philo or Pilate or Josephus

[18] *The Problem of Jesus* (New York, Kenedy, 1955).

had happened to be present in that room where Jesus appeared, none of these would have seen anything at all." Christ gave to his apostles and disciples these experiences of his risen body as signs that led them to their act of faith in his resurrection; objective perceptions indeed, but of a unique presence, to which they bore true but unusual testimony.

The body of Christ belonged to another order, and was free from the limitations imposed on us in this spatio-temporal existence. A similar existence will be given to our bodies. Can we feel our way any further in describing the characteristics of this mode of being? "All this," writes M. Guitton, "reminds me that I am not quite sure what a body is." He then shakes our complacency by asking: "Are the ideas of space and time, of volume and mass and life, necessarily associated with the idea of body? They certainly are, if the body is only matter. But if matter is assumable by spirit which we see it is even in our present existence, does it depend fundamentally on space-time and biology? Can we not conceive the possibility of the body's being no longer subject to space, no longer submitting to it, or treating the physical world as an instrument?" That seems to me personally to over-spiritualize the risen body and to be philosophically somewhat dubious. Admittedly, there is less confidence nowadays in what is held about the constitution of the material universe. That perhaps should make us at least more cautious in dogmatizing about conditions in the renewed universe of the future.

The more traditional approach to the conditions of our risen existence is to distinguish four endowments given to resurrected bodies: impassibility, splendour, agility and subtlety. This enumeration has been a commonplace in theology since the thirteenth century. Though not in a universally consistent way, it is often connected with the text of St. Paul already quoted (1 Cor. 15.42–4). It is a mistake, however, to ascribe to Paul this Scholastic analysis.

Splendour and agility need little comment. Splendour means that the glorified bodies will offer unblemished beauty to the sight. Most are led by the transfiguration to affirm further that our bodies will possess a supernatural radiance, the bodily brightness of our spiritual glory. Agility is an aspect of our freedom from the material limitations of this present existence; it has been affirmed since the fourth century. It indicates the ease with which we will be able to move from place to place. Authors disagree about the mechanics of it. St. Thomas, and most with him, think that the body will be transferred by an act of will, but in a way that will still involve movement through the intervening space and some lapse of time. Suarez hoped to dispense with both those requirements.

Subtlety bears several different meanings. For some, it is the ability to pass through other bodies. Strange how the one endowment everyone seems to associate with the risen body is quite uncertain! Christ passed through the closed doors of the upper room, but was that due to the habitual condition of his glorified body or to a particular miracle of divine power, as many of the Fathers thought? At any rate, such an endowment of co-existing locally with other bodies cannot be affirmed with certainty and would render the conditions of existence very complicated in the renewed but still material universe.

Subtlety has another meaning for St. Thomas. It indicates the basic gift of the glorified body which makes perfect its union with the spiritual soul. There is achieved an integration of man's nature, and the material side of it is put into perfect harmony and rhythm with the spiritual. The glorification of the body excludes the imperfections which flow from its materiality. These encumber the spirit in its natural union with the body. In the resurrection, matter is made perfectly subordinate to spirit; it becomes malleable in its association with the spiritual soul. If it is the meaning and purpose of the body to be the expression of the soul, and its medium in activity and communication, then the earthly body is but an imperfect body, and the body in the full sense will be the risen body. The human body is formed by spirit; subtlety will allow the spirit and its divine life full sway in its perfecting of matter, so that this may become an apt co-principle in its life.

It is necessary to distinguish several elements in the gift of impassibility. The first is immunity from all bodily evil. Clearly affirmed in Scripture, this is also something bound up with the meaning of redemption. Suffering and death came into this world by sin, and Christ came to deliver us from these evils as well as from sin. Tradition, both patristic and Scholastic, then goes on to affirm a second element in impassibility. There will be no need to guard the risen body against corruption by taking any measures to keep it in being. Its incorruptibility will be an impossibilty of corruption, and not a mere external preservation through God's Providence. This intrinsic incorruptibility will free us in our risen life from all concern with the necessities of our present material existence, such as food, drink and sleep. These will cease to be essential requirements for our bodily life.

The Scholastics pursue this line of thought even further and introduce a third element into impassibility. They bring the movement of bodily life to a standstill and will not allow any internal change in the risen body, except the qualitative changes involved in sense knowledge. This fits in with the medieval conception according to which material things fall into two groups, heavenly and sublunary. Heavenly bodies, such as the stars, are, it was thought, in no way subject to intrinsic change but only to local motion. The risen bodies must share in such a perfection. Besides, all substantial changes in the world are due to the movement of the heavens. This will cease in the renewed universe, and consequently so will the changes, including those of the human body.

This last element in impassibility has been re-examined recently by Fr. de Broglie,[19] and he sees in it a very questionable hypothesis. The point has quite a wide bearing. It concerns the restoration of our bodily life after the resurrection and the physiology of the risen body. What is called vegetative life is the fundamental life of a living body. It involves many different operations: those connected with eating and drinking, the activities associated with breathing and the circulation of the blood, and so on. All these manifestations of bodily life can be reduced to two basic forms of activity, namely assimilation and disassimilation in regard to the various substances profferred to the living organism. Can we suppose that the risen body is utterly deprived of these activities? The Scholastics had no idea of the wonderful complexity and harmony of the life of the body, with the life of all its innumerable cells, such as this has been revealed to us by modern science. Now that the intricately woven pattern of incessant change in the human body has been displayed to us, is it possible to conceive any longer a living human body of marble-like immobility? The existence,

[19] *De Fine Ultimo Humanae Vitae*, pp. 282–94.

too, of a sense-life is jeopardized by such a conception, since the two levels of life seem inseparably connected. The problem then faces us: can we reject the Scholastic conception of impassibility and maintain that a vegetative life continues in the risen body?

From the theological point of view, the problem is tied up with the discussions about the eating and drinking by the risen Christ. The Scriptures tell us that after his resurrection Christ ate and drank with his apostles. Was this real eating and drinking? Many, like St. Thomas, think that no vital assimilation of the food and drink was involved; it was not then in the full sense an eating and drinking. Others maintain that there was an exceptional and miraculous assimilation. St. Augustine, however, understood it as a real eating with assimilation, and he attributed to all the risen a true and habitual power of eating and drinking. An examination of the patristic tradition leads Fr. de Broglie to assert that it is not unanimous over the power of eating and drinking in the blessed, and its authority obliges us only to exclude any need for food and drink. The Scholastic teaching is due to their false physics. He concludes then that one is allowed to hold, and he clearly favours the idea, that there will be a true vegetative life in the risen body, with the various activities of assimilation and disassimilation. To put it in another way, there will be eating and drinking and all that organic life we now see to be the basic life of a living body. At the same time, there will be no need for food and drink, because the blessed will be able to suspend at will the common laws of human life and live above them when they so desire. And if anyone objects that the risen body will be corruptible, if there is to be a continual change and circulation of matter within it, he answers that the incorruptibility belongs to it as a body, and not to its individual cells and elements.

In the remarks of M. Guitton previously quoted and in this opinion of Fr. de Broglie, we see two different trends in recent thinking about the resurrection. M. Guitton so stresses the transformation of the body that one fears for the truly bodily character of the resurrection. On the other hand, Fr. de Broglie so stresses the possession of a true body with its life that he aggravates disturbingly the difficulty that many thinkers find with the resurrection: how to conceive as everlasting a thing and a life that seem essentially transitory. His ideas are very attractive, until one remembers that such a life has to be conceived as eternal. Was it perhaps more than false physics that made the Scholastics give to the risen body and the renewed material universe something of the immutability characteristic of a spirit in possession of its last end?

Our gropings before such problems should not make us forget the importance of the resurrection of the body in Christian teaching. What matters is not the speculative analysis of the resurrection but our faith in it. Our belief in it is in fact our belief that man in all that he is has been saved. It is our belief that salvation comes to us from the risen Christ. It is our belief in the cosmic extent of God's saving plan. The risen body is our solidarity with the re-created universe in Christ Jesus.

CHAPTER XX

THE END OF THE WORLD

The most surprising thing about the end of the world is that we Christians are supposed to want it, to look forward to it. It is an object of our hope. The early Christians longed for it and were impatient at its delay. This is strange to our present mentality. Why the change of outlook? If the first Christians desired the end of the world and we dread it, it is an easy guess that our notion of the end does not correspond to theirs. The event must have a different meaning for us than it did for them.

How do we think of the end of the world? The thought that first comes to mind is that everything will go up in smoke and flame; all will be destroyed. We associate the end with some natural, cosmic disaster. When scientists utter some gloomy foreboding about the break-up of the present system of the universe, we identify that break-up with the end of the world. Or again, we associate it with some ultimate destruction willed by man. When we envisage the possibility of a hydrogen war wiping out mankind, we identify this with the end of the world.

But isn't this an odd outlook for a Christian? Someone, surely, could object: "What about God's plan for the universe? What about God's plan for mankind? Is all to be destroyed? Are creation and redemption to end in meaningless catastrophe?"

The usual answer is very unsatisfactory. It is to say: "Oh, but men will survive the destruction, some to go to heaven and some to hell; everlasting life will take over from this universe of time, with rewards for the just and punishment for the unjust." Why is this not enough?

What is missing is the cosmic significance of Christ's work. We cannot dissociate the victory of Christ from creation with its purpose nor from human history with its purpose. Christ did not save men by taking them out of a created universe which would end in ultimate annihilation, nor by snatching them from human history which would be an empty drama due for annulment in final ruin. On the contrary, the salvation brought by Christ means that in him this created universe will reach the purpose for which God created it and that in him human history will find its meaning and fulfilment.

The early Christians realized all this, and for them the end of the world meant, not final catastrophe, but the triumph of Christ. They identified it with the Second Coming of Christ. But why a *second* coming?

The death and resurrection of Christ already marks the beginning of the end of the world. By those saving acts Christ introduced into this world and into human history the final order of things. The new creation has begun. We already have eternal life. We enjoy already the life of the world to come. We live in the last days. No wonder the first Christians were impatient for everything to be settled quickly. But the ascension of Christ and the promise of his return made it clear that the end of the world would only come about in two stages.

The present age is the first stage. The final order of things now exists, fully in Christ himself but only in a hidden, incomplete way in the rest of creation. This is an intermediate period. The reason for it is to give men the opportunity of associating themselves freely with the new creation and of co-operating with its gradual penetration into the old. When all is ready, at a time known only to God, Christ will come again. His return will mark the second and ultimate stage.

The Second Coming of Christ will bring into the open the new order that now lies hidden. It will show the meaning of human history and how God has been present in it, directing it to his purpose. Christ will bring all to completion. His return is the end of the world, not in the sense of the destruction of all, but in the sense of the final fulfilment of all. By it will be achieved all that God set out to do when he created this universe and man, all that he planned when he sent Christ to save man and the universe with man. All that is good and valuable in creation and human history will be taken up into the final order. Nothing except sin will be excluded. This will be the triumph of Christ, which was the reason why God created this world and is the end towards which he is directing all things.

We can see now why Christians must hope for the Second Coming. If we believe in Christ, can we do anything else but hope for the day when his work will be completed? We are like men in the last stage of a war. The decisive battles have been won. We are waiting impatiently for the time when we can enjoy in peace the fruits of the victory. Christ has fought and won the decisive battles against evil, but there is still some mopping-up to be done. We long for the day when all this will be finished and we shall enjoy in undisturbed peace with him the fruits of his victory. The Second Coming will mark the end of the intermediate period and bring the day when we can share the tranquil but ardent rest of God.

The return of Christ cannot be identified with any natural catastrophe or any disaster contrived by man. The popular ideas on this are wrong. The coming of Christ will be a free intervention of God at an hour known only to him. We have but a glimpse of his plan. We do not know enough even to guess at the time of Christ's coming. It will be sudden and unexpected. There is no reason to associate it with any natural event, and as for man's folly and its results, God will see to it that men do not upset his plan. Only when Christ will have come shall we see how the time chosen is suitable for the perfect accomplishment of God's purpose.

Our failure to long for the Coming of Christ is a great loss to our Christian life. It means a failure to grasp the cosmic extent of Christ's work. We think of our religion as simply an affair of our individual happiness. That happiness is part of God's plan, but his plan embraces much more than that. Our destiny is but part of a magnificent plan that includes in its wonderful sweep the whole of creation and the whole of human history. The work of Christ will not be complete until all creation has been brought into subjection and until human history guided by the action of God has reached its full unfolding. The Second Coming of Christ marks this triumphant climax.

Again, our failure to look to the Coming of Christ makes us

unable to appreciate properly the meaning of human history or to judge rightly the achievement of human progress. We divorce all this from the work of Christ. Either we condemn it entirely or we divide our life into two parts, one for this world and one for the next. The truth is that what men do contains two elements intermingled. There are the results of men's sins, the fruits of pride, injustice, weakness and lack of moderation; all this will have to be purged away. But within history there is also the action of God and his grace. This is the factor that will determine the ultimate destiny of this order and all that is good will be taken up into the new creation.

We must not put our trust in men and their plans. We must not think that men can decide the future of the universe. That has already been decided by Christ. He will return to take possession of what is his. Meanwhile we must live in the hope of that coming, and our prayer should be that of the first Christians: "Come, Lord Jesus."

THE RESURRECTION

When Christ comes again we shall all rise from the dead. These bodies we now have will be given back to us, this time for a life without end. What about those who are alive on the last day? Will they all die and come to the resurrection through a quick experience of death?

The question is debated among Catholic writers. Some think they will pass through death to the resurrection; others maintain they will undergo the change into the state of the resurrection at once without death. The discussion centres on the interpretation of several scriptural texts (1 Thess 4.15–17: 1 Cor. 15.51–52: 2 Cor. 5.2–4) and the meaning given to them in tradition. I think personally that the opinion that they will not die fits in better with the teaching of St. Paul, but the point is unimportant.

What is important is that all men without exception will receive the new conditions of bodily life which are the result of the resurrection. Everyone will rise from the dead, the wicked and the good, the damned and the blessed.

But we are not interested here in the damned. It is enough to notice that their bodies will endure for a life without end. The body of the sinner enters into his sin and it will enter into his punishment. However, our concern now is with the wonderful mystery of the resurrection of the just.

When we ask what it means, our first reaction should be to point to the resurrection of Christ. What will happen to us is what happened to Christ. The resurrection of Christ is the cause and model of our resurrection, and our new, risen life will be a sharing in the risen life of Christ.

But there is more to it than that. In a way we already share in the risen life of Christ. We do not often think in this way, but in fact our Christian life, our life of grace, is an incomplete share in the life of the glorified Christ.

Baptism is a resurrection. If we want to understand it, we have to compare it with the resurrection of Christ and see our baptism as a taking place in us of what happened when Christ rose from the dead. Our Christian life is a life on a new level of existence, and, when we ask what that new level is, the answer is that it is the level of the risen life of Christ which we shall enjoy in full at the end of the world. We are already living on a level that is above the level of the things of this earth.

This new life, which we have here and now, is given not only to our souls but also to our bodies. We have developed the habit of speaking of saving our souls or of the life of the soul, so that it is necessary to insist that Christ came not to save our souls but to save men.

Man is not a soul that by misfortune has become stuck to a body, but a living unity of body and soul. Even in talking of the Christian life we cannot leave out the body. When we live our Christian life, we live it in body and in soul.

But even this is not quite true, because our bodies and our souls do not exist and act side by side but have one life together. When we act as men, we act as body-souls, the two making one whole or unity, and that is the way we live our Christian life.

The sacraments affect us as men, and their effects penetrate our bodies as well as our souls. Christ told us that it was because we were nourished on his flesh and blood in holy Communion that our bodies would rise from the dead.

We can see now why the salvation brought by Christ would be incomplete without the resurrection. The blessed in heaven are not fully men but disembodied souls. They have received the vision of God and have thus received their eternal happiness. They are already the blessed. But their happiness is incomplete until the resurrection, because only after the resurrection will they enjoy their eternal happiness, not merely as souls, but also as men.

They have to wait for this until the resurrection on account of the way Christ has given us salvation. He has not given it to us so that we escape death but so that we overcome death. As Christians we already share the resurrection of Christ, but that does not mean that we shall not die; it means that we shall conquer death by rising again from the dead. There is planted in us the seed of the resurrection. Our bodies have part in our Christian life and in the effect of the sacraments.

The result of this is that, although we die and our bodies corrupt, death cannot gain the victory; the seed has been planted, and when the time comes our bodies will rise from the tomb. Then our share in Christ's resurrection will be complete, and death will be no more.

To that extent our Christian life continues in an unbroken line and death cannot interrupt it or destroy it. Jesus said: "I am the resurrection and life; he who believes in me, though he is dead, will live on, and whoever has life, and has faith in me, to all eternity cannot die" (John 11.25–26, KV).

What will our risen bodies be like? Once again we must turn to the resurrection of Christ which is the pattern and cause of ours.

We shall rise with these bodies we now have. It was his own body that Christ took from the tomb. But although we shall be given back our same bodies, these will be changed. This change is difficult to grasp. Wait and see, is really the only answer we can give to questions about them.

A few hints can be gathered from the resurrection of Christ. Our bodies will be real bodies with human shape and features but not subject to the same conditions that govern bodies we know. The physical laws we experience will not apply in the same way.

Again, our bodies will shine forth in glory. We have an example of this in the transfiguration of Christ. After his resurrection he limited this effect in order to make easier contact with his apostles, but we can say that in some way the glory of eternal life will be made visible in our very bodies.

Further, our risen bodies will be completely free from even the possibility of suffering or harm.

But perhaps what is most important is that they will be entirely subject to our higher faculties. Our nature is disordered through sin. Our bodies should be the expression of ourselves and should be fully subordinate to that spiritual activity that distinguishes us as men. They still are to a certain extent. Think of the way the face of a person, its lines and features, express the character of the man; consider how all our life here involves bodily energies.

But our body is often an encumbrance; it hinders us when we try to rise to higher things. It is often an unworthy image of our spiritual selves. After the resurrection the body will be perfectly malleable in its relation to the spiritual soul. It will express truly what we are and be a help, not hindrance, in our spiritual activity.

We should long for the resurrection. It is the fulfilment of all our hopes. At the same time, it is well to remember that we already have the beginning of our risen life. Our bodies are sacred even now. By a truly Christian life we must foster the seed of glory within them and not degrade them by sin.

THE LAST JUDGEMENT

A very revealing sign of how individualistic our religious outlook has become is the fact that many Catholics do not see why there should be a last judgement. Each man is judged at death, they say, what then is the point of the last judgement?

This is to limit our religion to an affair between the individual and God. It is to forget that the Christian message tells us of a divine plan that embraces the entire universe and the whole course of human history. Our individual destinies must be seen in the setting of that plan. The Scriptures teach us that.

The particular judgement at death is a truth of our faith, but it is only implicitly taught in the Bible. On the contrary, the last judgement is a constant theme in both the Old and the New Testaments.

"The Son of Man will come hereafter in his Father's glory with his angels about him, and he will recompense everyone, then, according to his works" (Matt. 16.27, KV). Christ will come again to judge the living and the dead. He will come to bring the final establishment of the kingdom of God, and that will mean the final separation of the good and the evil. Then will there shine out for all to see the goodness, justice and mercy of God, the glory of Christ and the holiness of the just.

God has already made known to us his goodness, justice and mercy, but much in this world weighs heavily on our minds. Why has God allowed such power to evil? Why do the good suffer and the wicked prosper? Why is there such cruelty in the animal kingdom?

We know so little of the plan of God that, despite all that we can say, these questions still baffle us. All will be made clear in the last judgement when we shall see the completed pattern of God's work, a work of goodness, justice and love.

It is Christ who carries out this work of God. During his life Christ was mocked and rejected; he is mocked and rejected by many even now. When he comes again, it will be with the glory that is his due as Lord and King. His splendour will bring joy to those who have accepted him and confusion to those who have despised him.

And the just will share his glory. So often they are trampled upon in this world. But then? Listen to the Book of Wisdom:

How boldly, then, will the just man appear, to meet his old per-secutors, that thwarted all his striving! And then, in what craven fear they will cower at the sight of him, amazed at the sudden reversal of his fortunes! Inward remorse will wring a groan from those hearts: Why, these were the men we made into a laughing-stock and a by-word! We, poor fools, mistook the life they lived for madness, their death for ignominy; and now they are reckoned as God's own children, now it is among his holy ones that their lot is cast (5.1–5, KV).

What will be the norm of that judgement? By what standard will everything be measured? It will be love. Not love in the ordinary, human sense, but love in the sense of the love of God which has been given to men as their life and destiny.

God did not create for us the things of this world: not for riches, pleasure, earthly power or honour. These have their place, but it is a secondary one. God created us to share his life. He made us so that we might be taken up into the family life of God and become his children. He wanted us to be united to him in that love which unites the three Persons of the Trinity.

We receive this love already in our lifetime and our lives will be judged according to their conformity to it. And since this love has been given to us by Christ and in union with him, Christ himself can be called the standard by which we shall be judged. How far do our lives correspond to Christ? How do they appear when we look at them in the light of Christ?

The love of God is binding upon us. It might seem strange to have an obligation to love someone, but we must remember that here the offer of love comes from God. God is the one to whom we owe our existence, and he it is who has established the order of creation. We are free to reject God's offer to share his life, but if we do so we inevitably exclude ourselves from the one destiny for which God made us and put ourselves outside the order of love which governs this universe.

Our lot will be eternal unhappiness, because we shall be cut off from God who alone can satisfy our longing for happiness. That is what is meant by the pain of loss. We shall also be out of harmony with creation, in conflict with it. That is what is meant by the fire of hell.

All those who spurn God's plan will be separated from the kingdom of the blessed in the final reckoning, and the world will be purged of evil. The battle with sin will be over and the just will enjoy eternal rest in the possession of God and the enjoyment of his life.

How will the last judgement take place? We all know the way it is usually described. The blowing of the trumpet, the gathering of all mankind, the placing of the sheep on the right and the goats on the left, and so on. Even the place of the judgement has been given, the Valley of Josaphat to the east of Jerusalem.

All this is symbol. It is a pictorial way of teaching us the essential truth, and a literal understanding of these details is not demanded by our faith. What we must hold firmly is that Christ will come as judge, that the good will be finally separated from the evil and that the justice of God and the glory of Christ will be made manifest when the completed plan of God is revealed for all to see.

The last judgement has its preparation in history. St. John teaches us that in a sense the judgement is already taking place. The first coming of Christ with its continuation in the sending of the Spirit is bringing about a separation in this world between good and evil. Men are taking their stand in relation to Christ. Christ and his Church spell salvation for some and condemnation for others. Those who accept Christ already receive eternal life. Those who reject him are already condemned. The choice made becomes irrevocable at death.

The last judgement will not bring any reversal of the particular judgement. It will manifest it and confirm it. And then the destiny of each individual will be seen in the setting of the whole plan of God. The process of division that has been taking place in history will be completed in the final establishment in glory of the kingdom of God.

On what side are we taking our stand? Do our lives place us with the sheep or the goats? The acid test is our love of our neighbour. Not any kind of love but a love in which we see God in our neighbour and love him for God's sake. We do not see God. How are we going to love him?

He has given the answer by pointing to our fellow men and telling us that what is done to them is done to him. When Christ described the last judgement, the one cause he gave for blessing or condemnation was love of our neighbour (Matt. 25.31–46). This world would indeed be Christian if instead of selfishness, avarice, injustice and hatred there were mutual consideration, generosity, justice and love.

NEW HEAVENS AND NEW EARTH

Oddly enough, many people are convinced that according to Christian belief this world will be utterly destroyed when the end comes. This is odd because it is part of our faith that the world will not be annihilated but glorified.

What does the end of the world mean for man? It means the end of this familiar form of human life, its destruction if you will, but it does not mean the end of man. His life will be changed and man will continue in all that he is, body and soul, living in a new state, the state of glory.

The same is true of the material world. God does not and will not annihilate any of the creatures he has made, but all will be changed. The present state of the world will come to an end—in that sense it will be destroyed—but this same material world will continue to exist in a new state, the state of final glory. It will be transformed so as to become a suitable dwelling-place for man with his glorified risen body. There will be new heavens and a new earth.

Although this has always been the belief of Christians, it is true that the most striking passage in Scripture on the subject can be easily misunderstood. It is in the Second Epistle of Peter and runs as follows:

> That same word [of God] keeps heaven and earth, as they now are, stored up, ready to feed the fire on the day when the godless will be judged, and perish. . . . But the day of the Lord is coming, and when it comes, it will be upon you like a thief. The heavens will vanish in a whirlwind, the elements will be scorched up and dissolve, earth, and all earth's achievements, will burn away.
>
> All so transitory; and what men you ought to be! How unworldly in your life, how reverent towards God, as you wait, and wait eagerly, for the day of the Lord to come, for the heavens to shrivel up in fire, and the elements to melt in its heat! And meanwhile, we have new heavens and a new earth to look forward to, the dwelling-place of holiness; that is what he has promised (3.7–13, KV).

What first makes an impact in that text is the description of the final destruction, the conflagration in which everything will be burnt up. We tend to overlook the mention of the new heavens and earth. Examined carefully and seen in the light of other passages, the text does not teach that after the last day there will not be any world at all, as if after the resurrection men were to exist by themselves without any dwelling-place, but that this world will pass from its present condition to a new condition in which all that is due to sin will have been purged away.

Will there be a final conflagration? Is this present world to end in an enormous bonfire? We are not obliged to think so. The description in the Epistle is drawn from two sources. The first consists of the ideas of the time about the end of the world.

Then as now it was a common idea that the world would come

to an end by fire. The writer simply used this idea to get across his teaching that this present order was coming to an end and would be subject to the final judgement. We are not required to accept the details of the description, any more than we are required to accept the ideas about the world used by the author of Genesis when he teaches us the doctrine of creation.

But there is also another source for the description. Fire is an age-old biblical symbol for the judgement of God. God's judgement is a fire that burns what is evil and purifies what is good. The key point in the passage is that this world will be judged.

We need to keep this judgement in mind when we ask what will survive the day of the Lord. The present achievements of men are for the most part an intermingling of good and evil. Sin unleashed the forces of evil in this world. Original sin with its effects has made it impossible for man by his unaided human powers to achieve in any permanent, stable way a life of ordinary moral goodness. That means that any lasting human achievement requires the grace of God. There can be no true progress outside the setting of the kingdom of God. The attempt to establish a new order on earth by human knowledge and human resources is an illusion.

On the other hand, the redemption of Christ is already working in the world and exercising its saving influence throughout the entire range of human activity. There is a true progress. When the end comes all human achievement and progress will come under the fire of God's judgement. What stands the test will pass into the new order, what is but dross will be consumed.

The final transformation will be the redemption of the world. The saving power of Christ extends to the material universe which is to share in the glory of the new creation. St. Paul writes:

If creation is full of expectancy, that is because it is waiting for the sons of God to be made known. Created nature has been condemned to frustration, not for some deliberate fault if its own, but for the sake of him who so condemned it, with a hope to look forward to; namely, that nature in its turn will be set free from the tyranny of corruption, to share in the glorious freedom of God's sons. The whole of nature, as we know, groans in a common travail all the while (Rom. 8.19–22, KV).

Sin has had its repercussions on nature, but this too is destined to share in the coming order of the resurrection.

Our curiosity is anxious to know what this new order will be like. It must remain unsatisfied. People have made guesses, but it is difficult to choose between them. In general there are two trends among those who write on the subject. Some stress the difference from this present world and sometimes so speak of the subordination of the world to come to the power of the spirit, its penetration by the forces of the spirit, that one wonders whether they sufficiently recognize its permanently material nature.

Others stress the likeness to the present universe; they speak of plants, animals and so forth in such a way that one wonders whether their imagination has not led them astray. No harm can come from dreaming a little on the subject, provided not too much importance is attached to the dreams.

Another mention of the new heavens and the new earth is found in John's description of the new Jerusalem:

> Then I saw a new heaven, and a new earth. The old heaven, and the old earth had vanished, and there was no more sea. And I, John, saw in my vision that holy city which is the new Jerusalem, being sent down by God from heaven, all clothed in readiness, like a bride who has adorned herself to meet her husband (Apoc. 21.1–2, KV).

The new Jerusalem is the symbol of the community of the blessed. It reminds us that as we work out our salvation together here below, so we shall enjoy our happiness together in the world to come. Part of our joy will come from being together and sharing our lives with others. God will make for us a new dwelling-place which will reflect our inner harmony. A Christian harmony among men can begin to renew the universe here and now.

INDEX